Manufacturing Morals

Michel Anteby

Manufacturing
Morals

The Values of Silence in
Business School Education

THE UNIVERSITY OF CHICAGO PRESS

CHICAGO AND LONDON

MICHEL ANTEBY is associate professor and the Marvin Bower fellow in the organizational behavior unit at Harvard Business School. He is the author of *Moral Gray Zones: Side Productions, Identity, and Regulation in an Aeronautic Plant.*

The University of Chicago Press, Chicago 60637
The University of Chicago Press, Ltd., London
© 2013 by The University of Chicago
All rights reserved. Published 2013.
Printed in the United States of America

22 21 20 19 18 17 16 15 14 13   1 2 3 4 5

ISBN-13: 978-0-226-09247-8 (cloth)
ISBN-13: 978-0-226-09250-8 (e-book)
DOI: 10.7208/chicago/9780226092508.001.0001

Library of Congress Cataloging-in-Publication Data

Anteby, Michel, 1970– author.
    Manufacturing morals : the values of silence in business school education / Michel Anteby.
        pages   cm
    Includes bibliographical references and index.
    ISBN 978-0-226-09247-8 (cloth : alkaline paper)
    ISBN 978-0-226-09250-8 (e-book)
    1. Harvard Business School—Faculty—Social conditions. 2. Socialization—Case studies. I. Title.
HF1134.H4A58 2013
650.071'174461—dc23
                                        2013016592

♾ This paper meets the requirements of ANSI/NISO Z39.48-1992 (Permanence of Paper).

Penser le silence c'est, en quelque sorte, l'ébruiter.

EDMOND JABÈS

Contents

Preface

"After studying a factory, why not write an ethnography of HBS?" joked my doctoral thesis advisor. We had met for coffee on my last day in New York City before moving to my new job as an assistant professor at the Harvard Business School (HBS). She knew I was addicted to fieldwork and foresaw that, despite the heavy teaching schedule awaiting me, I would need to get my fix. The school-ethnography idea was one of a dozen or so we batted around as we discussed possible projects. At the time it hardly registered on me.

After a few months in Boston, I began to see that she might have had a point. I had just completed a dissertation about an aeronautics factory and was surprised to find some parallels between it and my new employer. For one thing, the size of the student body (close to two thousand full-time students) called for the kind of standardization typical in large manufacturing settings. A sharp division of labor also seemed to prevail between faculty and support staff. And many processes at the School, including the steps required to prepare and teach courses, reminded me of a well-designed production line. Yet even then I discarded my advisor's suggestion and pursued other projects. I began, nonetheless, writing diary entries about my experience at the School that would later become field notes for this study. (I had developed the diary habit much earlier, in various settings, without academic intentions.)

Preoccupied with finding field sites exotic enough to sustain my interest for several years, I started scouting in the Boston area and began meeting with local business and labor leaders. Intriguing leads emerged from these conversations, but my interactions often centered as much on the School I had joined as on the sites these leaders worked in. My interlocutors would invariably inquire how I was doing at the School. After several such inquiries, I asked a slightly more experienced colleague if she got similar questions. "Regularly," she told me, and added with a smile that she always gave the same reply: "HBS is doing fine." Her switch from the individual to the collective level—from I to HBS—made us both laugh, and it stuck with me.

I like to believe that her reply led me to study the School's socialization of its faculty members and the possible implications of such socialization for student education. But that would be too easy an ex post facto rationalization. I have always enjoyed observing social patterns and reconstructing larger systems from their bits and pieces. (My older sister, who saw me in action early, says I have the soul of an anthropologist.) From the first day I set foot on the School's campus, I became intrigued by its stark contrast with the scruffier urban university environment I came from. As a new faculty member, too, I felt a need to figure out fast what my more senior colleagues already grasped that I did not yet fully comprehend. I could not avoid analyzing the School's setting.

At the Harvard Business School, the sheer number of students forces a routinization of the educational and sense-giving pursuit. Approximately nine hundred MBA students are admitted each year. For two years of their lives, they are immersed in a cohesive, shared endeavor. Though visitors might view the School as a semipublic and transitory setting, students experience it as a more durable and private space.[1] Most students eat, learn, sleep, and dream on campus, and their social life typically revolves around campus activities. Over the course of a typical week, they read a large number of instructional materials, discuss them in small groups, and then attend classes in which the materials are further analyzed. As this socialization unfolds, the School's roughly two hundred faculty members act a bit like ballet masters in an ongoing choreography. Though faculty members reside off campus, they also become socialized into the overall composition being performed. This intensive socialization process creates a certain social insularity, leading in turn to a distinct collective perspective.

The School's insularity is reinforced by the river that separates it from the rest of Harvard University and from the city of Cambridge. (The School is bounded on its other sides by a stadium, a railroad yard, and several acres of less-developed grounds.) The School's separateness brings to mind the islands that Bronislaw Malinowski described in his account of his time in the western Pacific.[2] Some of the surprising practices I initially encountered in the course of the School's daily life seemed to me as exotic as Malinowski's experiences in the Trobriand Islands. Finding exoticism at home was not what I expected when I joined the School. These early surprises became my daily fix; this book is their depository and outcome—an inquiry into the organizational underpinning of moral pursuits.

INTRODUCTION

Routinizing Morals

My pen, which is accustomed to figures, is unable to express the
march and rhythm of consonance; therefore I shall try to only
record the things I see, the things I think, or, to be more precise,
the things we think. Yes, "we," that is exactly what I mean, and we,
therefore, shall be the title of my records.

EVGENY ZAMYATIN, *We*

On a sunny day in July 2005, I was inducted into the "we" of the Harvard Business School's faculty. That day, a staff member guided me to my newly assigned office and introduced me to my faculty assistant. The assistant had prepared everything for my arrival, from paperclips to colored markers for the office whiteboard. My few old belongings barely filled a drawer. Two books that every incoming School faculty member received that year proved, in that sense, quite handy. Both were large and colorful, their green and yellow covers pleasing to the eye. More importantly, their titles—*Education for Judgment* and *Teaching and the Case Method*—seemed appropriate for a rookie's office.[1] I placed the books on an empty brown shelf; the setup now looked a bit brighter and more complete.

Despite these efforts, my office still felt quite silent and empty. When I swung my door closed, outside noises suddenly vanished. I knew other faculty probably experienced a similar silence, and I wondered how others filled that void. Maybe a plant would help? Or perhaps something more meaningful? I made a note to rummage through my belongings at home for something appropriate. Luckily, my colleagues regularly dropped by to welcome me and volunteer their help. They offered tips ranging from where to find food on campus to the names of people I should meet and events I might want to attend. Their visits also helped fill my new space. That day marked the start of my socialization into a unique perspective, one with more moral undertones than I ever expected—and one that remains, to this day, partly mysterious to me. The early juxtaposition of my silent office and my colleagues' vocal incursions foreshadowed, in an uncanny way, this book's main argument.

This book asks how moral conduct is encouraged in organizations and points to *vocal silence* as a possible means of upholding morals. I will specify below what the term entails, but it is probably sufficient, for now, to know that such silence creates a structured opportunity for friction between an individual's unspoken assumptions and the noisier collective he or she belongs to.[2] In vocal silence, an organizational member is left "alone" to make decisions, yet also hears whispers of a more distant collective guidance. Little did I know that day in July that such silence would prove so central to a faculty member's life and to the making of morals.

*   *   *

Manufacturing Morals examines an organization's attempt to promote morals via routines. Morals are shared understandings in which humans' highest aspirations and dreams come to fulfillment, and the underpinnings of many, if not all, collective human pursuits. Whether in everyday settings or at critical life junctures, morals allow us to distinguish right from wrong and good from bad.[3] They guide and justify thought and action in all arenas of social life.[4] The term *moral* is here defined as what a given community deems appropriate.[5] As an example, if a typical policeman on a given force believes "laying low" and making no waves is the best way to behave on the job, then such behavior would be labeled moral within that community of police officers.[6]

Between abstract morals and concrete individuals lie intermediary groups entrusted with ensuring proper socialization into those shared understandings. The families, schools, and faith communities we grow up in are obvious examples of such intermediaries.[7] Informal assemblies on sidewalks or street corners, or at neighborhood restaurants, can also act as intermediaries.[8] But many other entities, including professional groups and work organizations, also participate in the socializing enterprise.[9]

Scholars have studied this phenomenon in a range of organizations, from the Paris Opera to the World Bank.[10] Such entities offer their members an affiliation intimate enough to pervade the core of their everyday lives, yet distinct enough from any given individual for members to envision themselves as part of a broader pursuit. While such entities do not always achieve their goals, they often foster shared views among members.[11]

The existence of socialization dynamics in organizations is in itself no surprise; all of us who work in organizations have experienced them.[12] Every organization develops a distinct perspective among its members, consisting of the "patterns of thought and action" exhibited by members in response to specific internal organizational pressures.[13] Yet certain organizations, specifically those characterized by John Van Maanen as harboring "cultures of orientation," go beyond that and *purposely* aim to produce a particular perspective, often with moral undertones.[14] These organizations try to exert "normative control" by attempting to shape the experiences, thoughts, and feelings that guide their members' actions.[15] Most schools and universities exemplify such cultures.[16] Civic groups and nonprofit organizations typically aim to develop such cultures, as do many government agencies and for-profit companies. [17]

This book presents extensive research on the manufacture of morals in the context of one such organization. Few organizations aim to produce a shared perspective or set of morals as deliberately and consistently as the one presented here. And few have been doing so for as long, close to a century. The study looks at the mechanisms and conditions whereby such a distinct pattern of thought and action emerges, and addresses the difficult question of the routinization of morals.

The Problem with Routinizing Morals

Manufacturing Morals tries to answer the question that the sociologist Robin Leidner posed at the end of her 1993 study on the routinization of everyday life. Having shown that standardized interactions in the insurance and fast-food industries appear to conflict with, but do not rule out, sincere self-expression and personal connections, Leidner concluded, "We may wonder whether civility, trust, and personal integrity can be written into the scripts."[18] By scripts, Leidner meant a set of tasks that can be performed without significant conscious decision making on the part of those involved or of higher authorities in the organization—what others have labeled routines.[19] She does not address the steps that would be entailed in writing morals into these scripts or routines.

Put otherwise, Leidner asks whether morals can be transmitted in an organizational setting via scripts and routines. Moreover, does the process of scripting morals modify them or perhaps even destroy them? If so, how can morals endure? The founders of the Harvard Business School probably did not frame the organizational pursuit in terms of morals and routines, but the School, I will argue, is a pertinent setting in which to examine such questions. When I began this project, I did not intend to pick up where Leidner left off. Yet the analyses presented in the following chapters help answer her concluding question by showing how an organization goes about fostering a particular moral perspective via routines.

Morals and routines have traditionally been viewed as mutually exclusive. Indeed, past scholarship has noted the difficulty of writing morals "into the script." Max Weber hinted, for instance, at the inherent tensions between morals and routines. According to Weber, an individual's "exemplary character" and associated "normative patterns or order" are antithetical to routines.[20] Because character presupposes individual volition, the notion of routinizing character seems like a self-contradictory proposition. A person cannot simultaneously be deemed responsible and blindly follow a script. Weber's conception of routines as mainly constraining forces that crush individual character explains why he saw this paradox of agency and structure as largely insurmountable.

Similarly, Leidner's doubts about the coexistence of morals and routines rest on an acceptance of routines as involving virtually no decision making on the part of participants.[21] As she notes, "The efforts of organizations to routinize human interactions violate important cultural standards about the status of the self, standards that honor authenticity, autonomy, sincerity, and individuality."[22] The same could be said of the individual's ability to act morally (seemingly) independently, that is, to pick a proper course of action in the absence of external guidance or even gentle nudging.

Since routines are mainly seen as inducing automatic reactions, they can easily be understood as antithetical to the essence of morals. By shifting responsibility from the individual to the organization, routines and rules are de facto disempowering. Carol Heimer elaborates this point by noting that organizational members' responses are made "essentially irrelevant by the obligation to follow organizational injunctions."[23] Put more bluntly, organizations that rely heavily on rules and routines are often depicted as "vast systems of organized irresponsibility."[24] In such a view, morals and routines are seen as incompatible. A study of faculty socialization at the Harvard Business School offers an opportunity to revisit this assumption.

Methodological Approach: A Faculty View from Below

At its most basic level, this book presents an ethnography of work—one aiming to populate an account of a particular setting with the lives of (some of) its working members.[25] The study provides an account from the standpoint of a worker (here, a junior faculty member) of how a distinct organizational perspective is manufactured at the School.[26] In that sense, the study documents a view from below that hopefully echoes, if it does not completely represent, the perspectives of other untenured faculty members.[27] Since an organizational perspective often serves as a solution to internal problems created by particular organizational pressures, the key to uncovering such a perspective lies in identifying its members' *recurring* problems and solutions.[28] Thus this book favors these problems (e.g., how to dress and how to lead a class discussion) over others.[29] Hence, the study focuses primarily on internal dynamics.[30] As in Norbert Elias's study of princely courts, the goal is to decipher the particular internal etiquette that binds School faculty members together.[31] I rely on analyses of specific internal practices to capture what the moral pursuit entails and how faculty members are enrolled in it. Theories of morals-as-practices inform this choice.[32]

The total-participant position is ideal for examining the links between morals and practices. Indeed, it is only by virtue of having taught several years at the School (particularly in its MBA program) that I have been able to observe the making of a "proper" faculty member.[33] In the same way that the ethnographer Julian E. Orr was able to write about technicians' lives because he had worked as a technician, my work at the School enabled me to see the organizational process from the inside. Also, my inexperience forced upon me an urgent desire to adapt and learn the "manufacturing" process, rather than to take it for granted. The book thus documents an initiation into a new setting: a typical ethnographic data-collection strategy. The data for this study consist primarily of journal entries and field notes taken during my five years (at the time of collection) as an assistant professor at the School. (See appendix for a detailed description of my data and methods.) The entries and notes document in local terms a School faculty member's life in a given time and place—what Jack Katz refers to as a "worker's ethnography," which often captures the anxiety of a novice.[34]

Just as studying a physician's initiation can teach us something about how physicians educate their patients about medicine, studying a faculty member's initiation can provide some insight into how faculty members educate their students on their topic of instruction.[35] When studying organizations engaged in interactive work, such as service providers and universities, two populations typically coexist: those directly employed by the organization (e.g., faculty members) and those to whom the organization caters (e.g., students).[36] Faculty members are not the only components of the machinery that "mints" students, but they are probably the representatives of the universities with whom students spend the most *focused* time during their course of study.[37] In that sense, faculty members are also crucial employees, instrumental in upholding a given perspective.[38] Indirectly, they transmit the organizational perspective to individuals they repeatedly interact with. In this study's context, these individuals include men and women who will go on to lead major corporations.[39] Thus, assuming some cascading socialization dynamics and given the profile of School graduates, the study might also help us gain a better grasp of corporate morals.[40]

Conducting a study of a setting in which one is deeply embedded is not without challenges. For example, writing from the perspective of an untenured junior faculty member might suggest that I was at the mercy of my senior colleagues' whims and therefore lacked autonomy.[41] Issues of objectivity, conflicts of interest, and career pressure can be seen as interfering with data collection and analysis. These are valid considerations, not to be dismissed swiftly. To quote the opening of Pierre Bourdieu's study of French academics: "By taking as our object of study the world in which

we are implicated, we are forced to encounter a certain number of fundamental epistemological problems."[42] Bourdieu warns readers about the
difficulty of detaching oneself from the "indigenous" experience and emphasizes the importance of doing so in order to "reconnect" with the object of study. I went to great lengths to ensure distance *and* involvement
(see appendix). The reader can judge whether the detachment and recon-
nection succeeded.

My choice of setting and method does impose some obvious limitations. First, the study does not have much to say about the extent to which
faculty members become socialized. It can only document a *process* of
socialization, not its outcome. Second, the study does not reflect the views
of more senior School faculty members or of other faculty subpopula-
tions undergoing such socialization.[43] For instance, a clear limitation of
my approach is that it does not directly capture female faculty members'
experiences at the School. Third, the study is not about students' firsthand
experiences at the School. Others have much more directly captured and
analyzed those experiences.[44] The study does, however, document some
of the inner workings of a distinct higher-educational pursuit.[45] Whether
the research project has been successful from the perspectives of administrators, students, or other faculty members is for them to assess. At the
very least, they might discover an alternate view of their daily setting.[46]
Familiarity with the study's setting is, however, not required to read this
book. The less you know, the more exotic the journey will be. Moreover,
the setting serves only as a pretext for a broader inquiry.

Main Argument: Vocal Silence

The findings presented in this book rest on a dynamic view of routines
and suggest a largely overlooked way to routinize morals—one that moves
beyond Weber's agency and structure dilemma. From a theoretical viewpoint, the dynamic nature of routines has often been neglected.[47] As Martha S. Feldman and Brian T. Pentland remind us, not all routines exclude
participants' discretion.[48] Even filling out forms, a typical routine, allows
a good deal of discretion. Police officers can, for instance, selectively include or exclude pertinent details in their arrest reports.[49] Similarly, hiring

and budgeting routines can take on various meanings depending on who performs them. Individuals' active engagement in routines introduces dynamism into apparently mundane organizational life.[50] Thus, routines do not always coincide with "irresponsibility." Moreover, some routines (like vocal silence) not only permit but promote individual discretion. Such routines refrain from fully stabilizing what is ultimately assumed to grow from an individual's private judgment.

What does vocal (organizational) silence entail? Organizational silence is defined as a routine that requires *significant* decision making on the part of those involved, *with little direct guidance* from higher authorities.[51] For instance, a routine that calls for an instructor to grade students' assignments without higher authorities having specified any evaluative criteria qualifies as organizational silence. Similarly, a routine that calls for doormen to screen visitors for security risks without higher authorities specifying what such concerns might entail constitutes organizational silence. More broadly, whenever a routine calls for an individual to pass a judgment or make a call without specifying precisely how to do so, the routine embodies organizational silence.

By vocal silence, I mean that the routine is embedded in an organizational context rich in normative signs. Indeed, the absence of direct guidance from higher authorities does not equate with the absence of any guidance. Past scholarship has correctly noted that organizations harbor many *indirect* signs suggesting normative views.[52] Anything that is perceptible in a given setting can be a sign, whether intended as a form of communication or not. For instance, the ways other members talk about the organization or convey particular expectations to each other all indicate what conduct is considered proper. Signals, by contrast, are observable phenomena intentionally displayed for the purpose of shaping the receiver's impression and raising the probability of select outcomes.[53] Unlike (direct) signals that tell members precisely what to do, (indirect) signs point to what might be doable.[54] Hence, an abundance of signs can render any organizational behavior articulate, regardless of its apparent intent. Signs are the vocal elements of vocal silence.

We know that a prime function of silence is to allow for ambiguity.[55] Vocal silence still permits ambiguity, but also partly restricts it. Such relative silence encourages some disagreement while simultaneously constraining variation in outcomes. Instead of resolving the tension between agency and structure, vocal silence aims to partly preserve it. Indeed, members' participation is necessary to solve the silent conundrum.[56] The coupling of discretion and rigidity creates, within limits, the seeds of internal dissonance.[57] Since little seems set in stone, various potentially distinct views can coexist in these routines. In that sense, vocal silences allow for the repeated, seemingly private reenactment of morals in apparent voids.

Whether a model of vocal silence offers opportunities for awakening or the mere illusion of awakening remains open to debate. At a minimum, it encourages the perception of self-determination to prevail. Autonomy becomes partly reconciled with adherence to shared understandings through members' experience of individual discretion. Hence, a model of "inverted principal-agent" control, in which agents are ostensibly free to decide the course of their actions yet partly controlled by the principals surrounding them, might prove to be the key to large-scale moral pursuits.[58] (An agent ends up with fewer degrees of freedom than most economists might assume.) More specifically, by managing the tension between individual decision making and collective aspiration, vocal silence can provide a solution to the puzzle of routinizing morals. I will ground this argument in the context of the Harvard Business School.

Study's Context: The Harvard Business School

A medical school, a nursing school, or a school of social work might seem better suited than a business school as a site for research on socialization into a given moral perspective, since those settings more visibly train for professions with strong normative underpinnings. But the skill set taught in many elite American business schools, including the one I studied, would be quite limited were it not for its social component. If the goal were only the acquisition of technical skills, vocational schools could (and historically did) easily supplant today's elite university-affiliated business schools.[59] Rather, the education offered by faculty members at many leading business schools taps into what students become and involves socialization into a new, or at least a newly salient, perspective—one that I will argue is eminently moral in nature.[60]

Not all business schools embrace such goals or are as explicit about it as the one I studied. The moral trope is probably more prominent at the schools that Debra Schleef describes as "high-ranked."[61] Moreover, not all high-ranked business schools embrace the same model.[62] Thus the findings presented in this book do not apply to all business schools, let alone all organizations.[63] The book's findings do apply, however, to any organization, academic or not, that aims to promote a certain normative view of society among its members. Examples include organizations as diverse as the Girl Scouts of the USA, the Church of Jesus Christ of Latter-Day Saints, and the Whole Foods supermarket chain.[64] Historically, many elite US colleges also belonged on such a list. "In America," the historian Daniel Boorstin writes, "the college became a place concerned more with the diffusion than the advancement or perpetuation of learning." Boorstin points out that "each of the three earliest colleges—Harvard, William & Mary, Yale—was founded to support the established church of its particular colony," suggesting that from the outset such colleges engaged in socialization alongside education.[65] Likewise, I posit that the emergence of elite US university-based business schools was primarily a socialization endeavor, if not a *civilizing* project in the sense that Norbert Elias has employed the term, to characterize undertakings that promote selected behaviors.[66]

The historical milieu from which business schools emerged—US society in the nineteenth century—generated in part the moral imperative found in many elite US business schools today. As Charles Perrow explains, the manufacturing elite that was emerging was a motley bunch that included gentlemen with landed wealth and wealthy merchants, but also farmers, small businessmen, and craftsmen. "Indeed, the emerging elite could be almost anything, as long as they were white and not Irish."[67] As Perrow concludes, "There were few established traditions that might be blindly followed." In that context, an aspirational socialization project on the part of the emerging elite was hardly surprising. As Rakesh Khurana points out, "Just as the case for science as a vehicle for ordering society and achieving social progress was sometimes conflated with an argument for science as an intrinsically moral activity, the language used by the academic [business school] entrepreneurs promoting managerial science sometimes implied that it, too, was essentially a moral and ethical vehicle."[68] The conflation of managerial science and morals helped cement the need to de-

velop schools that would ensure proper training of this growing segment
of society.

The mandate of these elite business schools, in other words, was to
teach not merely how to run a business, but also how a business *should*
be run.[69] And this moral imperative was endorsed by many early figures
central to university-based business education.[70] The Harvard Business
School's first dean embraced such a view and defined business as the "activity of making things to sell at a profit—decently."[71] The use of the term
decently underlined his hope for developing a heightened sense of responsibility among businessmen. Similarly, the School's second dean viewed
the development, strengthening, and multiplication of "socially minded
businessmen" as a central goal of business education.[72] "The multiplication of men who will handle their current business problems in socially
constructive ways" also became the goal of other business schools. Elite
business schools found a language to explain and justify their pursuit.
Their faculty members became keepers of this language.

The establishment of the Harvard Graduate School of Business was true
to this spirit. In 1908, Harvard University's president justified the decision to launch the venture by noting that "business in its upper walks has
become a highly intellectual calling." The invocation of a calling attributes
a sacred nature to the endeavor.[73] The notion also lends not only personal
but also societal significance to students' future work.[74] Other evidence
confirms the framing of business education as a sacred, almost religious,
path, likening businessmen to ministers. At the dedication of the School's
new campus in 1927, the chairman of General Electric predicted that the
Harvard Graduate School of Business "will do its utmost to guard against
an illiterate ministry of business when our present ministers shall lie in
the dust."[75] Clear links were being drawn between the School's goals and
morals.

Repeatedly over the School's history, the moral project was reiterated.
At the School's founding, Harvard University's president explained that,
given the enormous growth of the business sector, "a definite forward
step" had to be made "in sustaining the ethical standards [of business]."[76]
The School's first great benefactor, George F. Baker, president of the First
National Bank, was also quite explicit about his overarching goal. "My life
has been given to business," Baker explained in 1924, "and I should like

to found the first Graduate School to give a new start to better business standards."[77] With time the School's goals broadened, but the moral imperative remained prominent. In 1963, for instance, the School's catalog listed "character" and "integrity" as qualities of a "good administrator."[78] More recently, in 1992, the dean quoted an alumnus's disappointment "at how frequently the graduates of some of our finest business and law schools were involved, in one way or another, in the cases being brought before the SEC [Securities and Exchange Commission]." The dean invoked this observation to support his conclusion that "surely the school had a bigger responsibility and a role to play in all of this."[79] Specifically, the role of everyday moral practice caught the attention of successive School administrators.[80]

Promoting better business standards was, however, not the School's only, or even its main, objective. As the historian Alfred Chandler notes, the initial course offerings indicate a more immediate preoccupation with training, in sufficient numbers, managers capable of working for increasingly complex multinational enterprises.[81] Moreover, the School's moral ambitions were repeatedly challenged.[82] As early as 1930, critics questioned the moral claims of the endeavor. What skills, for instance, were really being promoted, besides selling, buying, accounting, and trading?[83] In the 1970s, two close observers of US education remarked that the field of business administration was "less immediately focused" on broad social problems than were other academic disciplines and was not particularly intent on changing the normative order of society.[84] Notwithstanding such critics, the intent of the School's administration to promulgate higher business standards cannot be entirely discounted. A moral agenda motivated the School's creation, at least rhetorically. This book attempts to understand how a perspective that embodies such standards is produced and routinized today.

Outline of the Book's Contents

In the chapters that follow, I detail the model of vocal silence that incoming junior faculty members encounter at the School. The book's organization gradually draws the reader deeper into the School's inner "plumbing" by looking at how the various organizational pieces combine to solve the problem of routinizing morals; it then extends the solution to other contexts. By the end of the book, I hope, readers will be able to apply its findings to their own contexts, and to understand the hopes and limits of routinizing moral pursuits.

The first two chapters show how the School's working context (both physical and academic) points to a particular view of the world. Chapter 1 is a guided visit to the School's physical environment. It suggests an attempt to transform a densely populated community into a more ordered one and points to the harmonious coexistence on campus of distinct populations, such as faculty, staff, and students. Thus, the harmonious, stratified small town as a natural setting for activity is perhaps the first and most evident vocal background at the School.

Chapter 2 shows that the ordering enterprise extends to the academic labor market as well. The promotion of a distinct perspective within the faculty is shown to rely essentially on assessing performance according to a fairly School-specific formula. Many other schools and universities enforce a "publish-or-perish" model that outsources the assessment of their faculties' performance to guardians of academic subfields, but the School's parallel focus on managerial relevance adds complexity to this assessment. Indeed, relevance is regarded as almost sacred and fully as important as scholarship. Many incoming junior faculty members find the School's scholarly norms to be at odds with those that were inculcated during their training. They gradually grasp, for instance, that conducting *relevant* research is different from simply conducting research. Similarly, the emphasis on disseminating research findings to a broader audience, including nonacademics, is novel for many newcomers. By creating a new metric to assess academic purity, the School promotes a fairly vocal view of business scholarship.

The next three chapters document how, despite such vocal cues, the School goes to great lengths to script relative silence in otherwise well-oiled faculty routines. With respect to teaching and other activities, *all but* morals appears to be scripted. Chapter 3 describes a typical teaching session from start to finish and documents the School's many supporting routines designed to facilitate skillful in-class delivery. From pre-teaching faculty group meetings to pre-session reviews of which students to call on during upcoming class discussions, much organizational effort goes into ensuring the consistent delivery of courses. In contrast to matters of delivery, a session's take-away—particularly its moral lesson—is relatively free of direct organizational guidance.

This combination of rigidity and discretion also characterizes key organizational artifacts supporting classroom teaching, namely case teaching notes. Chapter 4 reports on an analysis of a random sample of teaching notes from the first-year MBA curriculum. First-year MBA students are divided into subgroups, called sections, with close to ninety students each. The section provides a highly social small-world experience in which faculty members are partly entrusted with students' learning. All sections follow a similar curriculum. The teaching notes that accompany most class sessions help faculty members prepare their courses and might predetermine outcomes. Analysis shows, however, that while much is scripted in these notes (e.g., the leading question with which to open the discussion of a case), the overarching purpose of the cases remains largely unspecified. In that sense, teaching notes support the development of partially discretionary behavior among faculty members.

Teaching is not the only arena where vocal silence prevails. Chapter 5 delves more deeply into faculty members' nonteaching activities to better understand what perspectives might be favored by the School. Besides teaching, for instance, faculty members are expected to patrol continued community membership. They are charged with deciding which students who "hit the screen" (i.e., underperform academically) should be deemed worthy of continued membership. In addition, faculty members are expected to command proper earnings when taking on external jobs (e.g., consulting engagements). By proper earnings, I mean either earnings high enough to align with the School's prestige or, when the work is deemed "worthy," no earnings at all. Again, faculty members enjoy discretion when deciding which students are worthy of membership or what faculty work merits forsaking compensation. Both routines also refrain from stabilizing what proper behavior might entail.

Given the uncertainty surrounding faculty members' discretionary behaviors, chapter 6 examines the "quality control" needed in such an organizational model. Vocal silence only functions because it is left to the discretion of "known" individuals in a context rich in indirect signs. This chapter shows that, to achieve consistency, the School historically relied on a cadre of mostly internally trained faculty members—individuals whose highest academic degrees were conferred by the School or by Harvard University. Once such faculty members were brought in and promoted, the School's administration needed only to focus its efforts on course preparation, delivery, and maintenance, with less attentiveness to overall goals. Increasing the hiring of externally trained faculty helps expand the educational endeavor but also creates complications for a system that, almost by design, does not explicitly specify normative views. Changes in faculty composition that are too dramatic can easily undermine the School's capacity to manage quality control and lead to slippage in the preferred perspective.[85] Without collective efforts focused on the contents of morals, the prevailing understanding of what proves moral can gradually shift. That said, the School's context still harbors many vocal signs to bound what happens in a faculty member's "private" discretionary realm.[86] Combined, these signs delineate limits within which discretion is exercised. Overall, such an organizational model of vocal silence creates some ambiguity, which allows, within limits, multiple viewpoints to coexist.

The book's conclusion revisits the question of the hopes and limits of routinizing moral pursuits in light of the above analyses. I also discuss the study's implications for our understanding of higher education and corporate morals. First, I summarize the vocal silence solution to the problem of routinizing morals. In doing so, I also specify key attributes of the vocal silence model, many of which can be viewed both as organizational strengths and as shortcomings. In light of the study's findings, I argue that depending on one's understanding of the nature of the moral project, vocal silence might or might not be the best way to organize a social community. More specifically, I argue that while moral orders—or compliance with shared understandings—tend to require voice, moral pursuits—or the (re)discovery of these understandings—often rest on partial silence.[87] Thus, under certain circumstances, vocal silence might be more generative than its muteness suggests.

The goal of scripting "civility" and "decency" in organizations is highly appealing since it contains the hope of scaling up a desired moral pursuit, and thus the potential to affect a large number of people. At the same time, such scripting is often resisted since it is thought to destroy morals.

(Morals, in this view, need to be internalized to be authentic.) My hope is that the study's findings will help move the debate beyond this stalled dichotomy.[88] By focusing not only on what routines dictate, but also on what they permit, this book provides a novel lens with which to analyze morals and organizational routines. Routines do not merely constrain; they can also enable. Scripting vocal silence might seem like a risky solution, partly because it relies on the hope that, at the individual level, the desired perspective will almost magically emerge. Furthermore, scripting vocal silence might seem costly to some organizational members, since it curtails the possible range of morals. An apparently risky and costly solution may nonetheless be the price to pay for morals to endure.

ONE

A Footbridge to
the World

Up and up we sailed, way up at first, to get "the lay of the land"
and make note of it. . . . "Let's make the first trip geographical," I
suggested. "Spy out the land, and drop back here for more gasoline.
With your tremendous speed we can reach the range and back all
right. Then we can leave a sort of map on board—for that relief
expedition."

CHARLOTTE PERKINS GILMAN, *Herland*

It is seven-thirty in the morning. On my walk to campus, several streets
lined with two- and three-story wooden houses gently curve toward the
riverbank across from the School. My alarm clock is set for six-thirty, but
on teaching days an alarm is rarely necessary. I instinctively wake up at six;
the anticipation of the upcoming class session is a potent enough alarm.
Oarsmen practicing on the river occupy the foreground; behind them are
the School's main buildings, notably the library, which towers over the
campus. From afar, the size of the campus is imposing, the view strikingly
beautiful and impressive.[1] Crossing the Charles River to reach the School
on sunny days is like walking into a postcard.

Many paths lead to campus. The one I take, officially known as the
John W. Weeks Bridge, is commonly called "the footbridge" because it is
for pedestrians only. The footbridge's vicinity is messier than other parts of
the campus and the town, contrasting sharply with the neatness to come.
Colonies of wild geese generously fertilize the riverbank, and their loose
feathers dot the grass. Overgrown shrubs call for attentiveness to where
one sets one's feet. Also, in warm weather a few individuals, probably

The "unsafe" John W. Weeks footbridge. Photo by Catherine Hammond.

homeless, sleep near the footbridge. "Watch out for the footbridge," I was advised early on. "It's not safe. You don't want to go there." Yet it is the most direct route from my house to my office, and a regular flow of human traffic and an emergency call box linked to the university's central police dispatcher provide me a sense of enough security.

Having cleared the river, a pedestrian endures one final annoyance before reaching campus: the burst of noise and exhaust from cars speeding under the much shorter span that extends the bridge across a major traffic artery. But entering the quiet and tidy campus renders this last stretch almost worthwhile. The sudden contrast is welcome; it highlights what the campus has to offer: a separate, insular, ordered, and fairly vocal world.

* * *

The architect who oversaw the competition to build the campus rightly noted that the winning plan did not "open up the whole group [of buildings] to public inspection from outside."[2] Indeed, the campus forms a rather cohesive, closed community, and approaching on foot makes one feel lucky to be part of that community. As George F. Baker, the campus's main financial underwriter, had hoped, one is struck by "an atmosphere of quiet, good taste appropriate to an old university."[3] Such an atmosphere results from the assembly of distinct physical elements—all combining to form an ordered setting.

Physical layouts and their usage patterns provide critical cues to understanding social behaviors. They signal not only what behaviors actually occur but what behaviors are encouraged. The aesthetics of the layout can be seen as a manifestation of underlying theories of social behavior. For instance, similar assumptions drove the rise of European modernist architecture and the development of scientific management.[4] As Mauro Guillén, who studied these developments notes, an architectural aesthetic is "not necessarily a rational element, but it is a rationalized one."[5] That is, distinct social orders become consistent with specific aesthetics and vice versa. Aside from its often perceived inherent beauty, I am beginning with the School's physical setting because aesthetics point to ways individuals are expected to behave.

A Small, Quiet Town

The campus's plantings and buildings contrast sharply with the banks of the nearby river. A pedestrian entering the campus suddenly encounters perfectly trimmed lawns and impeccably maintained buildings. Regardless of the season, the grounds are pristine. Landscaping crews are constantly at work trimming trees, mowing grass, patching holes in the pavement, and shoveling snow. In winter, before the first snowfall, the corners of the main lawns are marked with colored wooden sticks so snow-removal teams will know where to halt their golf cart–size plows. In the fall, leaves are meticulously assembled in piles at a distance from the main paths and then trucked out of sight. All the paths linking the periphery of the campus to its main buildings, such as the library and faculty offices, are invariably cleared to facilitate circulation.

The quiet that reigns on campus is surprising given its size and density. With more than thirty-four acres of land devoted exclusively to the educational endeavor and a daytime "permanent" population of close to thirty-two hundred—faculty, staff, and MBA and doctoral students—the campus feels

A leaf-cleaning crew on campus. Photo by Erin McFee.

like a small town.[6] (This number excludes the more than nine thousand yearly executive-education enrollees, who typically spend only a few weeks on campus, as well as residents of student housing who are unaffiliated with the School.) The prevailing impression of quietude is partly due to the fact that all shipping and receiving takes place at a centralized location on the periphery of campus. From that location, all incoming and outgoing goods (including food and trash) are dispatched underground without disrupting life on the surface.

The campus is closed to most motor vehicles, a rule that encourages face-to-face encounters along the walking paths. Taxis, and often black limousines, patiently wait for their clients on the campus' margins. As the campus master plan explains, the restriction on vehicles "was designed to optimize the sense of being in a landscaped pedestrian precinct."[7] Most traffic disappeared from campus in the 1980s, and "scores of trees and thousands of flowers where cars and trucks had once dominated" now dominate the landscape.[8] When a car does enter the campus, bystanders see it only briefly. Campus roads are strategically curved so that no extended stretch of asphalt is visible from any point on campus. Such visual shielding of the bystander's perspective helps provide "as much domestic feeling as [is] reasonable" to the grounds.[9]

These scaling strategies have been integral to the campus's design, both at its inception and today. When students first moved to the School's current location, the idea of a small residential community already prevailed.[10] Much effort was deployed to achieve a small-town feeling despite the fairly large student cohort (521 students in 1926).[11] For instance, each student residence used to have its own dining room. Though the annual entering cohort has almost doubled since the 1920s, a communal atmosphere has been preserved.

To place this in the context of other community studies, the campus's daytime population is approximately one-quarter that of the early number of residents in Herbert Gans's study of a US suburban community that he called Levittown (3,221 versus 11,861), yet the campus occupies less than 1 percent of that suburb's total area (34 acres versus 4,928 acres), making for a much denser, more intense living environment.[12] To offer another reference point, the campus houses approximately as many daytime occupants as the housing complex in Boston's South End studied by Mario

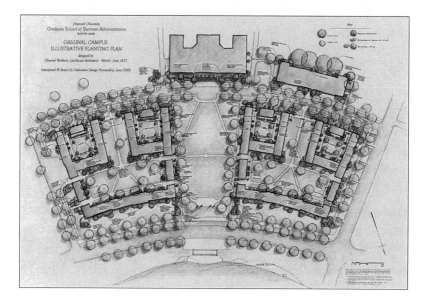

The original communal Campus Master Plan. From "The Original Landscape Design of the Harvard Business School, 1925–1927" (Halvorson Company, 2000).

Luis Small (with 3,000 people) but occupies almost twice its 20 acres.[13] Put otherwise, the campus is comparable in population to a small town or a neighborhood in a large city, and to the latter in area.

Unlike most towns and neighborhoods, the campus has, however, almost no signage to guide visitors. Benefactors' names (like Bloomberg and Morgan) adorn buildings, but apparently more to recognize the donors' generosity than to provide orientation.[14] Temporary signposts are selectively erected to guide new arrivals at the start of a new school year or a new program, but they are removed within days, once their purpose is achieved. In a residential community, it is assumed that community members know where they are going. On average, some 70 percent of students reside on campus. Second-year students are slightly more inclined to live off-campus than first-year students, but many remain on-site. In executive-education programs as well, most participants board on campus.

The School's residential feel explains why its grounds represent for students not just their weekday environment but also their nighttime and weekend environment. For students, the School is sometimes characterized as "a twenty-four-hour, non-stop educational experience."[15] Moreover, until the late 1950s, many faculty members resided on campus, especially unmarried instructors.[16] Today, only the School's dean maintains a dedicated on-campus residence. Still, the notion of a residential campus, envisioned shortly after the School's creation, persists.[17]

Small towns provide many opportunities to interact, and I invariably bump into individuals I know (including students) on my way to work. Even on the far side of the river, before reaching campus, such encounters are frequent. Students typically wear an outer jacket emblazoned with the School's crest, their graduation year, and their section affiliation, and so are easily spotted. (Each entering MBA cohort is divided into ten sections of approximately ninety students each, designated with a letter and their graduation year, for example, Section B 2010). I quickly learned to greet most, if not all, people close to campus. Elementary politeness and the slim chance of failing to recognize a current or former student dictate the behavior. The number of people one "knows" quickly grows. A faculty member who teaches two sections a year will have taught approximately 360 students by the end of the second year.[18]

Once on campus, encounters follow more predictable patterns. At specific

The silent library tower. Photo by Han Lei.

hours, notably before the start of class periods, orderly flows of people move smoothly from one location to another. Despite some modifications, the campus paths originally designed "to convey pedestrians directly and unambiguously from origin to destination" still do so quite effectively.[19] To ease circulation and shorten waits at the dining halls, class periods for different student groups are staggered. Second-year students' earliest classes begin at 8:30 a.m., for instance, whereas first-year students typically start at 8:40 a.m. (The two-year MBA curriculum consists of a series of first-year required courses and second-year electives.) One might expect to hear the library's tower bell at the start and end of each period, but a tolling bell would invariably disrupt classes in progress; thus the tower rules silently over campus.[20]

Despite its silence, the library tower embodies the School's history, and in particular its shifting relationship to Harvard University. During the period between the School's founding and its move to the current campus (1908–1926), the School's collections were held at Harvard's main library. Yet "some members of the University who never had become reconciled with the establishment of what they termed a mercenary enterprise" resented such commingling.[21] (More virulent critics suggested that the university disown its Graduate School of Business and let it become the "Boston School of Business.")[22] A dedicated library on the School's campus diminished these criticisms. The library's current bell is a replica of an earlier bell, part of a set of eighteen bells made in Russia for Harvard College, that was sent to the School when it became apparent that two of the bells were too similar in tone to be sounded together.[23] That some deemed the School's books unwelcome at the university library and that the School was considered an appropriate home for an unwanted bell suggest an initially tenuous position within the university. Almost seventy years later, a School alumnus helped secure newly consecrated bells both for the School and for Harvard College. (The acquisition and consecration of the new bells occurred upon the return of the original bells to Russia.) This time around, the School was instrumental in helping the college secure its new bell, one indication of its improved standing vis-à-vis the university. A commemorative plaque in front of the School's library informs passersby of this history.

Shaping and Taming Nature

Passing the library in the morning, I often spot new plantings. Flowering annuals are replaced after their blooming seasons with later-blooming annuals. Plants without leaves are rapidly and mysteriously unearthed. Even the sudden appearance of full-grown trees—blocking the view from the campus of a new building on the School's periphery that clashes stylistically with the rest of the campus—comes to seem almost normal: shaping nature is an activity that most people at the School gradually come to expect. School members' ability to spot such changes underlines the care with which grounds are maintained but also suggests an acquired taste for expecting neatness.

That most flowers on campus are white is not a mere gardener's whim. White, according to the Olmsted brothers' initial landscaping plan, contrasts pleasingly with the buildings' red brick and echoes their white painted trim.[24] White-flowered shrubs and trees such as Japanese barberry, white fringe trees, and yellowwood allow the buildings to stand out, and the sheer variety of plants provides "a measure of informality and diversity to the rigid forms created by the buildings."[25] The sight of visitors photographing flowering trees and rabbits perched on the grass hardly registers on most campus occupants. Tourists replicating the postcard that is the campus blend into the landscape and validate its beauty.

Quiet mornings offer many sightings of rabbits and New England squirrels. They roam around in search of food like other rabbits and squirrels, but a running joke has it that the School's squirrels are regularly shampooed.[26] Nobody believes this, of course, but it is hard not to look at them more closely when they stand upright in the grass. They do look well groomed with their shiny fur. Despite their implausibility, jokes, like myths, often capture uneasy truths and tensions about the setting to which they refer.[27] The pretense that squirrels, by simply residing on campus, become pampered echoes in an uncanny manner the School's overt endeavor to create a "transformational experience" for its students.[28]

After a few months, the grounds' neatness becomes so familiar that any disturbance immediately catches the eye. Early one morning, for instance, I spotted something unusual in the grass: a small, white object disturbing the regularity of the lawn.[29] It was flat, narrow, and pointed, and turned out to be a collar stay. I was surprised that such a nuisance had not yet been removed. By noon, when I passed the same spot, it had disappeared. Other times, I spotted "disturbances" that turned out to be purposeful. Another morning I noticed in the grass what looked like a large bike lock attached to the leg of a heavy wooden bench. I remember first thinking it strange that someone would forget a bike lock there. But the next bench along the path also had a lock attached to its leg. They had been put there to prevent theft. They also prevent the benches from being moved, thus ensuring their orderly placement.[30]

Order and neatness are further enhanced on campus by the architectural similarity of building facades. With few exceptions, the School's buildings are built in a neo-Georgian architectural style. Their facades, redbrick with white painted trim, evoke the nation's beginnings.[31] One focal point of the architectural plan, besides the library, is a large student center described by its architect as "unmistakably *Harvard*" and by other observers as "a very nice country club."[32] At the building's dedication in 2001, the architect explained that "a university had to have its own brand, just as a corporation or a product does." For campus residents and visitors alike, the School's brand is easily recognizable. Though reminiscent of other New England college settings, it stands out as perhaps more imposing and cohesive. With twenty-nine buildings totaling 1.2 million square feet, the sheer volume of red brick, white trim, and surrounding white flowers is imposing.[33] The architectural consistency of buildings dating from 1926 and more recent additions conveys cohesion and suggests purposeful efforts to shape and tame nature.

Ensuring Neatness Indoors

Within seconds of entering a faculty office building, one forgets the human density outside. Two sets of doors—green painted wood outside, glass inside—keep temperature changes at bay. A faculty or staff identity card is needed to enter the buildings outside of regular hours, making them fairly secluded.[34] A small food cart and the soothing sound of a fountain greet arrivals at the main faculty building, Morgan Hall. Named for the nineteenth-century banker John Pierpont Morgan, it houses close to 170 faculty members and about half as many faculty assistants and other support staff. All faculty buildings are adjacent to the library; faculty members belonging to the same academic unit, such as finance or marketing, are clustered on the same floor.

The cart can cater to the occupants' food needs for the entire day. It serves mostly coffee, along with fruit, pastries, and oatmeal in the morning; soup, sandwiches, salads, and a few more elaborate dishes at lunch; and more coffee and cake in the afternoon. The card that gains one entrance to the building can be also used to pay, making cash and credit cards unnecessary on campus. Before heading to their offices, occupants pass a large mosaic, surrounded by a fountain, on the ground floor of a three-story atrium. Because the mosaic measures almost five hundred square feet, its design can be fully grasped only from several stories up. (It used to line the bottom of a public bath in ancient Antioch.) At its center, the sea goddess Tethys gazes serenely. Like the library bell, the mosaic was not originally intended for the School; it was meant for the university's Fogg Museum, located across the river at Harvard College, but its size precluded installation there. After decades in storage off-campus, it was acquired by the School in 1989 and installed a few years later. Morgan Hall was one of the few university buildings large enough to accommodate it.[35] The mosaic conveys a sense of timelessness in the campus's densely populated environment and causes most newcomers to pause.

As I enter my office on the third floor, I hang my coat in a closet large enough for several suits, drop my bag on the couch, check the light on my phone for waiting voice-mail messages, and log in to my computer. The default screen saver, Harvard's Veritas crest, greets me. My office is typical of a professor's office: a desk, a chair, a bookcase . . . and seating charts. During teaching semesters, these large color printouts, twenty-four by thirty-inches, adorn most faculty members' walls, usually directly above the desk. Each chart provides a visual representation of an amphitheater-like classroom, from the instructor's perspective. Its purpose is to help the instructors identify their students. Seats are assigned, and each seat on the chart bears a student's name and photo. The charts look like blowups from a high-school yearbook or a wanted poster in an exceptionally busy police precinct. They are printed several days before the start of classes, and their arrival signals the imminent start of a new semester.

The addition of some of the School's standard features, namely size and neatness, complete the picture. The offices are large, fully 250 square feet.[36] For visitors, the impression of size is heightened by the presence—in every office, regardless of its occupant's rank—of a sofa large enough for three guests and a wooden coffee table.[37] The sofas are fairly uniform: firm with textured fabric in matching blue, gray, and green tones. Visitors perceive them as luxurious amenities, but faculty members joke that these couches are provided so they can sleep at the office during snowstorms or other unexpected events. The subtext is that, whatever the circumstances, classes must be held. Some visitors comment on the couches, others on the wood paneling in many offices, still others on the prestigious brand of office chair. What signaled luxury for me was the fact that my office dwarfed all of the places I had called home during my years of graduate school in New York.

Most faculty and staff members quickly come to expect neatness, not only outdoors but in their offices. Visual disturbances, such as dirty windows or worn carpets, rarely appear, and when they do faculty assistants promptly contact a custodian or a supervisor to resolve the issue. Missteps tend not to be repeated. The preferred way to contact custodians is via their supervisors (present during the day) since the School's cleaning crews work during the late evening and night hours. Despite my sometimes odd work hours, I have never seen the office cleaning crew except on paper.[38] Pictures of three School custodians appear in a book about the university's service workers. The captions list their names and the exact hour when their photos were taken: Amadeo Lopez, 2:18 a.m.; Larry Segura, 3:30 a.m.; Phil LeBlanc, 6:30 a.m.[39]

Custodians are not alone in their efforts to keep offices neat. Colleagues and students also pitch in to make sure that appearances are maintained. As an illustration, after a few years at the School, a junior colleague's office walls remained suspiciously naked. A visit from his mother offered a more senior faculty member an opening: "So, are you planning to move?" he asked, with a smile, gesturing at the bare walls, in the mother's presence. Shortly thereafter a framed piece of art, sent by the mother, appeared on the office wall. Students also play their part in embellishing offices: first-year students and participants in some executive programs commonly give faculty members end-of-semester gifts.[40] Many of these gifts, such as class photos or a copy of a classroom teaching case signed by the entire class, arrive already framed, as if intended as office adornments. (Such gifts also signal a faculty member's popularity.)

Another idiosyncrasy of the School is the speed and professionalism with which offices are "turned around." The precision of the process reinforces the sense of order on campus. The day before my scheduled arrival on campus, I dropped off some items at my new office and found the carpet torn up, the walls being repainted, and the furniture being replaced. The following day the office was pristine, and a metal card holder on the door stood ready for my name.[41] Had I been moving from another office on campus, its layout would have been photographed to facilitate the exact repositioning of stacks of paper on a desk and books on shelves. (In a typical year, more than 15 percent of faculty members already at the School change offices.[42]) All of these changes proceed smoothly without interfering with other activities.

Disentangling Human Traffic

On teaching days, particularly when I am on the 8:40 a.m. shift, I stop at my office only briefly before heading to class.[43] If several faculty members are teaching the same case at the same time to different sections, it is customary to round up colleagues and walk to class together. (First-year students attend all of their classes with other members of their sections; thus the same material is taught simultaneously in several classrooms.) Ten minutes or so before the start of classes, these small faculty groups can be seen heading toward classrooms. These brief walks are opportunities to fine-tune the teaching plan, catch up on recent developments pertinent to the case—such as the company's stock price or the case protagonist's new job—or simply to loosen up before class. When such faculty groups cross paths, they acknowledge each other but avoid small talk so as not to disturb their own or their colleagues' concentration.

As soon as students spot, at a distance, faculty groups walking together toward the classroom building, they know that classes are about to begin. In cold weather or rain, however, spotting such groups is not as easy, since many faculty members use the system of underground tunnels that serves as a protected pathway between offices, classrooms, and other campus buildings.[44] These tunnels were originally created to supply the old dormitory dining rooms from a central kitchen.[45] Students typically use the tunnels that run from their dormitories to classrooms; faculty members stick to those leading from their offices to classrooms; and executive-education enrollees sometimes use them too, often to reach the athletic facilities. Those in one category typically encounter members of others only in the tunnel under the library. Thus, faculty members' knowledge of the underground system is at best partial.[46]

During the day, small errands and routine activities are easily performed on campus and provide some opportunities for various campus members to come together. The campus offers all of the services one would expect in a small town or city neighborhood; alongside housing, dining, and office facilities, there are a post office, sports facilities (tennis courts, a gymnasium, an indoor running track), a multidenominational chapel, a day-care center, and several notaries.[47] The School was also the first graduate school at Harvard to have its own full-time physician.[48] While the School relies on external assistance for medical emergencies, a small on-campus medical team provides routine care. The sense of belonging to a complete, if not a total, institution is pervasive, particularly among students who live on campus.[49]

Social distinctions among campus members prevail as they do in any small town. Dining practices exemplify such distinctions. Lunch is served starting before noon and coincides with renewed traffic on campus. Most students eat lunch at a large cafeteria located in the student center, but the faculty's options are more varied and exclusive. In addition to the options open to students, they can choose among a faculty dining room ("the Commons") on the library's ground floor, a more upscale faculty club on the executive-education side of campus, and, during the summer, weekly lunches in the dean's garden.[50] All three venues are open only to faculty members and their guests.[51] The faculty dining room, in particular, is also meant to promote a sense of community among faculty members across units.

The existence of distinct, non-overlapping worlds on campus first came to my attention early on when I tried to guide a visitor to my office. He called me by cell phone to say that he was on campus but lost. Upon inquiring where he was, he described his surroundings. "I see the sculpted head of a woman on a large stone base," he said. "There's also a small patch of grass and a few small brick buildings." I recalled no such sculpture and even asked if he had crossed the river, skeptical that he was actually on the School's grounds. When I asked him for the name of any building within his view, he named my own building. I met him downstairs, still puzzled as to where he could have been. He pointed to a sculpture located at a distance in the middle of the students' housing quarters—an area of campus I rarely visit.[52]

Some buildings, like the gymnasium and the chapel, are meant to serve more integrative functions, but the degree of integration they achieve varies. Arguably the most democratic spaces are the campus athletic facilities, and in particular the gym.[53] Students, staff, and faculty all use it, but interaction is usually kept to a minimum. During a typical hour in the weight room, no one seems to be chatting. Weightlifters concentrate on

An ordered state of mind: in the HBS library. Photo by Catherine Hammond.

their machines and often wear earphones. In other rooms, such as those equipped with cardio-fitness equipment, users typically read cases or papers while working out; they may acknowledge each other but usually refrain from longer conversation.[54] The chapel, by contrast, is a more social setting. Most activities within its walls are student- or staff-driven, with some faculty participation, but attendance at events tends to be fairly homogenous. For instance, a series of end-of-day live musical performances seems mainly to attract staff members, not faculty or students.[55]

At the end of the day, students may briefly intersect with faculty and staff heading toward their cars. Schedule and destination differences produce a de facto sorting of campus members into distinct flows. The vast majority of faculty members with parking permits use a particular daytime lot, which is used by almost no students. (Students who live on campus prefer another lot that allows overnight parking.[56]) My route home often brings me back to the footbridge, whose narrowness promotes social commingling of a kind more common in the world beyond campus. Many graduate students, executive-program participants, and visitors use the footbridge, but few faculty members seem to rely on it for their commute. Crossing it often reminds me of the existence of a messier, outside world.

* * *

The School's buildings, gardens, tunnels, and offices embody a well-established order, always undergoing gradual revision but also deeply ingrained.[57] In that sense, a visit to the School's campus—its access routes, its greenery, its dining halls and tunnels—starts to capture some of its organizational perspective. Above and below ground, inside and outside its buildings, the School's physical layout is a constant reminder of how to behave. The size and constant turnover of its residential community dictate a need to shape behaviors purposefully and repeatedly. The campus's neatness, quiet, and neo-Georgian architecture are what visitors notice, but a less visible ordering process is also at work. Though the School encourages informal interactions among faculty, graduate students, executive students, and staff, they remain quite rare; daily activities, efficient arrivals and exits, and scheduling constraints all discourage such mixing.[58] A fairly harmonious, small-town community with its distinct populations is experienced daily.

Physical layout, space, and other tangible features are often taken for granted in organizations, but they are embodiments of norms and expectations. Physical elements are not a fixed blueprint and can allow for variation, yet they also provide many cultural signs.[59] Shaped spaces act as depositories of specific social histories and as outcomes of repeated purposeful efforts. The meticulous ordering of trees, shrubs, and other plantings in the gardens of Versailles, for instance, suggests a ruler's political aspirations to extend his order abroad.[60] Similarly, American middle-class family life cannot be clearly understood without a detailed description of the characteristic single-family house with its family room facing the backyard.[61] The physical layout of a community or neighborhood cannot be dissociated from its social organization.[62] It is often hard to disentangle whether occupants shape their physical environments or physical configurations determine occupants' behaviors. Robert Park, a founder of the Chicago school of urban sociology, clearly favored the latter proposition. His assertion that "mind" is "an incident of locomotion" captures his outlook.[63] In Park's view, locomotion, or purposeful movement in a given material setting, shapes the mind (i.e., how individuals think). Setting aside questions of directionality, the interplay between mind and locomotion is difficult to refute.

Throughout this book, the campus is compared to a small town, but it also shares a crucial characteristic with larger cities, particularly their aspiration to embody and even create a "state of mind." The city, Park writes, is more than "a mere constellation of institutions and administrative services. . . . The city is, rather, a state of mind, a body of customs and traditions, and of the organized attitudes and sentiments that inhere in these customs and are transmitted with this tradition."[64] As this chapter suggests, the campus's physical setting displays the efficacy of the School's ordering project—or, to put it another way, its ability to favor a certain "state of mind." Orderly, neat, quiet spaces do not merely facilitate the pursuit of the educational endeavor; they embody it. Orderly small-town communities provide the template and goal for the pursuit.

The regularity of the campus's layout and functioning can prove quite comforting and attractive. That the lamps on the outdoor lampposts are turned on twenty minutes *before* sunset in winter and cars are barred from the outdoor parking lot at night (despite the absence of apparent other demands on the space) conveys a sense of timeless order. In these and other instances, physical order, if not moral order, infuses campus life. The footbridge over the Charles captures crucial aspects of this effort to create order. There is some basis for perceiving it as unsafe; though crime reports are difficult to track at such a granular level, some do indeed suggest a need for caution.[65] But beyond considerations of safety, the bridge serves as a passageway, to the tamed campus setting or the unruly outside world; it keeps some people in and keeps others out.[66] The bridge represents the School's necessary link to the outside world and its desire to regulate the incoming flow. Beyond its physical layout, the School's embrace of order extends, as the next chapter will make clear, to its faculty members' labor.

TWO

Reshaping
Academic Purity

Living as we do in the closing year of the twentieth century, enjoying the blessings of a social order at once so simple and logical that
it seems but the triumph of common sense, it is no doubt difficult
for those whose studies have not been largely historical to realize
that the present organization of society is, in its completeness, less
than a century old.

EDWARD BELLAMY, *Looking Backward, 2000–1887*

"Just a few more days before our packets are due. Is yours done?" asked
Peter, a junior faculty member in the midst of a promotion review, when
we ran into each other on campus.[1] "My statement still needs a last round
of feedback from colleagues, and then it should be ready to ship," he added.
"I need to make sure everybody's on the same page." This meant that a few
senior members of his unit still had to read his statement to reach agreement on how to frame his work for other School faculty members. The
statement is a short document summarizing a faculty member's research,
teaching, and service activities. Along with his or her publications and
works in progress, it forms the main part of a promotion packet. I too was
waiting for feedback before handing in my packet. "Almost done," I said,
in the hope that saying so would make it happen.

The ritual of submitting a review packet occurs as regularly as influenza
in an untenured faculty member's life. The main difference is that its timing is more predictable. The packet provides an opportunity to shape the
past and future selves that an academic wants to be known for in the scholarly community. Each year, during the week when packets are due, carts

A stack of green boxes ready to be filled. Photo by the author.

carrying multiple sets of materials—copies of articles and book chapters, résumés and statements, typically in green filing boxes—roll past faculty offices and down the elevators in Morgan Hall. The materials end up in a basement room one level below the dean's office before being distributed to internal and external reviewers. When Peter's boxes were carted away, his faculty assistant cheered. She had spent two months meticulously collating, indexing, formatting, and copying all of the materials.[2] Peter's comparable relief would hopefully come a few months later; review decisions are typically announced around April and December.

* * *

A variant of the green-boxes ritual is standard practice in most academic settings, but at the School the process also embodies the enforcement of a peculiar kind of academic purity—a norm strikingly unlike that to which faculty members trained elsewhere, even by other faculties at Harvard University, are socialized during their studies.[3] At most US research universities, evaluation of faculty members' performance is based "almost exclusively on publication of scholarly books or articles in professional journals."[4] Performance is associated with published research and its national and international recognition by one's peers.[5] Advancement at the School also depends on scholarship, but here the standard transcends traditional definitions of scholarship. Here the goal is to produce *relevant* scholarship.

The School's emphasis on relevance results from nearly a century of efforts (the lifetime of the School) to reshape the definition of academic purity—a historical process akin to that evoked by Edward Bellamy in this chapter's epigraph.[6] As the social anthropologist Mary Douglas reminds us, the distinction between pure and impure imposes "system on an inherently untidy experience."[7] The equation between relevant scholarship and purity is, however, at odds with what most outside-trained academics define as academic purity.

Assessing Relevance

Brown-bag seminars, conferences, weekly electronic broadcasts listing the topics of faculty members' new research, and ordinary interactions on campus all offer informal opportunities for faculty members (both junior and senior) to assess each other's relevance. Every few years, however, candidates for promotion or contract renewal are assessed more formally by their peers, potentially culminating in a tenure review. (Typically, the School and the university give candidates nine or ten years to prepare for a tenure decision.)[8] At all of these decisive points in a junior academic's career, senior School faculty members need to be convinced of the quality and relevance of the candidate's work.

Unlike the traditional publish-or-perish test applied in most US academic settings, the School also relies on a test of "managerial relevance," often referenced using the more enigmatic expression "fit," as part of the evaluative equation.[9] The School's administration conceptualizes business administration as a practice akin to legal or medical practice. The perceived uniqueness of the set of managerial challenges embodied in this practice justifies using relevance as an indicator of faculty performance. In management scholarship generally, including outside the United States, relevance is frequently invoked.[10] That being said, relevance often serves a largely symbolic (almost token) function.[11] At the School, by contrast, research that helps advance business practices is seen as a highly valuable contribution to the organizational mission, and the notion of relevance reinforces the focus on practice. As an illustration of the centrality of practice at the School, consider a failed attempt to modify a course's title: some faculty members tried to retitle the "Administrative Practices" course as "Human Problems in Administration," but the move was resisted by most other faculty members, who deemed human problems less important than administrative practices.[12] Outcomes deemed relevant (here, practices) need always be at the forefront of the educational endeavor, and analytical lenses (such as human problems) must be subordinated to those outcomes.

Many junior faculty members grapple with managerial relevance at key moments in their careers at the School. Consider the feedback I received during my first formal review, three years after arriving at the School. For the three-year review, which also serves as preparation for future reviews, a few senior colleagues solicit their peers' views on the junior faculty member in question; it is the only review for which external letters are not required. The colleagues then draft a letter to the candidate summarizing their shared assessment; they also meet with the candidate to offer help with his or her development over the ensuing few years. The entire exercise is reminiscent of concerned parents preparing their child for an ultimate contest—in this case, one that will involve the entire tenured faculty and select outsiders.

My assessment letter, an excerpt of which follows, nicely expresses senior faculty members' preoccupation with (and, sometimes, disagreement about) relevance. It also highlights the School's basic evaluative framework. "There is a strong sense that your work . . . is managerially relevant," the letter states, after praising my progress and commenting positively on the quantity and quality of my work. "However, there is a desire among some of us for you to further demonstrate this relevance, through whatever means you prefer." "Just to be clear," the letter continues, some faculty members "are satisfied that they themselves can see these connections; others, however, feel very strongly that you go the next step and demonstrate the managerial relevance of your scholarly work." I admit having felt, upon reading this passage, a bit tense. Was the letter communicating that my work was managerially relevant or not? Moreover, what kind of demonstration was expected?

Junior faculty members know that they will be assessed for promotion and tenure by a primary and a secondary audience, whom they are allowed to select from among three distinct audiences: scholars, educators, and practitioners. One might write primarily for educators and to a lesser degree for practitioners and want to be evaluated by those audiences, or, alternatively, one might address and wish to be assessed by scholars and secondarily by practitioners. Relevance, however, seems to transcend these categories. Even from faculty members who select scholars and educators as their two main audiences, managerial relevance is expected (though neither audience consists of managers per se). This tension leaves many junior faculty members wondering what relevance really means. According to senior faculty members, relevant scholarship should "anticipate or deeply understand some of the most fundamental challenges of our times," but its nature still often proves elusive.[13] When I asked another senior colleague what *relevance* signifies, he smiled. "You should know better than to ask that question," he said earnestly. "If relevance were to be defined, it would lose its plasticity. Not defining it is what makes relevance *relevant!*"[14]

The School's administration has made numerous attempts in written documents to specify its expectations for faculty, but the interpretive flexibility accorded to the standard of relevance allows the administration to assess any candidate's work on its terms.[15] Such flexibility is not uncommon in academia. As early as the 1950s, studies found that shielding junior faculty members from the criteria by which they were evaluated was standard practice in many US academic settings.[16] The ability to see purity where others do not—in the context of the School, to look at work that outsiders would be unlikely to view as relevant and designate it so—is core to sustaining any value system.[17] Distinguishing purity (that is, relevant work) from impurity (nonrelevant work) might seem like a simple call to make, but it entails a shared understanding of a candidate's work, an understanding reliant on a faculty member's ability to signal relevance.

Demonstrating Relevance

The most obvious way to demonstrate relevance is to do so in the field. Professors of management practice who have worked in industry before joining the School (often in leadership positions) are by definition relevant. Those teaching at the School tend to be former high-level executives at prominent firms, whose past successes suggest evidence of their ability to understand and overcome key managerial challenges. By contrast, the vast majority of the School's incoming junior faculty members, particularly those with limited industry experience, accustomed to interacting largely with other academics, need de facto to prove their relevance.

Theoretically, there are many ways to demonstrate relevance, but for junior faculty members the most common one is to publish articles in managerially oriented outlets such as the *Harvard Business Review*.[18] I recall my excitement the first time I was approached by the *Review* for a possible contribution to an upcoming issue. (Within weeks of my arrival at the School, I received an e-mail solicitation sent to a dozen recipients.) Naively, I asked a more experienced colleague what to do—or, more specifically, what kind of work I might want to see in print. "Good luck if you can get them interested in what you do," he corrected me. "They're the ones deciding what they want and if they want it, not you!" It became clear that faculty members do not simply decide what they want published in the *Review*. The editors—who are professional journalists, often with advanced graduate training, but not practicing academics—make the calls. Faculty members have to jockey for inclusion of their work in this "in-house" outlet.[19] The routine requests for submissions sent to faculty members are somewhat deceptive. I was and would remain in the position of applicant. Only if the work was deemed relevant enough would the relationship be reversed, and even then, as a senior colleague noted, only temporarily. "I got lucky once," he said, "but I don't know what will happen next."

Nothing feels more wounding than to be deemed irrelevant, but this not infrequently happens. Many junior faculty members' pitches to the *Review* seem to go cold. Occasionally, a faculty member is individually solicited for a contribution. A phone conversation typically ensues, questions are asked, and the decision arrives, usually a few days later. When the decision is negative, the subtext is obvious: the work is not interesting or relevant enough for the *Review*'s readership. The editors are often right when they make these calls: a negative reaction on their part is usually triggered by a faculty member's inability to explain plainly why his or her findings should matter to individuals outside the field, let alone to practicing managers.

The *Review* editors also make a habit of pushing authors to spell out the implications of their findings up front. Most new faculty members' prior training in doctoral programs hardly prepares them for this practice.[20] Qualifying the implications of one's findings is integral to a research write-up for virtually any scholarly publication, even if doing so dilutes its impact. Furthermore, the *Review* editors, in their roles as assessors, do not employ the peer-review process typical at academic journals, which is thought to guarantee quality. Alternative definitions of quality are at stake in these highly dissimilar, and almost competing, editorial processes. Because *both* types of output are expected from the faculty, the definition of academic purity gradually shifts.

Publishing in managerially oriented journals is not the only way to demonstrate relevance. Another is to write course materials (cases, teaching notes, and module notes) that colleagues and students deem relevant.[21] Providing solutions to actual business problems (such as creating a new financial instrument or an operational innovation) can also be coded as relevant. And it appears that the greater the demand from businesses for a faculty member's services, the greater his or her perceived relevance: being retained as a consultant to prominent organizations, serving on select corporate or nonprofit boards, and teaching in executive-education programs all suggest being highly in demand, and by extension highly relevant.[22]

The relevance test is perhaps most conspicuously on display during the School's annual Faculty Research Symposium. This event, inaugurated in 2003 and attended mostly by faculty members, features keynote speakers from the School's faculty. Untenured faculty members, often working on new topics at crucial career-transition points, are ideal candidates to speak. A small group of tenured faculty members selects the presenters, based on recommendations from each unit represented at the School.[23] On average, nearly half of all presenters are untenured members of the faculty.[24] Presenters need to reach out to faculty members across multiple units in order to pass this test and be deemed relevant beyond the circle of peers who are already knowledgeable about their research topics. Presenters' colleagues typically attend to show support and occasionally to ask helpful leading questions. The stakes involved in such presentations run high. "Wish me luck," an untenured presenter asked me before heading for the venue. "Break a leg!" I replied and made sure to be in the room for his talk.

Scholars and Popularizers

Reaching a broad audience also calls for venturing beyond the School's boundaries, and not just by publishing articles addressed to managers. When a radio crew visited my office to interview me, I remember being pleased at their interest, yet also thinking that I was ill prepared. I had never done a taped interview before. The program's host, a sound engineer, and a representative from the School's external-relations team all entered my office. Unfamiliar with School practices, I politely asked if the external-relations officer wanted to join us. To my surprise, she said that was the plan; I nodded in approval and pulled up an additional chair.

Midway through the interview, the host asked me a question on an unfamiliar topic; I hesitated, then said that the question went beyond my area of expertise. As I articulated that sentence, instantly, I felt that I had failed to live up to the interviewer's expectations or, more uncannily, to the School's expectations. Many School faculty members were constantly being quoted in various media outlets, but my doctoral training had not included any guidance on interacting with the media.[25] Facility with the media was apparently expected from me and, by not providing an answer, I had missed an opportunity to be quoted.

The radio segment aired some time later and generated some buzz. Current students, colleagues, and friends heard it, or heard about it, and even some former students contacted me. While some audiences were quite attentive to such exposure, others, particularly academics at other institutions, were notably less responsive. Many School colleagues congratulated me on the segment, but despite my listing it as media coverage on my curriculum vitae, no external colleague ever mentioned it.

Gaining public recognition is not only a novel pursuit for many junior faculty members but one that can initially elicit ambivalence. Working to gain public notoriety goes against deeply ingrained academic norms. In the US academic world, F. G. Bailey explains, one who attempts to "popu-larize" his research is typically seen as "someone so intent on success that he is unwilling to wait through the labors of slow recognition that is the best most scholars can expect."[26] The frequency of calls for public scholar-ship in academia only underlines the weight of the structural forces that coalesce to discourage it.[27] "The contempt in which a 'popularizer' is held comes about for several reasons," Bailey continues. "Firstly, he is using discoveries of other people to make money or reputation for himself: the fact that special talents are needed to market stuff (so that in fact he does add something) is usually ignored. Secondly, in the process of populariz-ing he is likely to dilute and distort: the fact that dilution may be a neces-sary price for the dissemination of knowledge is ignored. Thirdly, at the back of all this lies a dominating myth among academics about their own superiority. Knowledge, for whatever reason accessible only to a few, is by that very fact superior to knowledge accessible to anyone."[28] For traditional US academics, therefore, having a large public following can carry nega-tive connotations.

At the School, however, being viewed by the media as an expert, or the go-to person for a given topic, is seen as possible evidence of relevance. Whereas articles, chapters, and books are the conventional vehicles for communicating with one's academic peers elsewhere, talks, seminars, classroom presentations, and media citations or appearances are venues for addressing the School community and the larger world.[29] Junior fac-ulty members thus learn to navigate a primarily oral culture, quite distinct from the scholarly culture with its emphasis on the written word. Learn-ing to communicate with the public via the media is an important step in gaining relevance.

Media citations also facilitate conversations among the School's aca-demic units. For instance, faculty members in marketing and finance can sometimes rely on sound bites to start conversations. "Congrats! I just read a piece in the *New York Times*: very interesting" is a common overture, to which the reply might be "Thanks! They got most of it right, even though they only reported part of the experimental manipulation." Such an ex-change of appreciation and distancing is typical of junior faculty members. The translation process—within and outside the School—often forces members of a given subfield to reduce and simplify their findings to a core message. The clever methodology employed, the theories explored, and the unique scholarly challenges surmounted to achieve the goal hardly register with journalists. But despite the shortcomings, a conversation is started, planting the seeds for potential relevance.

Negotiating Caste and Subcaste Membership

The School's focus on relevance calls for assessment criteria quite different from those of disciplinary departments and most other business schools. Faculty members are asked to produce something (relevance) that most of their peers elsewhere are unlikely to recognize as fully legitimate. The sociologist Diana Crane has used the concepts of caste and subcaste to describe tensions between academics' double affiliations: with the educational institutions they serve (castes) and with the "invisible colleges" of academic peers in their disciplines (subcastes).[30] Generally speaking, subcastes dominate academic life, but at the School the priority of the caste (the School) over the subcaste (the academic disciplines) is integral to the ordering project.[31] Ever since the School was founded, efforts have been made to distinguish its endeavor from a strictly disciplinary pursuit, particularly as exemplified by the university's disciplinary departments.[32]

For those readers less familiar with traditional academic assessment procedures and to provide contrasts to the School's practices, consider the case of a typical large, research-based university. Most departments in such universities maintain lists of the journals and presses that their members consider the most highly respected in their subfield. These journals and presses are then rank-ordered by level of prestige in broad categories (A-level outlets, B-level outlets, and so on). The resulting list constitutes an imperfect but often fairly consensual proxy for academic quality in those settings.[33] Such a definition of quality is used not only at US institutions but increasingly abroad as well.[34] What has been called the Americanization of academic research is evident, for instance, in many European and Asian settings, where reliance on "top-tier" publications and citation impact (i.e., how many times a publication is cited in other publications) as proxies for quality have become the norm.[35]

In the life cycle of an aspiring tenure-track faculty member at a typical research university, promotion to the next grade level (such as associate professor with tenure or full professor with tenure) is contingent on a fairly predictable combination of research productivity and quality. Oftentimes, teaching and service to the university or the profession also play a role in promotion decisions, although probably to a lesser extent in many major research universities. Thus, a junior faculty member at a typical research university can specify quite accurately what is expected if he or she is to reach the next professional level, namely, to publish a certain number or combination of pieces in various levels of outlets. Predictability in such an environment is high, and publishing in such outlets is widely thought to reflect the quality of a scholar's work.

In order to publish in such journals, academics need to convince editors and reviewers of the quality of their work. Editors at academic journals and presses are typically the most prominent and often the most knowledgeable members of an academic subcaste. (They are full-time faculty members who volunteer their service to help regulate a given academic community.) In any given subcaste, it is the editors and their trusted reviewers who make or block academic careers. They are often the "high-producers" in the invisible college, as Crane explains, since editors typically attain their positions by first having published work in the very outlets they later oversee.[36] Thus, aspirants to higher academic echelons traditionally depend on editors for their progress and ultimately their employment. As David Riesman irreverently noted half a century ago, "Scholars who enter a field because of what it can do for them in career terms (rather than because of what they can do for it) often end up as members of intellectual blocs—gatekeepers insisting on tolls to be paid to their field."[37]

Enter now the school or the university. Every ambitious research-university administrator attempts to build what is called a caste. Prestigious institutions try to assemble unique groups of respected scholars who might attract bright students and wealthy donors. A successful university ends up creating what Arthur Stinchcombe labels a *monopoly*, in the sense that no other university can easily duplicate its particular combination of resources.[38] Such combinations, in turn, are thought to attract even greater resources. By insisting on relevance, for instance, the School is in part attempting to create a unique, nonreplicable combination of resources. Once a caste is sufficiently established, it can bestow prestigious

caste-specific degrees (such as an HBS diploma) that command more resources (donations and tuitions) from its various constituents.

But no school or university can ignore academic disciplines, or subcastes, completely. In faculty tenure decisions, for instance, the stakes are
high, since errors are difficult to correct. Thus schools and universities
rely heavily on candidates' external colleagues to help assess internal and
external candidates. The Harvard Business School is no exception; external letter writers (some from disciplinary departments) are invited to comment on faculty promotion and tenure decisions. And most schools and
universities rely on disciplinary departments to train their future faculty.
As an example, in 2009 close to 45 percent of the School's "ladder faculty"
(tenure-track and tenured faculty members) had been trained in disciplinary departments.[39] Disciplinary training includes, for instance, doctoral
studies in history and economics. Nondisciplinary training, by contrast,
encompasses, for example, doctoral studies in strategy and accounting.

At the School, the senior faculty's assessment of the candidate is, however, perceived to carry more weight relative to external assessments than
is the case in other settings. In practice, this does not mean that external
peers are consulted less. The number of requests for outside letter is typically equal to or higher than at most other institutions. In the 1970s these
dynamics prompted a longtime faculty member, Fritz Roethlisberger, to
distinguish between *locals* and *cosmopolitans* at the School—that is, between
faculty members with local (caste) and national (subcaste) orientations.[40]
The School's mix of locals and cosmopolitans required paying equal attention to both constituencies. Still today, such balance is maintained. For instance, the current policy of barring School faculty from receiving external
grants somewhat insulates faculty members from external pressure. The
rationale for this policy is that it "allows the faculty to pursue the research
opportunities [with] the greatest potential to create new knowledge and
advance the practice of management," since the School generously funds
most of its research.[41] But the policy also limits opportunities for external
academics to formally assess a scholar's "value," since fund-granting bodies are mostly staffed by peers.[42]

It is therefore not surprising that the relations between the university's disciplinary departments and the School are sometimes tense.[43]
In the words of the School's dean, the "center" of the university, namely

the Faculty of Arts and Sciences, sometimes views the School as "Outer Mongolia."[44] This attitude is not unique to Harvard; professional schools at many other universities experience similar tensions. Business schools and schools of education, for instance, are often accorded second-class status by core disciplinary faculty members.[45] In that regard, the School's acquisition from Harvard College of a large wooden table where the entire Faculty of Arts and Sciences was said to have met regularly, and the installation of the table in the School's main faculty dining hall, carries a quasi-symbolic meaning.[46]

Diffuse tensions between the School and academic subfields are not novel. Roethlisberger's memoir, published in 1977, already highlighted this recurring theme.[47] "The cultivation of this big garden [the School]," he wrote, entailed "some implicit polarities." He went on to explain that "no individual professor could grow 'his thing' unmindful of the other things being grown in the garden. He had to relate his corn to his colleagues' beans and show how in combination they produced the diet required for this person who was . . . *not* an economist (macro or micro), *not* a sociologist (concrete, general, or abstract), *not* a psychologist (clinical, social, or pure), *not* an anthropologist (physical, cultural, or social)—in short not any kind of specialist at all." Specialists at the School were expected to serve the School's pursuit (and, incidentally, to be males).[48] Since then, the gender composition of the faculty has changed, but the expectation of service to the School's pursuit remains.

The ensuing tensions are still sometimes apparent. The titles that faculty members list on their business cards illustrate this point. Once on board, all faculty members—whether economists, psychologists, or political scientists—are expected to become generalists in business administration. In the same way that schools of law and medicine have professors of law and medicine, the School needs professors of business administration. Upon my arrival at the School, I found that my assistant had already arranged for School letterhead and business cards. My card read "Assistant Professor of Business Administration." I was not surprised, since that was my job title. Within two years, however, I changed offices and needed new cards. When I was asked how the card should read, it occurred to me for the first time that I might have some leeway. Upon closer examination, I discovered that the School housed many "assistant professors," "associate professors," and "professors," but that only a few added the qualifier "of business administration" on their cards. In fact, only 29 percent of those who had leeway did so in 2009.[49] I opted for the common omission.

Such details may seem trivial, but they highlight the ways in which competing definitions of academic purity play out at the School, and the small ways in which some faculty members juggle them. The concern for appropriate titles, I later learned, was nothing new. In 1942, when Wallace Donham resigned as the School's dean after twenty-three years but remained on the School's faculty, he petitioned the university's board of overseers for a change in title from the George F. Baker Professor of Business Economics to the George F. Baker Professor of Administration. The change expressed his desire to align his title with the School's main goal, the teaching of business administration.[50] The new title also distanced him from a disciplinary affiliation and suggested that he had embraced an alternate evaluative framework.

The tensions between the School and the academic subcastes are most evident in the evaluative framework applied to junior faculty members. Running two "races," the internal relevance race and the external scholarly race, embodies these tensions and is often seen as a necessary condition to be granted tenure at the School.[51] Few traditional research institutions seem to assign as much weight as the School does to its internal race. Even fewer such institutions would presume to convince outsiders of the internal race's importance and embark on an attempt to reshape a field's purity. Academic purity is classically understood to result from the cumulative efforts of hundreds of scholars at dozens of institutions.[52] As Harrison White reminds us, in discussing sociology, "Certainly no one department is large enough to mount work on the scale of an invisible college."[53] Yet in some ways the School has attempted to do exactly that by enforcing a form of purity that is often viewed outside as heretical.

* * *

Most faculty members, regardless of academic environment, are expected to run multiple races. At most universities, both teaching and research are expected. "Perhaps the leading problem for the individual faculty member," Theodore Caplow and Reece McGee note in their study of US academia, "is the incongruity between his job assignment and the work which determines his success or failure in his own discipline." As Caplow and McGee go on to explain, faculty members are "hired to teach" (the caste race) but their success depends primarily on the pursuit of their "private professional interests" (the subcaste race).[54] Effective teaching is assumed to translate in part into high student ratings; the weight assigned to these ratings is at the discretion of the school and the university. By contrast, successful pursuit of private professional interests is assumed to lead to peer-reviewed publications, which is at the discretion of the discipline.

Multiple races are also being staged within the confines of the School, but with a key difference compared to most other business schools and disciplinary departments. First, the weight assigned to the School's pursuit is perceived by many junior faculty members to be greater than in many other settings. Second, the criteria used to assess performance within the School seem less familiar than at many other settings. Teaching is highly valued at the School, but the emphasis on relevance adds complexity to the pursuit. Introducing relevance as a key perceived variable in the review of faculty members changes the nature of the internal race.[55] Because academic careers are partly shaped by organizational contexts, the race's setup matters; its vocal cues influence individual decisions. Over time, faculty members learn to adapt to organizational demands and to the noise that surrounds them.[56]

As the green boxes containing the review packets are carted off to the basement room for future distribution, the candidates under review return to their daily activities. These activities are akin to those of their colleagues in most other academic settings: teaching, collecting and analyzing data, writing up findings, reviewing, and so on. The main difference is that at the School faculty members' output must ultimately be deemed relevant. At most universities, intra-institutional behaviors mostly consist of rituals, while action, excitement, and intimacy, to use Harrison White's terms, flourish along academic disciplinary lines; at the School, by contrast, action, excitement, and intimacy are also expected within the School itself.[57] The whispers of such expectations help shape academic purity and guide the way business scholarship is pursued and ultimately how faculty members teach.

THREE

Preaching in Silence

"Well," said he, "let us take one of our units of management, a commune, or a ward, or a parish. . . . In such a district, as you would
call it, some neighbours think that something ought to be done
or undone . . . a neighbour proposes the change and, of course,
if everybody agrees, there is an end of discussion, except about
details. . . . But supposing . . . a few of the neighbours disagree
to it . . . arguments pro and con are flying about."
WILLIAM MORRIS, *News from Nowhere*

I am standing in what is commonly called "the pit" at the center of the
classroom amphitheater, in front of ninety chatting students, waiting to
begin teaching my first class at the School. As the clock at the rear of the
room approaches the session's start time (8:40 a.m.), the class falls silent.
I have never seen so large a crowd go silent so quickly and in such a coor-
dinated way. The session is about to begin.

Despite my summer preparation, I realize at that moment that I am
still somewhat clueless about what to do. I follow the reassuring advice of
a senior colleague: "When you start feeling butterflies in your stomach,
don't think about it too long. Remember that the students are feeling the
same way; just jump in and start the session. All will go fine." I mumble,
"Welcome to the Harvard Business School," and realize simultaneously
that my voice does not carry far enough when the classroom is full. (I had
practiced, but in a sparsely populated room.) "It's an honor to be teaching
your section this year," I add, much louder. "The best introduction to this
course is the case you prepared for today, so let's jump right into it." Had

I better understood the demands of the performance I was embarking on, I might have felt even more scared.

* * *

At the broadest level, teaching at the School is a bit like a performance, one in which most moves and steps are rehearsed many times before class. This chapter attempts to make explicit what the performance entails, particularly in the required first-year courses in the School's MBA program— the program I am most knowledgeable about, having taught in it for four years.[1] The account suggests a sense of uniformity across the different sections' classroom experiences by describing the shared routines that surround each phase of the teaching process: preparation for course delivery, the teaching sessions themselves, and post-session maintenance like interacting with students outside the classroom and updating teaching materials.[2] But it also emphasizes the premium placed on customizing the experience, by encouraging students' "discovery" in the classroom, for example, or allowing for a variety of case discussion conclusions. Striking a balance between routine and novelty permeates teaching at the School: this is a balance that new faculty members need to pick up fast.[3]

Though some MBA students attend preparatory workshops in quantitative methods or English-language skills, and all students attend an initial case-teaching session, classroom norms remain in flux on the first day of classes. Students still barely know each other, but it is probably the new instructor who feels most lost. Luckily, many organizational routines guide the rookie on this journey and contribute to ensuring some teaching uniformity at the School. Effective socialization of faculty members is highly reliant on choreographing the teaching performance, an enterprise that consumes much organizational attention.

Common Dressing Rooms

Seventy or so faculty and staff members sit silently in a large room with chandeliers and tall windows. Dimmed lights and the thin white curtains masking the windows lend the gathering a somewhat exclusive flavor. The faculty head of the first-year required MBA curriculum welcomes everybody to a new academic year. This is the kickoff meeting for the faculty members who will be teaching first-year courses.[4] All of my "shift mates" are present—those who will help shape the students' experiences; those who will turn over the classroom to me; and those to whom I will hand off the classroom. (Students stay put in one classroom throughout the first year; faculty members rotate in and out.)

The sight of all my fellow instructors is humbling. The collective presence dwarfs any one of us; the stability of the institution seems assured. Novelties in the curriculum, procedures to follow when problems arise, and community values are all discussed to ensure consistency.[5] In some ways, the meeting resembles a morning kickoff meeting in any large, routinized work environment, the main difference being that this meeting occurs only once a year rather than daily. Afterward, the process is delegated to the "course heads"—faculty members who oversee the delivery of a given course (while teaching one section of it).

Course heads are senior faculty members, mostly tenured, charged with ensuring that all of the instructors who deliver the same course are on the same page. Under their guidance, typically six or seven instructors meet around a large table several times a week to discuss upcoming cases. Each class session focuses on a given case. Cases typically describe a decision point faced by a single protagonist. They are generally cowritten by School faculty members, run fifteen or so pages, and are meant to capture "universal" workplace challenges.[6] Students usually must decide on specific action plans and defend the pros and cons of their decisions. (New cases are constantly being produced, but older ones are also frequently used.) At each meeting of the instructors, one member is usually assigned to walk the group through an upcoming case and his or her preferred teaching plan. Few other business schools have student cohorts large enough to justify such teaching groups; even at other schools that strongly value teaching, preparation is usually individual, or at best an apprenticeship with a more experienced colleague. At the School, by contrast, new faculty members step into a well-oiled collective apparatus.

Teaching plans from previous years, some of which date back a decade, are circulated. Though each faculty member is free to teach as she or he wishes, the norm is to try to adhere (at least once) to the plan.[7] These teaching plans evoke a sense of reenacting a past performance. "Show the video from 1 minute 00 seconds to 4 minutes 06 seconds," one plan instructed. "When the protagonist's nickname is heard, pause and ask the class, 'Does he deserve that name?'" The plans specify to the minute the series of questions and probes that work best in a given situation. "Pull down the center-front board to discuss the action plan," advised another plan. "Hide calculations on the right with the top right-board." (School classrooms have nine blackboards, arranged in sets of three, that can overlap; often there are two additional side boards.) The final piece of advice was meant to ensure that the instructor ended the session with certain boards visible and others hidden.[8] At the teaching group meetings, plans are sometimes revised to suit the specific timing of the case and the dynamics of the class. For instance, "At this point in the semester, students traditionally get anxious about their summer internships," reminded a senior colleague. "Some of their section mates already have jobs." The plan was modified slightly to take the students' probable mood into account.

My own inexperience became obvious during one of my first teaching sessions. The session was attended by a senior colleague, whose plan on the case I had relied on to learn my part. (Class visits are common practice at the School and among the many ways that senior colleagues support junior faculty members' development.) At a crucial transition point in the session, I wrapped up the discussion and announced that we would now watch a video of the case protagonist. I proudly pressed the Launch button on my media console—a computer screen from which the instructor can control the lights, the screens, the volume, and an in-class voting system (convenient to tally pros and cons). Only then did I notice that the screen was still retracted and the lights were still on: I purposely avoided my colleague's gaze as I corrected the misstep with two quick taps on the console. During our later debriefing, he pointed out gracefully that I still had some minor logistics to master.

Following the teaching plan helps avoid such missteps. Listening closely to other faculty members' accounts of their experiences with a case is also useful. In addition, the more recent practice of screening prior years' taped sessions provides new instructors with a sense of what to expect. (Small classroom stationary cameras can record any session on demand.) Institutional memory is readily shared. That few instructors sign the teaching plans they circulate to the teaching group reinforces the principle that teaching "recipes" belong to the School, not to any given individual.[9] Despite the lack of clear attribution, I gradually learned to identify plans' likely authors by format. Because some authors' teaching styles suited me better than others, I recorded the probable author's name on each plan. My own plans are typically handwritten and succinct, and they sometimes include embarrassing reminders of my blind spots: a "smile" notation up front to remind me that I tend to look a bit too solemn when entering a classroom; a "speak louder" reminder prior to my discovery that I could attach a microphone to my tie.

Teaching plans also indicate potential pitfalls in a given session and ways to avoid them. One plan noted, for instance, that a student with a background in law had pointed out that some of the material in a case centering on a trial was procedurally incorrect. To preempt questions that might derail the class discussion, the plan suggested identifying students with law backgrounds and possibly stating at the outset that the material might not coincide exactly with US legal procedure. A list of comments from prior users of the teaching plan followed, covering most other derailments the case could occasion and ways to handle them. Reading such comments is akin to reviewing a list of aircraft operating procedures for responding to severe turbulence.

Despite all this preparation, moments of unscripted student "discovery" represent a coveted goal. The use of the term *pasture*, with its religious undertones and suggestion of contemplative thinking, to refer to the main segments of a teaching plan expresses this aim. A typical description of such a segment might be "In this pasture, the goal is to have students become aware of the complexity of handling cross-national acquisitions." Common pastures include analyzing a firm's performance and developing an action plan for a firm's leadership. New faculty members are commonly advised that the best way to foster discovery in a pasture is to speak as little as possible. Thus, the rule of thumb is to elicit at least four or five student comments before stepping in. An instructor often intervenes in class debate to make key teaching points at transitions or at the end of a session; the goal is internalized learning and discovery, which are difficult outcomes to rehearse for. Everybody understands that fostering such outcomes requires a combination of expertise and luck. Even the custodians who erase the boards at each changing of the guard (between consecutive class sessions) wish incoming instructors good luck.

Individual Dressing Rooms

Along with meeting in teaching groups and sharing teaching plans, faculty members also prepare their sessions individually. Though choreographed and performed privately, these are School-specific routines in which much uniformity still prevails. Whether at home or at the School, time is always set aside to review a case and fine-tune a session's teaching plan. Some faculty members recommend doing this the evening prior to the session, so one can "sleep on" any insights or outstanding questions. Others deem it better to review right before entering the classroom, so the effort remains fresh in the mind. Regardless of when and how the preparation is done, all faculty members would agree that every session needs to be prepared. (Only those who have taught a same case many times can sometimes omit this step.) While not showing up to teach a session might be the ultimate taboo, not "prepping" a case for a given session ranks probably a close second.

Dressing the part is another step in one's individual preparation. Academics tend to pay little attention to their attire, but most senior School faculty members have a clear sense of proper dress in the classroom.[10] Like guests at luxury hotels or colonial administrators, they are well dressed and quite attentive to their appearance.[11] Many entering faculty members receive a call from an "executive clothier" within a few weeks of joining the School.[12] (The clothier has long done business with the School's faculty but is not on staff.) When I received the call, I recall thinking that the person calling was probably a tailor. "Soon you will start to teach," he told me, "and you need to be properly dressed. I have worked with many HBS professors and I can help you make the transition." "You'll need a certain number of suits," he explained. "You might also need to attend formal events that will require a different set of clothes than your daily attire." (I was soon to discover that this meant faculty social events.) The clothier offered to help me find a limited number of color and fabric matches to "facilitate" my life.

Help was indeed needed. With close to thirty teaching sessions looming, two or three per week over the course of the semester, a large wardrobe would be required. "Go to Brooks Brothers for shirts and suits," a pragmatic colleague advised. "You can never go wrong." This was good advice, but I could have used more specific guidance. Color choices, for instance, must be partly dictated by practical considerations.[13] Solid black shows chalk marks, and lighter-colored fabrics lack the decorum expected in the classroom. Nonsolid dark colors are therefore a common choice for suits. After some trial and error, faculty members often end up wearing similar clothes, thus, ensuring a certain visual uniformity in the class delivery (for men, a light shirt, a gray or blue jacket, and a bright tie are typical).

Another step in individual preparation entails reviewing the seating chart to select students to call on in the upcoming discussion. Students who want to participate raise their hands, but typically more than enough hands are raised. Given that participation is graded, it is important for students to be given equal opportunities to enter the discussion. (Class participation generally counts for half of a student's grade.) Thus someone who has not spoken for several sessions often gets priority. In addition to the large color seating charts adorning the walls of most faculty offices, smaller, session-specific printouts of the seating chart serve as calling reminders. These printouts are automatically generated after each session, once a faculty assistant or instructor enters the names of those who just spoke and some comments on their interventions.[14] Colored circles classify students for the coming session (green for the "call list," orange for second-priority students, red for those who have already participated often), and instructors often add their own idiosyncratic annotations, such as happy faces to signal students with relevant case experience. My own calling patterns initially ended up very different than I had hoped. Many students I wanted to hear from did not speak. Others who had already spoken proved quite aggressive at again entering the discussion. This invariably resulted in an epidemic of green circles on the next session's calling chart. Keeping the epidemic under control is an unexpectedly daunting and tiresome task for inexperienced faculty.

A faculty desk with seating charts on the wall. Photo by the author.

Memory exercises facilitate the calling routine. Most faculty members memorize some of their students' names and faces before the start of the semester via online or paper "class cards" bearing their names, photographs, and other biographical information. A student's undergraduate institution, past employer, and home region, for instance, might jointly create a memorable portrait. Tricks are then used to memorize seats and faces. Some faculty members hand-copy students' names and the seating chart to imprint a visual memory of the section's layout. Others browse students' online or printed profiles. I make flashcards listing students' names, with my own cues to their memorable attributes written on the back (e.g., "looks like my cousin Roni," "square glasses," "long hair"). The cards make the exercise feel a bit like a trivia game. Memorizing students' names and faces prior to the start of classes can mean that strangers begin looking (unilaterally) familiar. Once, right before Labor Day, I killed some time by flipping through my flashcards while waiting for a visitor at the Boston airport. Suddenly I saw someone I believed to be in my deck walking out of the gate. I held up the card to compare the photo to the person who had just exited. My notes read "enjoys karaoke, sideburns, from Arkansas." Bystanders looked at me suspiciously, as if I might be tracking a criminal. It was a false match. I returned the deck into my pocket.

When, in my office, minutes before heading to class, I review the session's annotated seating chart and students' names, the fleeting associations triggered by such exercises come to mind and generate relevant cues for class discussion. Where on the seating chart will I find the former Disney employee who might be able to comment on organizational culture? Who has lived in Michigan and might be familiar with the automotive industry? What are the names of the students who listed football as a hobby and might support competing teams? (All these students get smiley faces on my calling chart.) Such apparent trivia can significantly enrich the class discussion.

With students' faces swirling in my mind, I head to the restroom mirror to adjust my tie. The gesture reminds me of a comedian checking his makeup before taking the stage. Upon exiting, I generally bump into colleagues who will be teaching the same case the same day. Some are known for coming up with new and improved teaching plans during the walk to class.[15] For instance, a suggestion might be to flip an action pasture before the analytical one to force students to take a stand up front. In a matter of minutes, one has to decide whether to use the new plan or stick to the previous one. In that sense, the walk to the classroom often constitutes the ultimate dress rehearsal. Students use the phrase "cracking the case" to mean figuring out what a case is about, but before this happens, the instructors also need to crack the case (not to mention the sequence of cases). This largely happens in the teaching groups, but it occasionally continues on the way to the classroom. These discussions also catalyze the energy to launch a session. Thus walking alone to class is often dreaded. Small groups of neatly dressed instructors carrying copies of the case, a teaching plan, and annotated seating charts are a common sight on campus.

Working the Pit

Once in the classrooms, male instructors traditionally remove their jackets before starting to teach.[16] Removing one's jacket signals that the session is about to start, and also that teaching is laborious. "Working the pit" requires keepings tabs on many moving parts. A colleague advised me, for instance, to "listen to the noise students make when they start moving on their chairs." The seats in first-year classrooms rotate on metal poles affixed to the floor. "Too much squeaking," he said, "and you know that students are becoming impatient." A silent room signifies perfect attention. In practice, tracking an ongoing exchange, thinking about the next pasture, and listening to the chairs is a complicated juggling act. This example suggests the efforts and level of attention expected when delivering courses at the School.

While teaching, an instructor needs to be paying attention to several simultaneous mental movies or tapes. The course-structure tape tracks how the concepts covered in the current session relate to other parts of the course. The case-specific tape tracks discussion of the day's case, particularly students' pro and con arguments and the ad hoc cliques that often form to defend given courses of action. A third tape notes the minute-to-minute comments of each participant. This last tape is "purged" immediately after class, when the instructor (or a faculty assistant) summarizes the classroom comments for purposes of assessing students' class participation later on. A successful instructor usually can convey complete attentiveness to each student's remarks while keeping the discussion rolling effortlessly and weaving the concepts under discussion into the overall flow of the course. Needless to say, such multitasking requires practice and dexterity.

Attentiveness in the classroom also matters because good teaching is valued at the School. Good teaching means, by and large, teaching that students appreciate. Students rate instructors at the end of each semester, but before then most faculty members find that emerging from a session that did not work feels almost shameful. Years of average performance, with no visible signs of progress, can take a toll on any instructor. First-year students' ratings are only seen by the individual instructor and the course head, but the average rating of all ten sections of a given course is shared with all those who teach it. A personal sense of underperformance is usually sufficient motivation to try to do better next time. Yet even for instructors with high ratings, the desire to improve remains a strong norm. Figuring out how to best teach a case often helps the entire teaching group improve its collective performance.

The most basic step in mastering teaching is probably learning to avoid technical glitches in the classroom. Particularly when case protagonists (often CEOs or leaders of large firms) come to campus, such glitches are to be avoided at all costs. During one such a visit, a video simulcast had been arranged so that students in other sections could also hear the CEO. (Two or three sections typically discuss a given case during the same time slot.) The protagonist was visiting a colleague's classroom, and the stream was to be broadcast to large screens that would be remotely lowered in the other classrooms, including mine. A member of the audiovisual staff at the back of my classroom was counting down the minutes left before "going live" and signaling me with hand gestures. Even so, this being my first simulcast, the dropping screen surprised me and cut me off midpasture. I made sure this did not happen again.

Luckily, regardless of an instructor's skills, the design of the classroom also influences how classes unfold. The curve of the amphitheater encourages students to look at each other, to converse, and ideally to challenge each other's arguments. Steps leading to the top rows on either side of the classroom even allow the instructor to climb up and out of sight occasionally, promoting exchanges among the students. (Senior colleagues invariably encourage rookies to use the steps.) Also, the nine distinct boards, particularly the three central ones, help structure a discussion into distinct pastures. Belief in the importance of the classroom layout is such that replicas of an HBS classroom have been built abroad to allow for the duplication of the teaching experience in the few instances when executive-education programs are conducted off-site.[17]

Many organizational routines, such as teaching group meetings and teaching plans, promote a fairly uniform class delivery, but the instructor still needs to "work the pit"—that is, lead and customize the discussion from the center of the classroom. Actual classroom teaching is paradoxically the most and least closely overseen activity at the School: many hours go into collective preparation, but the instructor is ultimately alone in front of the students. Downplaying the prepared aspects to allow students to shape the session, while properly conveying the teaching materials and leaving room for discovery, is the stated goal. Discovery often comes about via novel insights, comparisons, or personal examples. Students are quick to notice this. As an article from the students' newspaper appropriately remarks, "strong" comments are those that "advance the discussion" or

A re-created HBS classroom abroad: International Senior Management Program, Vevey, Switzerland, 1978. Baker Library, Historical Collections.

"infer from someone's observation and challenge someone's conclusion with evidence." By contrast, comments that "take the discussion back to a point discussed 15 minutes ago, restate an existing comment or take a lot of air time with little substance" are considered "weak."[18]

After class, instructors often swap "war stories," reciting word for word strong comments so incisive or moving that they made the class fall silent, killed a weak argument, or brought the section almost to tears.[19] These moments constitute badges of honor for faculty members: evidence of internalized learning. When discussing a fraud case, for instance, a student openly acknowledged that she had taken part in a dubious accounting practice. Her remark lingered in the classroom for what seemed like minutes. The section saw that day that, under some circumstances, "good" people can exhibit very poor judgment. When I recounted the exchange to colleagues after class, many nodded in approval. "Good work," one exclaimed.

Instructors are gently advised to develop repertoires of methods and skills to elicit strong comments, but some core elements seem to transcend repertoires. For instance, reinforcing productive comments and helping stumbling students articulate their arguments are common to many repertoires. In the School's ideal class session, the students, not the instructor, voice compelling arguments and articulate the lessons learned. In that sense a slightly underarticulated argument that gradually takes shape with the input of other students often proves more valuable than a polished, prepared one. Another way to foster strong student comments is to broadcast videotaped segments of past case discussions. When case protagonists cannot be present on campus, the norm is to broadcast videotaped segments of their latest visit in class. (A camera operator at the back of the classroom generally tapes sessions with case protagonists.) Reliving past sessions may seem contrary to the goal of internalized discovery, but its mimetic effect cannot be discounted. The video segments illustrate the nature of strong participation and showcase how best to contribute in the classroom.[20] Many such videos include question-and-answer segments, and the camera occasionally lingers on former students' attentive faces. But more generally, the real-time reactions of the instructor and section mates to student comments shape expectations for student participation. Section mates' occasional applause, or repeated references to a specific comment, as well as positive reaction from the instructor, signal helpful, if not high-quality, participation.[21]

Surprises are in a sense both feared and hoped for by the instructor. A case discussion with too many surprises (or too much discovery) can derail a teaching plan and its objectives. But a case discussion with no surprises (or no discovery) is also sure to fail. This partly explains why few instructors provide "direct" answers to students' questions; too much guidance might kill the discovery process. Faculty war stories capture both success and miserable failure, underlining the organizational centrality of the teaching task.[22] Many faculty members share horror stories with select colleagues, but some discretion is de rigueur since an instructors' reputation is at stake. The worst derailments—such as when an instructor overslept and failed to show up to teach a section—are rarely talked about.[23] Stories about prepping the wrong case, or having a student walk out of the classroom in anger, circulate more readily among trusted colleagues.

My own horror story involves an occasion when my simultaneous mental movies got entangled. After a student's unusually trenchant remarks on the day's case, I began a brief wrap-up: her arguments had been insightful

When no room is left for students' self-discovery. From Hank Levinson (HBS MBA
'56), *Casual Observer; or, Across the River and Up the Creek* (Cambridge, MA: Eagle
Enterprises, 1955), n.p. (12th page).

and her action plan viable, and she had summarized the gist of the case. I
remember being pleased with her and with myself. As I ended the wrap,
I thanked her for her insight and began assembling the papers spread
out on the desk in front of me: a ritual that signals a session's end. Ninety
faces gazed silently at me. Nobody rose. As the silence lengthened, I knew
something was wrong but not what it was. That morning I was scheduled to teach two sections back to back, one from 8:40 to 10:00 a.m., the
other from 10:20 to 11:40 a.m. It was 9:40 a.m., an hour into the first session; we had twenty more minutes to go. The student's astute comment,
coupled with my having encoded the second session's stop time on my
case-specific tape, led to the mix-up.[24] After a very long pause, I decided the
course had to continue. The teaching group, as always, had provided additional questions to relaunch the discussion if a case fell flat. I used one
of these questions, and after perhaps five minutes got a grip on what the
actual ending time should be.

Such derailments seem to go virtually unnoticed by students, and their rarity probably testifies to the efficacy of the many layers of preparation for teaching.[25] But the acute sensitivity to mistakes on the part of the faculty suggests the existence of an internalized delivery-derailment taboo, as well as a potent form of organizational regulation: self-control.[26] Because derailments are not meant to happen, they constitute news. It is not as much their consequences as their mere and infrequent occurrence that renders them memorable.[27] The day of my derailment, when the proper ending time (10:00 a.m.) approached, I again wished everyone a good day and again packed up my notes. The students applauded, as they routinely do at the School, to mark the end of a session.

Post-Session Maintenance

Just as maintenance is often required after products are delivered, each class session generates post-session activities. Cases and class discussions often trigger requests for more information. "What happened to the case protagonist?" is a frequent question, not always addressed in class. Sometimes students simply want to discuss specific points in cases that speak to their own experience. Such activities typically begin immediately after class, when certain students approach the instructor with follow-up questions or clarifications. (Other students disparage them as "pit-divers" seeking to increase their participation grade.)[28] If the case centered, for instance, on trading, a former trader might want to let me know how his trading room proved similar to or different from the one described in the case. Alternatively, a student with no trading experience might be curious about typical career paths in the industry. Most instructors field as many queries as they can on the spot, but the arrival of the next instructor, or the first instructor's having another class scheduled, often limits the time devoted to such questions. When time runs out, students are encouraged to set up individual meetings.

Afternoons are the usual time for meetings with students: classes have usually ended and instructors are too tired, by that time in the day, to concentrate on intensive labor. One afternoon in my first weeks teaching at the School, as I was talking with a student in my office, I heard a knock at my door. In keeping with School norms, the door was half open; my assistant entered and told me that my next appointment had arrived.[29] I did not recall another appointment so looked at her a bit puzzled, but thanked her. After the student left, I asked about the next appointment. (Appointments are usually scheduled by faculty assistants, who group them in batches for efficiency's sake. Slots of twenty minutes are typical.) My assistant told me that I had no more appointments. She had learned through working for many years with other faculty members to knock at the end of each time slot to indicate that the time was up. She was trying to help. As early as 1963, a junior faculty member had remarked on the need for such help: "Faced with the manifest impossibility of getting to know 180 men [two sections, all male at that time] . . . many instructors tend to discourage rather than encourage student contacts."[30]

As the semester progresses and grade anxiety rises, appointments with students increasingly center on class participation. The phrasing of requests for appointments suggests the students' growing anxiety. A typical request in week three: "Could we please meet to discuss my class participation?" In week six: "I am hoping that there might be a time when we can connect in the next week or two?" In week nine: "I was wondering if I could arrange a short (5-minute) appointment to discuss how to improve my participation?" The progression of these requests also suggests an awareness of the increasing demands put on the faculty at the end of a semester, as the students adjust their expectations accordingly.[31] Student meetings are generally instructive for the faculty and provide important feedback on a course's reception. Students' eagerness to engage with teaching materials can be quite rewarding and drives the faculty's future efforts, including case writing.

School faculty members are strongly encouraged to develop teaching materials such as cases and teaching notes. A key reason to develop such materials is that the case method is seen at the School not only as "a method of teaching, but also a method of research."[32] Writing a case usually entails finding a willing protagonist, framing his or her challenge in terms that are sufficiently detailed to convince an industry reader yet broad enough to interest a general readership, and obtaining approval from his or her company to release the case. (Most cases, even when identities are disguised, require a sign-off from the organization depicted. The only exceptions are purely fictional cases.) As with the delivery of teaching sessions, each step in the process of producing cases is codified. From assigning a case number to line editing, dedicated School staff members stand ready to contribute. Case writing, besides earning the author the recognition of other faculty members, can also carry financial incentives. Faculty-authors receive some royalties from sales of their materials outside the School (mainly to other business school students). Yet other School members' reactions are the real drivers of faculty members' efforts.

A standing ovation typically opens a class session devoted to a new case authored by the instructor. How the case is actually received within the School becomes evident, however, only at the end of the semester, when students assess each case as part of the online course evaluation. Its popularity

The campus at night. Photo by Catherine Hammond.

outside the School may be roughly inferred from the yearly summary of royalties that faculty-authors receive each summer. These data help in revising previously taught cases to make them sharper or in developing new cases for which there seems to be a demand: for instance, global or failure cases. How cases are launched and monitored suggests, if not a continuous production line, at least an organization with many well-specified routines. For faculty members, from the moment student names need to be memorized (in early September or January) to the time when course and case evaluations become available and new cases start to be conceived (late December or April), the impression of being shift mates working on a complex product is constant.

* * *

From the smallest details (the timing of the descending screen) to the biggest challenges (fostering internalized discovery), multiple well-oiled processes are in place to help instructors with their tasks. Every time instructors remove their jackets in the first-year classrooms, at 8:40 a.m., 10:20 a.m., and often again at 1:10 p.m., these gestures are the result of a flurry of processes that converge in that moment. The processes capture and codify the institutional memory and help instructors learn their craft. If a case has been well delivered once, replicating the steps that fostered its success is seen as the best way to ensure subsequent success (almost regardless of the instructor).[33] By contrast, relative organizational silence prevails on the conclusion of a session, the promotion of any given perspective in the classroom, and other such topics.

In other words, the content of what is taught is discussed in the teaching groups, but specifying the "normative" conclusions to be drawn from the case discussion is studiously avoided. Routines guide the proper delivery of classes, but their proper conclusion is left to the instructors' discretion.[34] As an illustration, when an early financial contributor to the School lobbied for explicit instruction in a "higher code of business morals" and the creation of an ethics course, the administration pushed back. Edwin F. Gay, the School's dean at the time, explained his decision not to offer such a course: "I believe with you that we should give some occasional lectures which seek to give our students some light on what is at present a very per-

plexing and not wholly solved problem." The difficulty, he added, is finding lecturers "at once practical and elevating, without being 'preachy.'"[35]

Then as now, preaching—of specific conclusions or any moral viewpoint—is seen as an ineffective mode of instruction. If anything, preaching in silence is the norm at the School. As a close observer of the School
recently noted, "Effective faculty mentors do not make pronouncements
from on high, for there is not blind acceptance of authority (even if held
in high repute) among these students."[36] Instead, faculty members are
encouraged to allow students to decide for themselves, based on the arguments voiced in the classroom.[37] Skeptics might contend that despite such
apparent ambiguity, School-specific norms still get conveyed in class. In
particular, the teaching notes faculty members rely on to prepare their sessions might contain specific guidance on what to teach. The next chapter
analyzes such notes to explore that hypothesis.

FOUR

(Un)Scripted Journeys

He showed me also, in one of his books, the figures of the sun,
moon, and stars, the zodiac, the tropics, and polar circles, together
with the denominations of many planes and solids . . .
JONATHAN SWIFT, *Gulliver's Travels*

Settling into my airplane seat after a short out-of-town trip, I pull out the documents I plan to read during the flight. At the top of my pile is the teaching note for the case I assigned my class for the next day. As often is the case, the Sunday end-of-day Boston-bound flights are quite full, and another passenger takes the seat next to mine and unpacks as well. Then he plugs in his earphones, takes out a pen, and starts energetically under-lining a document. I notice the School's logo at the top of his document: he is reading the Wolfgang Keller case, about a Greek brewery. My heart starts to beat faster; I expect to teach that case later in the semester, not tomorrow. He must be a student in one of the nine other sections of the course I teach, and this means I am probably off schedule.

Because students typically read cases only a day in advance, I swiftly conclude that I am prepping the wrong case. Session delivery mess-ups are among junior faculty members' recurring fears: walking into a class-room primed to teach the wrong case would be a nightmare. What luck to catch this potential derailment in time! It is not too late to shift gears before the next day. I feel like thanking him. Then I notice a second logo on the folder containing his copy of the case: the logo of the Massachusetts Institute of Technology. A sense of relief sweeps over me. HBS cases are

71

used in many academic settings, including MIT. Whatever class he is enrolled in undoubtedly follows a different schedule. His instructor is probably reviewing the Wolfgang Keller teaching note at the same moment I
turn to the teaching note about my next case.

* * *

Cases need to be digested to be taught well. "Read them and sleep on
them," advises an experienced colleague. Reviewing teaching notes is also
indispensable. Teaching notes are ten- to fifteen-page documents, available to School faculty members and registered instructors elsewhere, that
provide guidance on how to conduct a classroom session on a given case.
A teaching note is typically written by the faculty member who developed
and first taught the case. Organizational artifacts like these notes are consequential.[1] Like a trail or a sky map, a teaching note provides a lens through
which to see, read, and navigate the case data. And as an "exemplar" of
how the teaching session might proceed, a teaching note guides action in
subtle ways.[2] Alongside teaching group meetings, notes are the bedrock of
an instructor's preparation; if any norms exist at the School, notes should
capture them (at least in part). They are rich documents that capture the
accumulated experience of various instructors who have taught the case
and familiarize other instructors with the case's various usages. Teaching
notes can thus act as powerful socialization tools for junior faculty members, and by extension for students.

Many School courses also offer "course notes" and/or "module notes"
(notes on a subset of class sessions) that summarize classroom presentation of all or part of a course at a more aggregate level. But new instructors'
initial focus on day-to-day delivery of sessions guarantees that teaching
notes play a more central role in getting up to speed on new courses. The
notes allow for a scaling-up of the educational pursuit by codifying past
learning.[3] Even more than the cases themselves, teaching notes enable
junior faculty members to learn the tricks of the trade. In that sense, teaching notes constitute one of the backbones of classroom teaching.

So what do these notes tell us? Like the classroom experience described
in the previous chapter, teaching notes help us identify the more or less
stable components of the School environment. Though teaching notes offer
suggestions about how to teach a case, they mostly refrain from specifying

Students' mailboxes, to which teaching cases are distributed. Photo by Catherine Hammond.

what should ultimately be taught. They script the teaching process to a certain point but typically leave unscripted the broader teaching goals. In other words, the vast majority of notes describe the steps or techniques needed to execute successfully the recipe of the day without clearly specifying the resulting dish. This is not to say that teaching notes are not helpful. In fact, they set the stage for a strong discussion. Yet as a senior School faculty member reminds us, the case method does not focus on answers. Instead, it teaches students and faculty members to identify "great" questions that yield answers, almost regardless of what the answers might be.[4] The teaching model is meant to equip students analytically, and teaching notes help faculty members achieve that goal.

Scripted Teaching Steps

"Instructors should open the class by asking a student: 'As an equity investor with a long-term horizon, what grade—A, B, C, etc.—would you give the firm's senior executive team for their performance?' Next, poll the students for their grades, based on a show of hands. Expect very few As and most likely an even distribution of Bs, Cs, and D/Fs."[5] Instructors who rely on such an opening are likely to initiate discussion on a strong foot: immediately forcing students to take a stand is a proven route of entry into a case. Moreover, such an initial overture also pushes students to justify their assessments, at least in their own minds. Many variations on the assessment entry question populate the teaching notes: "On a scale from 1 to 10, how would you assess the firm's performance?" "If given the opportunity, would you want to work for this company?" These variations also illustrate the numerous leading questions found in the notes.

The vast majority of teaching notes for first-year MBA courses (72 percent of the notes used in all ten required first-year courses) contain leading questions that instructors can rely on at critical junctures to advance discussion. (See table 1 for an accounting of the teaching notes analyzed.)[6] For example, an instructor who wants to shift the focus of classroom discussion from what's happening inside a company to external dynamics might ask, "Who buys these products anyway?" or "Who are the company's customers? Should we care about them?" Such questions help redirect students' focus from one topic to another. They also draw on the transitions that have worked best in the past, and as such offer scripts for successful teaching sessions. Much effort also goes into honing a precise wording that unambiguously draws attention to an unexplored tension or encourages a transition to a different subject of conversation. Any slippage tends to trigger a sea of raised hands requesting clarification (justifiably). For instance, asking students to "assess a firm" without specifying what is being assessed (e.g., its performance) can easily lead down more discussion threads than a novice instructor ever imagines. It is often said that skilled instructors who are already familiar with a given case can walk into the classroom with nothing more than the three or four main questions spelled out on a sheet of paper (or memorized) and lead a class discussion successfully on that basis alone.

New and less talented instructors, and certainly many junior faculty members, generally welcome more help. This is why most teaching notes (62 percent across all ten courses) also include typical student answers. As an illustration, the author of one note explains that, when probed about

Table 1. Teaching notes overview, 2007–2008

	Number of cases	Number of notes	Percentages of cases with accompanying notes (%)	Number of sampled notes
Course A	38	17	45	6
Course B	33	21	64	7
Course C	20	13	65	4
Course D	19	11	58	4
Course E	29	25	86	8
Course F	26	19	73	6
Course G	26	16	62	5
Course H	31	23	74	8
Course I	29	20	69	7
Course J	26	19	73	6
Totals	277	184	66	61

Note: All ten required courses offered during the 2007–2008 academic year (e.g., finance 1, finance 2, marketing, technology and operations, strategy) are analyzed. A course on negotiation, also offered that year and since dropped from the curriculum, is excluded. A few simulations and alternate course materials (e.g., readings) are not included here.

their assessment of a case protagonist, "many students, if not most, will see him as a sincere and well-intentioned human being. He has strong convictions (perhaps too strong), pride (perhaps too much), and compassion (perhaps too blinding). . . . A few students, however, may contend that he is a bit of an egotist and perhaps even a bully." Armed with these insights, instructors can prepare themselves for possible scenarios that might occur in the classroom.

Though teaching sessions invariably differ, knowing typical reactions to given topics still proves handy. As another note's author, perhaps a bit blasé, remarks when referring to a case's action plan: "Students' answers are predictable: the largest numbers of students recommend some form of slap on the wrist and a smaller number recommend the outright firing of the protagonist. . . . Few of the students choose to do nothing. . . . There is a small but vocal group, however, that sees this as a watershed opportunity to 'walk the talk' on this question." The note encourages the instructor to spot and engage fairly rapidly with the vocal group, and possibly to rely on them to push back against the majority position. Notes never identify specific students, but students' pervasive generic presence in the notes' narratives vividly prepares instructors for the likely tenor of the classroom.

Despite teaching notes' specification of leading questions and typical student answers, classroom discussions often go off track. I recall wondering more than once how we ever got to some point. Small details in cases can easily spiral into full-blown debates. A protagonist's clothing, visible in a video, might lead to a discussion of power relations at work. The case's geographical setting could trigger debates about the pros and cons of urban renewal. A footnote in the appendix might even prompt a discussion of data validity. Possible tangents are almost limitless, and they shift with the composition of the class. Case discussions are in part projections of students' varied hopes and fears; as a result, teaching derailments are inevitable.

Minor derailments are often welcome surprises for instructors, since they inject adrenaline into case-teaching, but occasionally discussions can go seriously off the tracks. How to regain at least partial control of a class discussion, as sometimes proves necessary, is therefore a third common theme in teaching notes (present in 67 percent of cases across all ten courses). Case-method purists might praise partial losses of control as providing ideal learning opportunities for insight to emerge from conversations. But in practice, few junior faculty members feel at ease teaching a case without some guiding compass in mind. Teaching notes are written to assuage their fears by offering concrete ways to regain control of off-track or stalled discussions. For example, one note, whose author was once presumably caught off guard, advises, "If sentiment turns sharply negative, consider arresting the trend by saying: 'Wow: you guys are harsh graders! Let me remind you that this management team spotted these opportunities when the industry was not even formed. They built a business pretty much out of thin air. How could they be bad at what they do?'" Questions like this inevitably lead students back to consideration of the central issues of the case.

Similarly, when complex financial calculations pose a risk that ill-prepared students will slow down a session, another author suggests, "The calculations in the case are potentially quite complicated. To navigate through them smoothly, instructors may want to ask several student volunteers to submit their analyses the night before class. The instructor can then select a couple of students who have done the analysis well to lead the discussion. This reduces the risk that the class will get bogged down."

Students' study area to prepare for class. Photo by Han Lei.

The vast majority of teaching notes thus point out landmines specific to the case in question and suggest pretested remedies to avoid or disable them. The hazard is not eliminated, but the risk of stepping on it in the classroom is reduced. Some blasts will occur nonetheless, but emerging unharmed is evidence of a faculty member's teaching talent. Healed wounds and bruises are indeed marks of proper teaching, attesting to an instructor's valiant determination to lead students over arduous terrain.

High-Stakes (but Unspecified) Battles

While teaching notes specify clear methods and patterns with respect to the teaching process (namely leading questions, typical answers, and techniques for regaining control), their combined educational purpose proves less easy to assess. Three-quarters of all notes (75 percent across all ten courses) articulate specific teaching or learning objectives; typical examples are providing "an opportunity for students to make a capital budgeting decision," understanding "the role of an occupation in an employee's life," considering "the legal tools available to create and capture value from innovation," and realizing that "markets go through stages of growth." By focusing on discrete challenges in business life, the notes (and the cases they accompany) promote attainment of a set of skills in the service of a broader but largely unspecified edifice or goal.

In School classrooms, teaching notes transform the formless flow of business life into a series of objectified and diverse business challenges. Like the training of medical students, which favors seeing reality through the lens of symptoms, diagnostics, and treatment, the training of business students—as articulated in most teaching notes—encourages a view of corporate life as a succession of challenges that demand varied and tested resolutions.[7] By focusing on analytical tools designed to overcome challenges, the notes offer a rich repertoire that students can be expected to master. Via models, frameworks, and checklists, students gradually acquire technical breadth. The notes' stated goals in turn concentrate on ways to handle specific challenges. Thus the overlap between different teaching notes' stated goals is quite limited. Little overarching purpose can be gleaned from surveying those goals.

The stakes and significance of that overarching purpose are nonetheless repeatedly emphasized. If cases are not about life and death, they are certainly about winners and losers in a challenging mêlée; the majority of notes include narratives that refer explicitly to the firms' or the protagonists' success and/or failure (69 percent of notes across all ten courses). Success comes in many flavors and can be measured at many levels: most notably that of the protagonist (e.g., "The manager figured out how to operate in Asia, successfully adjusted his firm's business model, and is now poised for considerable success"), but also that of the workgroup (e.g., the chosen design "typically leads to improved worker morale and dedication, contributing to fewer worker grievances, lower worker absenteeism, and lower worker turnover") and the firm (e.g., "The product then achieved national distribution and several of the competitors mentioned in the case decided not to enter this market").

Failures are similarly described at all levels of analysis. Notes report that protagonists are forced to resign due to poor performance, that firms go into bankruptcy, and that the government is asked to commit costly financial resources to support struggling firms. The balance is a bit tilted toward success: notes that discuss only success (18 percent of notes across nine courses) are slightly more numerous than those discussing only

Students on their way to class. Photo by Han Lei.

failure (11 percent across seven courses). No clear contextual or individual factors (e.g., industry, setting, country, or the protagonist's demographics) seem to predict one outcome over the other; all settings and protagonists are given equal opportunities to win or fail. Only high-valence emotional states on the part of the protagonist seem to be consistently associated with failure in the teaching notes: rushed decisions, excessive anger, and rapid unanalyzed reactions tend to lead to failure.[8] Ill-planned actions lacking analytical underpinnings also seem invariably to fail.

Perhaps more importantly, business life is depicted as offering simultaneous opportunities and pitfalls. A substantial number of notes point out that the situation in question can result in either failure or success (40 percent across nine courses), underscoring that the course of action is by no means predetermined. The notes also prompt instructors and students to ponder the possible consequences of choices not made and paths not taken—always implicitly questioning whether the outcome might somehow have been different. In other words, notes assume a high level of individual agency. Case protagonists are participants in dramas in which confrontation with personal choice is the norm and carries heavy consequences.

The dramatization of corporate life is further reinforced by constant attention to real-life events. News about corporate clashes and their outcomes permeates life on campus. It is common to overhear a group of students discussing the latest market developments and leader successions. Student-led clubs routinely invite corporate leaders to campus to recount their stories. Instructors teaching first-year courses typically receive updates on the companies featured in the cases they teach from the member of the teaching group most familiar with the case being taught. Many instructors also keep up via the press. The *Wall Street Journal* and the *New York Times* appear every morning in most faculty members' mailboxes and then rapidly disappear into their offices. Faculty members also forward relevant news items to colleagues with an interest in a given company. And more than a few key players in past corporate battles, having joined the School as management practice faculty members, are visible and approachable presences on campus. Former practitioners of this kind represent living embodiments of the ups and downs of past corporate clashes.

Warlike terminology permeates several notes (18 percent across five

Dispatches from the field: the *Wall Street Journal* and the School's student newspaper, the *Harbus*. Photo by the author.

courses), further underlining how high the stakes are in protagonists' environments. The parallels between this terminology and the unsecure "liquidated" culture favored by Wall Street investment bankers are numerous.[9] In notes, companies "attack" markets, "declare fights" against other firms, and "engage in economic wars." At the same time, competitors in both local and global encounters are labeled "attackers," wrong moves are deemed "deal killers," and firms are described as vulnerable to "hostile takeovers." Some authors even suggest asking students questions like "What have been the 'weapons of war'?" and "How should the protagonist fight for survival?" In such unstable environments, clearly, no one is completely safe. Anybody can end up liquidated. Even the most storied companies can be brought down. Commenting on the "classic" quality of a studied case, an author explains that it exemplifies the situation of "historically successful companies that start to suffer performance pressures and appear (deceptively) to experience rebounds." Instructors reading the note understand that a battle is brewing, even if the case protagonists remain oblivious to what is to come. Between wins (here, rebounds) and losses (here, performance pressures), there is a battle in the making and its stakes are evident.

Yet what battles, exactly, are being fought? The battle's overarching goals typically remain ambiguous. One certainty is that the individual protagonists unmistakably lead these fights. In the same way that US corporations tend to position managers as agents of change, many notes depict protagonists as almost heroic figures.[10] Though success and failure are measured at multiple levels, such as winning promotions or increasing return on investment, teaching notes typically depict action as driven mainly by a solo protagonist (62 percent of notes across all ten courses), not by teams or groups. Battles tend to be characterized as individual, and the implicit hope is that students will identify with the protagonists. A large number of notes (39 percent in eight courses) suggest asking students to slide into the shoes of case protagonists. One, for example, offers the following question for the classroom: "Imagine you have oversight on this part of the business. Are you comfortable with what's going on?" "Do you want to be in a position that your firm is the subject of such a story in the *Wall Street Journal*?" Implicitly, organizational outcomes can be traced to personal decisions.

What do the teaching notes, in the aggregate, convey to aspiring instructors? Basically, the note reader comes to understand that cases portray high-stakes battles in which individuals face difficult and consequential business decisions. Notes cast business challenges as human problems. Proper judgment matters, since mistaken decisions in a warlike environment can have disastrous outcomes. By placing the individual at center stage, teaching notes also suggest that protagonists can guide their own destinies. This view of leaders as crafters of their own fortunes reflects a broader US managerial culture that favors what the sociologist Katherine S. Newman has called "meritocratic individualism," defined as "the notion that individuals are responsible for their own destinies."[11] This proposition carries moral assumptions about human behavior reminiscent of the secular version of the Protestant ethic described by Max Weber.[12] A perspective that looks to individual choices to win recurring battles in which individual and firm successes are conflated predominates in the School teaching notes.

Such an ontology transforms business outcomes into the result of individual struggles. Managers become part of a broader entrepreneurial group in which individualism and heroism prevail.[13] Structural social constraints are often overlooked in favor of a conceptualization of the world as composed of individual possibilities. Yet this outlook cannot be all-encompassing. Many, though not all, School students seem to aspire to engagement with something more than the mastery of technical tools to promote their own individual advancement. Teaching notes occasionally allude to such broader goals (e.g., creating jobs, bolstering a country's competitiveness, and the like). But the articulation of such social goals is mostly left to the imaginations of instructors and students.[14] Teaching notes essentially refrain from scripting such goals; almost by design, they allow multiple goals to coexist. This relatively hands-off stance leaves faculty members with the option, if exercised, to fill the gap.

A Glimpse of "a Good Life"

That the teaching notes refrain from articulating an overarching purpose does not mean that judgment is absent from these organizational artifacts. Over half of all the notes analyzed depict individual protagonists' actions as either correct or wrong (56 percent across all ten courses). Yet judgment is largely reserved for *the process*. When the protagonist is presented as following a correct course of action, note authors tend to stress that he or she followed the appropriate steps. For example, one typical note author comments positively on the fact that a manager consulted with his client before deciding to modify the nature of the longstanding relationship between his firm and the client's. Similarly, another author remarks with approval that the protagonist not only pursued legal action against a competitor but also tried to explore all other possible parallel actions, and goes on to praise the protagonist's ability to analyze all of his options.

By contrast, protagonists depicted as taking wrong turns usually ignore an important market signal, disregard vital information conveyed to them, or underestimate workforce inertia. In the unraveling dramas that ensue, they overlook key warnings signs. Though these notes' narratives convey some normative cues about what protagonists (and, by extension, students) should do or not do, such cues mainly pertain to steps, actions, and decisions, not overarching goals.[15] Correct and incorrect steps are frequently specified, but right and wrong outcomes are rarely articulated. Notes remain relatively silent on the overall direction of the path traveled by protagonists.

The first time I caught myself taking a strong normative stand in the classroom, I remember feeling quite strange: it was as if I had gone off-script and landed in uncharted terrain. The class discussion centered on a factory line; I asked what the line manager's worst fear might be. "A union," one student immediately retorted. By that, the student meant a strike led by the union that would stop the line; he elaborated on the negative repercussions of such an event. The class fell silent and no hands were raised. As a rookie, I was intimidated by the silence. I had not yet learned to wait for other students to pick up on the last comment. Instead, I stepped in and reminded the class of some pros and cons of unions in various countries and industries. My bias was evident: all of the students noticed it. If I were to update the teaching note accompanying that case, I would probably frame this episode as a potential classroom pitfall and suggest ways to restart the discussion.

The fact that the instructor's espoused overarching goals or moral stand are not part of notes or regular scripted course sessions is made particularly salient by what traditionally happens in the final session of a first-year course.[16] Every such course culminates in a special end-of-term session in which, in keeping with a longstanding tradition, the instructor is expected to share something more personal or idiosyncratic with the class. A student who experienced more than a dozen such sessions recalls their being "a departure from routine. Gone were the case-study discussion and the class's typical rhythm." Instead, the instructor was going to "tell us a story from his own life."[17]

Despite being told not to prepare a lot for the final session, junior faculty members probably think harder about it than about many case discussions. Senior colleagues reassure more junior faculty members by advising them merely to do something that day that feels right, but figuring out what feels right takes time. My first year at the School, I shuffled through memories and family photos I kept at home to trigger associations. I reflected on what had brought me to the School and what made me do what I do. This session is a rare occasion when instructors are given—by design—an opportunity to share more of their convictions with their students.

My memory of my first "last session" is slightly blurry. My prepared final remarks—captured in a one-page session outline I brought to class—began, "I thought I could speak about the thrills and angsts of being a new faculty member here, but you all saw it live so there is no need to explain." After delivering that line, I spoke about journeys—those we thought we were engaging in and those we ended up pursuing, those involving movement and those that require staying put—and about packing and unpacking one's bags. In retrospect, I doubt that my "story" was very clear or insightful, but it seemed appropriate for that moment. In subsequent years, depending on how I thought the course had gone, I tried to tailor the final session to the class's shared endpoint. In an effort to recast the course content in a longer time frame, I have sometimes shown reproductions of works of art or read excerpts from classic books that have inspired me. Some of these sessions fell flat. Others made me regret having set aside only these few last moments for such conversations. None felt completely normal.

There are obviously as many ways to end a course as there are instructors. Thanks to Daisy Wademan, who published a sample of fifteen such sessions, all delivered in 2001 or 2002, we can get a sense of what sort of thing is said. (She selected only stories that inspired her or had what she describes as a great impact on her classmates, but her sample seems fairly representative.) The stories were all different but at the same time expressed consistent themes. All addressed "how to create a better life— a *good* life—as a leader."[18] Some faculty members delivered words such as we associate with graduation ceremonies: "Have the courage to forge ahead. Listen to your passions. Consult your own internal compass. Think about yourself and the human condition. And then do something truly great." Others offered more practical advice, for instance, urging students to apply "techniques of connecting with people, staying grounded, being down to earth and approachable" in the workplace. Yet others focused on how to measure accomplishments; one faculty member recommended "measuring achievements in how you affect others . . . not in how you burnish your own résumé." Finally, some faculty members were more explicit and spoke directly to the School's stated pursuit. One asked rhetorically, for instance, whether we, as managers, should not "create our own code of conduct," going on to clarify: "Why not have a statement of mission for managers as a group, which outlines our highest standards of skills and responsibility?"[19] This phrase echoes, and even intensifies, the School's early "better standards" narrative.

These end-of-course sessions allow instructors to disclose themselves to their students more fully than ordinary teaching permits. They also serve a more symbolic purpose, offering examples of personal drivers of action completely outside the scripted boundaries of teaching notes. (Faculty members' stories are by no means exemplary; they often simply illustrate ways of deriving meaning from work.)[20] Despite their rarity, such moments provide glimpses into more or less explicit overarching goals. By populating that last session, and possibly others as well, with such "stories," most (if not all) faculty members fill the void left in regular teaching notes by conveying their own normative views.

By the same token, first-year students typically express their views of the instructor during the final session. The end of the semester provides them an opportunity to remind faculty members of what students value. In addition to often presenting a traditional gift (a framed class photo or a framed case), a class representative—the section's president or educational

The joy of receiving an end-of-semester gift. Photo by Pankaj Makkar.

representative, or a student with a particularly close connection to the faculty member—usually addresses the instructor briefly on behalf of the class. These remarks, which resemble a eulogy, typically comment on the faculty member's teaching ability and personal idiosyncrasies, but they also sometimes acknowledge the instructors' production of cases, as an excerpt from one such address demonstrates: "This semester you've outlined some paths to succeed. You've taught us to question, to plan, and to lead. . . . Your questions are tough, your class well-aligned. You've written two new cases—your T-shirt reads 'stellar.'"[21] The instructor who is also an author of cases is thus reminded that he or she produces pieces for semiprivate consumption. Like a book for select readers or a piece of art for exclusive viewing, cases and their associated teaching notes help School students develop a shared understanding of who they might become.

Cases are by far the most conspicuous organizational artifacts from students' vantage point. Teaching notes are a less visible, accompanying support of the cases and, more broadly, of the School's educational infrastructure. (First-year courses also include occasional exercises and group projects, but case-based teaching remains the norm.) The program of study proposed in the notes is one in which teaching and learning, and knowledge in general, is organized in purposeful ways. Without embracing a view of education as a form of social control, one can easily see how such organizational tools can both constrain and enable, thus simultaneously scripting and unscripting the educational journey.[22] When adhered to, teaching notes create a framework in which learning is discovered and constructed. Notes thus serve as what sociologists call "cultural anchors" or "handles" that allow for consistency in teaching.[23] More specifically, notes favor questions rather than answers and avoid stabilizing, at least in writing, any given normative view.[24] Thus, an adherence to relative normative silence seems to be a cultural anchor at the School.

* * *

Teaching notes assist in the enterprise of recoding human problems as business challenges and of emphasizing the individual capacity to succeed or fail at solving such challenges. These concepts are, most fundamentally, the permanent anchors that case-based classroom teaching revolves around. The individual-agency bias has been well documented across many business schools.[25] Both pervasive and frequently decried, it seems to exercise a fairly strong hold—as far as teaching notes suggest—in the School's first-year curriculum. What may distinguish the School, however, is the prevailing insistence on the high stakes of the decisions in question. Not only are individuals held accountable for outcomes, but the outcomes themselves are situated in a context of ongoing corporate clashes in which winners and losers are the norm. Furthermore, the outcomes are interpreted as fairly direct reflections of individual action. In the context of what the sociologist Michèle Lamont characterizes as the widespread US belief in "being what you want," business outcomes can be coded as evidence of individuals' ability or inability to want sufficiently strongly.[26] A key implication of this ontology is that students probably do not fear "falling from grace" (to use Katherine Newman's terminology) as much as they fear not "attaining grace" in the first place.[27] What makes the difference between attaining and missing out on grace is the individual's course of action.

Notes remain, however, fairly silent on the *direction* of such a course of action. The definition of "grace" thus remains quite amorphous. Though teaching notes typically articulate discrete business challenges, they mostly refrain from spelling out an overarching goal. Notes' apparent silence on key normative issues allows for a variety of goals to coexist within the confines of the School's broader perspective. It is individuals, and in particular faculty members, who help bring to the surface in this apparent silence such overarching goals. Yet the silence is only apparent, since these same notes contain many vocal cues as to what proper behavior entails. Nonetheless, a central question for the School administration is how to select people who will properly articulate goals and animate the apparent organizational voids (see chapter 6). Alongside such selection, constant efforts need be deployed to ensure continuity. The next chapter examines how new faculty members are socialized outside of the teaching process.

FIVE

Doing What Others Don't

The men . . . wear a slight covering, and above this a round hat a
little larger than the size of their head. In the fields they use caps,
but at home each one wears a biretta, white, red, or another color
according to his trade or occupation.

TOMMASO CAMPANELLA, *City of the Sun*

A few years after joining the School, I inherited a large framed etching that
had belonged to my grandparents, but it did not fit at home since most of
the walls were already taken. This made it a perfect candidate for my office.
The print, made in Germany in 1906, represents two men, in lieu of an
ox, laboriously pulling a plow guided by a woman. I brought it to campus
and asked around for a nail. "I'm sorry, we found none," my faculty assistant told me. "But don't worry, we can call maintenance. They will hang
it for us." She paused, suddenly sounding apologetic. "Actually, I believe
you are not allowed to put a nail in your wall. Maintenance folks are the
only ones who can do so. I'll place a job order." She smiled reassuringly.

Within twenty-four hours a maintenance person appeared in my office.
Not only did he look the part, he came equipped with a full toolbox. After
inquiring where I wanted the etching positioned, he measured the wall
from left to right and top to bottom to find the exact center. Once a pilot
hole was drilled, he chose among a selection of nails to find the "best
match" for the job. To underscore perhaps his expertise, he added, "You
don't want such a nice piece of art to fall, right?" I could only agree. What
I imagined as the rapid hammering of a nail in a wall became an elaborate

A job well done: the perfectly centered etching. Photo by the author.

project, complete with adding small touches of white paint to the "damaged" parts of the wall. I was impressed; clearly, I was not in the business of hanging frames or, for that matter, anything else on the wall. The result was a testimony to the risks of veering beyond one's assigned mandate. The episode illustrates the extent of the division of labor on campus, but also the presence of many organizational signs that shape behavior.

* * *

Any division of labor can first be seen as reflecting the differential distribution of technical skills, experiences, or capabilities among individuals. But it also points to what the sociologist Emile Durkheim referred to as a moral order, a way in which differing moral functions are distributed among members of society.[1] As fellow sociologist Robert Park noted in the urban communities he studied, the division of labor constitutes "a discipline" or "the means of molding character."[2] As tasks are distributed, character gets shaped. In that sense, looking at what is expected in practice of faculty members (and other School members) helps further clarify what type of character or perspective the School favors.

The expectation that faculty members not hang anything on their walls on their own is a testimony to such a division of labor. Besides teaching and research, faculty members are expected to engage in many other activities, both formally (e.g., grading) and informally (meeting students). At the same time, a variety of activities are deemed off-limits both formally (nonconsensual relationships with students) and informally (preaching in class). In that sense, faculty members' perimeter of expected action or inaction can convey what is not explicitly codified in other School routines, such as those surrounding proper research (see chapter 2). Examining what is encouraged or discouraged rather than what is written or said offers an alternate window into the School's perspective.

When individuals engage in given tasks, they trace jurisdictional boundaries that signal perimeters and mandates of competency.[3] Individuals not designated to operate within a given perimeter are generally deemed competent in *another* one and therefore are also reminded, by default, of what they should be doing. The division of labor impacts not only those engaged in given tasks (e.g., maintenance staff) but also those assumed, simultaneously, *not* to engage in these tasks (faculty or academic support staff). Thus, a "hollow" definition of what School faculty members are supposed to do can first be constructed based on what others, around them, are mandated to accomplish. While maintenance people intervene only sporadically in faculty members' lives, many other staff members provide daily reminders of task division on campus and of proper faculty behavior.

Carving out a Faculty's Role by Default

Early in my tenure at the School, when preparing an article for consideration by an academic journal with a unique bibliographic style, I asked a colleague who had published in the journal if proper formatting of references was required at the time of submission. His answer teasingly underlined my inexperience: "Remember you are now a HBS professor. Ask your assistant, she will do it better than you can ever do it. Also, that will allow you to focus on other things." The last sentence sounded almost like a reproach. "Other things" seemed a euphemism for more important things. Not only was I out of line, but I was also stepping out of my perimeter and potentially failing to deliver on other expectations.

My assistant indeed did a wonderful job of formatting the bibliography. Daily, the School's eighty or so faculty assistants make sure faculty members can do their work without the need to handle too many mundane details of academic life. Their role is similar to that of assistants in professional service firms. Each assistant works, on average, with three or four faculty members. Assistants typically handle many interactions with other School staff members (except senior administrators), update faculty members' electronic agendas, and make travel arrangements. If, for example, two faculty members meet in a corridor and agree to have lunch together, their assistants will determine the optimal day and time to do so. Similarly, faculty assistants handle a majority of student appointments.

While such assistance is not unexpected in resource-rich work environments, the suggestion, once, that my assistant bring me a snack between two teaching sessions in another building on campus caught me off guard. Why would I need to have snacks delivered? It seemed almost colonial. The downtime between the two sessions was twenty minutes. Yet after adding time to answer a few questions at the end of the first session and grading the first session's class participation, little time was left to prepare for the second round. After my first break, I realized that such assistance was no luxury. I was tired, hungry, and craving food. Going to the cafeteria to purchase a snack during that time often proved infeasible; vending machines also got mobbed; and returning to my office consumed too much time.

Though I declined the offer for assistance (preferring instead to carry my own snacks), I accepted many other offers, including the systematic opening of my incoming mail (unless marked confidential), the preparation of personal folders summarizing students' information prior to meetings, and the printing of local maps for orientation during travels. Any busy individual will recognize the benefit of targeted help. Such offers of assistance are extremely considerate; along with other School support practices, they also carve out, by default, the faculty members' expected roles. Such an environment helps focus faculty members on their "core" occupational tasks, particularly on teaching and conducting research.

In addition to my faculty assistant, a variety of other administrative

A faculty member deviating from core tasks? Photo by Catherine Hammond.

support positions at the School are meant to free faculty members from "nonessential" activities. Most visible, perhaps, are the research associates who help faculty members with many tasks. Each year, more than a hundred new research associates are hired, and most stay several years at the School. (Research associates typically work for more than one faculty member at the same time.) The fact that these individuals are generally full-time School employees and not students working on the side while they study (as is the case in most other academic settings) signals the extent to which the School supports its faculty.

Research associates are not the only ones providing assistance on a daily basis. Course assistants (one for each first-year core course offering), section chairs (a faculty contact person for each entering MBA student section), and educational representatives (or "ed-reps,"students elected from each section) likewise contribute to the infrastructure supporting faculty work. For any conceivable task, including developing interactive course content or new teaching plans, a School staff person can usually be identified and approached for help. And for unexpected needs, such as labor-intensive copying or data coding, a cadre of "floaters," or occasional support staff with no fixed affiliation, can be called upon for assistance. If anything, determining to *whom* I should turn for help is more difficult than obtaining actual help.

Many other teaching-related tasks are also streamlined or outsourced (though not grading, a point I will return to later). Historically, for instance, "scribes," paid by the School, would attend classes and take notes on student participation for faculty members for later review.[4] More recently, the launch of a student absence notification system illustrates this concern for streamlining noncore activities. On teaching days, I typically find a few automated messages in my electronic mailbox, all of which start, "Dear Prof. Anteby, Please note the absence below." Customized details follow: "Name of Student: Martha Jones [a pseudonym]. Date of Absence: 11/14/2008. Reason for Absence: Personal illness. Additional Information: I am so sick I will not be able to come to class today. Sorry for the inconvenience." For students, only one step is required to inform all faculty members of their absence. For faculty, the system efficiently informs us of who will not show up to class and what might be happening in a student's life. With all of these supports, the complexity of dealing with sometimes close to two hundred students at once—without any teaching assistants—is greatly reduced. The conspicuous absence of teaching assistants or teaching fellows underscores the fact that it is essential for faculty members to teach.

All is done to ensure that other (nonessential) tasks are properly allocated and performed. Dealing with students' serious medical and personal issues, for instance, falls explicitly in the category of faculty members' noncore tasks. "For medical emergencies, there is only one reaction to have: call 911." This message is part of a mandatory orientation for faculty teaching in the required curriculum. The orientation continues, "Emergency medical care is not handled on-site. First responses will come from trained emergency medical technicians." A long pause after *trained* underlines the faculty inadequacy for the task. Simultaneously, the speaker waves a telephone handset, with an unplugged cord, in the air to emphasize the point and repeats, "Call 911."

In other words, one should not attempt to do what one is not prepared for. If this message is not clear enough, the lesson goes on, "You are not a social worker, a therapist, or a marriage counselor." At that point, faculty audience members who have previously reached out in such a manner to students almost experience shame for doing so. (I duck my head.) "In a population of close to nine hundred students, issues will arise. People will have problems. Parents will pass away. Sickness will happen, and separations are bound to occur. When this happens, please make sure to tell your students we [the School's student support services] are here to help." In practice, many faculty members still reach out to students they perceive to be in need of support. Such efforts, however, are coupled with referrals to adequate services and professionals.

The freeing up of faculty time is further reinforced by the extension of the School's support to the realm of domestic life. Outside of work, a private concierge service is available to assist faculty members' in their daily chores.[5] A concierge can find a house-cleaning service, locate a vacation rental home, or order flowers for an anniversary. Time-consuming administrative issues such as obtaining local permits or visas can also be taken care of. Similarly, a concierge can handle home-computer repairs or house-maintenance issues. This support does not shrink the ensuing faculty's mandate but further signifies that it is to be defined in contrast to these other mandates.[6]

With most mundane tasks taken care of and many other tasks deemed off-limits, the School's new faculty member has little left to do but engage in what is not being handled by others. A faculty member utilizing all of the School's support would probably interact with few people besides colleagues, staff, students, and presumably family members. (This might explain why I felt a bit out of place on occasional rides using public transportation in Boston.) These work practices contribute to what sociologist Arthur Stinchcombe calls a sense of "organizational completeness," or the provision of all members' needs without the necessity for outside contact.[7] But in this context what is a faculty member left to do?

School faculty members rarely appear to be idle.[8] We already know that faculty members are expected to teach, produce teaching materials, and engage in relevant research (see chapters 2 and 3). I will not return to these previously described activities. Any faculty member can easily occupy all of his or her freed-up time working toward such goals. And if any uncertainty remains about what is expected on that front, the weekly "Faculty Research Publications" summary, an electronic message sent to the School's faculty, reminds readers where to focus their efforts. The messages tally the collective faculty research and teaching material output for a given week (such as new articles, books, and cases) and provide abstracts. Reading this update is enough to shame any dilettante into action.[9] Yet on top of these activities, faculty members engage in several additional key tasks—including patrolling community membership, serving the School, and commanding proper earnings.

Patrolling Community Membership

For Thanksgiving, and for many other holidays, various School residents are brought together to celebrate the occasion and build community ties on campus. One year, as I shared a meal with an MBA section I had taught, I recognized a student across the room, sitting at a smaller table with another faculty member. The student's presence, however, confused me. He had been in one of my classes but a year earlier. (On such occasions, meals are organized by section.) His section, however, was not there. While heading toward the buffet, I greeted him.

My former student told me what he had been up to, the subsequent courses he had taken, and his career plans for the future, all of these updates delivered in the most upbeat tone. I still could not figure out why he was in the same room as my current students. Upon inquiring what section was seated at his table, he told me in a quieter voice, "Section K." I had never before heard of a section K. To my knowledge, there were only ten sections, ranging from A to J. Seeing my puzzled looked, he explained that section K included all students who stayed a year longer and therefore graduated after their section mates. In other words, section K was an attempt to resocialize those students who decided, or were asked, to take a year off.

At the outset, all admitted students are deemed worthy to succeed. Colleagues tell incoming faculty members to remind any students who, early on, feel insecure in the School's environment that "admissions rarely go wrong." (Only about 10 percent of applicants are admitted.) "If you are here it's because you deserve to be here" is a favored encouragement to such students. This does not, however, prevent some from accumulating

Another form of patrolling. Photo by Catherine Hammond.

too many low grades during their first year. When this occurs, students are said to "hit the screen" and asked to take a developmental leave to gain more experience or work on select issues (such as class participation). The vast majority of these students seem to return a year later and graduate in three years instead of two.

The School's Academic Performance Committee oversees the cases of students asked to take a year off and examines the petitions they are required to submit to rejoin. The petition is a short reflection piece written by the student and addressed to committee members. "This is a bit like the Cultural Revolution," I said, trying to explain to a student who had hit the screen what to expect. "In order to petition to return, you need to signal that you understand what the issues are and that you are taking steps to address them. In other words, it's a self-critique. As long as you show genuine intent to improve, you should be fine." That was my (external) understanding of the petition process.[10] The student seemed slightly surprised, and in retrospect, the image of Chinese revolutionary guards was probably not the best one I could have come up with. That image, however, seemed to capture the essence of the exercise. As we crossed paths a year later on campus, we exchanged complicit smiles. He had been allowed to rejoin the community.

The question of community membership is central to the School's endeavor. The students' select absence and subsequent return signal to others that anybody can be put on probation and that, even once admitted, no outcome is assured. At the same time, the School probably needs the returning students more than they need the School. Their reentry illustrates the possibility of progress. Without them, the pursuit cannot claim that gains have been made. Reentry indicates that individuals can change enough to be redeemed. In that sense, reentry can be seen as the best example of advancing "better standards." Given the relatively short time students spend at the School, such events constitute rare markers of perceived longitudinal change.

Faculty members are instrumental in patrolling community entries and exits by providing the grades that constitute the student's academic record.[11] Unlike other academic settings in which teaching assistants or dedicated graders read papers or exams, School faculty members are the ones reading assignments and assessing participation to give grades. The academic record created helps inform the assessment of students' overall performance. Moreover, a forced grading curve is in effect at the School, meaning that a certain distribution of grades per section and per course needs to be respected.[12] The maximum frequency for the highest grade is 20 percent of a section (roughly eighteen out of ninety students) and the minimum frequency for the lowest grade is 10 percent of a section (roughly nine students); everyone else falls in between with the same grade.

An end-of-semester entry in my field journal highlights the challenge such a curve poses for instructors. "Time has come again to give my grades. Every faculty member, everywhere, does this, but in most settings there always are slackers who 'help' create a grade distribution. Here, students are overall studious, smart, and engaged. Thus, it's hard to pick the bottom ten percent. Typically finding three or four students who did not participate too much is relatively easy: they are the ones who wrote the weakest final exams, handed in minimal assignments during the semester, and mostly listened rather than participated. The main problem, however, resides in finding the additional students." Initially, many junior colleagues have similar difficulty in picking these additional ones.

The necessity for faculty members to identify the relatively weakest students, regardless of their degree of weakness, among a group of cohesive peers, is fairly unique to the School's environment. First, not all business schools have forced grading curves. But even business schools that do enforce grade distributions do so mostly for temporarily assembled student groups. In these other settings, students are not asked to bond as a class. Instead, they congregate in a course, spend only a few hours together per week, and then get ranked in that subject. At the School, students see each other hour after hour in a dozen courses, socialize throughout an entire year, and often develop close friendships, before being "curved." They are therefore ranked against those they know well, not strangers. (The practice is common as well in law schools.) Students are quick to pick up on these dynamics and understand that they are trying to outshine their peers. A student quote from the School newspaper explains the feeling: "No one wants to look foolish in front of a roomful of people they desperately want to impress."[13] Regardless of outside disclosure to potential employers, grade distributions are sorting and signaling mechanisms within sections.[14]

While grading proves important in any academic environment, the fact that at the School grading is done by faculty members and carries weight modifies significantly what is at stake. What students refer to as the "disappearance" of their peers, those asked to take a year off, does not go unnoticed in sections or at the School more generally.[15] Even though some students believe grades are somewhat randomly assigned, a pattern of lower grades across multiple courses is hard for students to fully discount.[16] A forced temporary exit follows repeated perceptions of weak performance. The origin of the forced grading curve goes back to 1941. As dean Wallace Donham observed that year, in about 15 percent of its admission decisions the School made "mistakes." (The current mistake rate seems significantly lower.) The School therefore had either to "scare these men out during the first year, or refuse them the chance to go on into the second year."[17] The consequences of a pattern of low grades during the first year are meant to correct these mistakes. By the same token, a pattern of high grades also receives School attention. Each year, the top 5 percent of graduating students are named Baker Scholars. These students tend to be seen as desirable candidates for positions as research associates, then doctoral degrees, and ultimately faculty positions (although this pipeline has narrowed over the years).

By making distinctions in student performance, faculty members de facto patrol continued community membership. Whether, when assessing performance, instructors take into account structural and contextual dynamics or consider individual agency alone to be at play, they ultimately need to hold students accountable and assign distinguishing grades. The School's grading policy depends upon and indeed guarantees uneven performance outcomes in large populations of students. Such variations uphold the consequentiality of what gets coded as individual decision making. Uneven outcomes validate the notion that individuals make a difference in their academic trajectory, one way or another.[18] And the faculty or a faculty subcommittee is entrusted with acting upon performance variations.

Serving the School

On most campuses across the United States, faculty members engage in service, both internally for their employers and externally for the profession. Many senior faculty members are asked to serve on internal committees (e.g., promotion committees) and in administrative positions (e.g., as program directors). Moreover, many faculty members hold editorial positions in academic journals and are active members of professional associations. At the School, these service demands seem to translate into senior faculty members' agendas filling up more rapidly than a beach at high tide. The premium put on the caste (i.e., the School) versus the subcaste (i.e., the academic discipline) might result from or explain this situation.

Academics in any setting are required to take on service activities, yet School faculty members also often repeat, not that they work for or at the School, but that they "serve" it. From teaching executive-education sessions to visiting alumni groups abroad, this service comes in many shapes. For senior faculty members in particular, serving often entails protecting junior faculty members from too high an administrative burden. The practice

Inside the School's chapel. Photo by Catherine Hammond.

of covering for junior faculty is common in many US research universities, yet at the School the one-to-one ratio of senior to junior faculty—the lowest of all Harvard University faculties and schools (excluding the dental school)—makes the relative cost of covering likely to be higher for senior faculty members. (The average senior-to-junior ratio at Harvard is 1.6 to 1 for professional schools and 2.6 to 1 for the Faculty of Arts and Sciences.)[19] With relatively fewer senior faculty members available to share the burden, the impression that senior School faculty members are quite busy is probably warranted.

At the same time, covering is a manifestation of a wider School expectation: the higher one stands in a social hierarchy, the more one is supposed to act purposefully—in this instance, by helping junior colleagues. Senior faculty members' deep involvement in School affairs is more than a surface impression. It also signals an organizational expectation and partially explains the sense of order felt on campus (see chapter 1). This expectation that one will contribute to the common endeavor permeates much of the School's operations and is constructed in stark opposition to the often-voiced notion of the self-interested behavior of executives.[20] In a sort of preemptive strike, School faculty members seem encouraged to disprove the corporate stereotype by enacting the opposite of the self-interested model of behavior. Such behaviors, and the notion of serving a higher goal, are meant to underline the educational hope.

Nowhere is the corporate counter-stereotyping more on display than during the annual student auction. Each spring, every section of first-year MBA students holds an auction to raise money for charity by soliciting "donations" from faculty. Upon first being solicited for an item by students I had taught, I turned to colleagues for advice. "Happens every year: don't lose sleep over it," I was told. The consensus among colleagues for a time-tested item was a dinner for four. "You might want to spice it up a bit, but overall it is a no-brainer." Someone else added, "Those who like you will self-select to bid on your item. At the end of the day, you all will enjoy it." A dinner it would be. When the student who was organizing the auction dropped by my office, I welcomed him and informed him that I would donate a "lavish" French dinner for four.

The organizer thanked me and immediately asked me what the minimum bid should be. I had not expected such a follow-up. I had read, however, enough literature on decision making to know that setting the bid too low could delegitimize an item (in this case, me), while setting it too high could signal an inflated sense of worth. I inquired what he thought an appropriate bid would be. "A hundred dollars sounds good," he answered with great assurance. "Assuming four students bid on your dinner, that's twenty-five dollars per person." I agreed the amount was reasonable. As he left my office, I remember thinking that the amount was maybe *too* reasonable, perhaps even cheap? Granted it was only a minimum bid, but was I properly serving the School?

While most ways of properly serving the School entail direct faculty labor (e.g., teaching and committee work), in this instance, as in many other US settings, money becomes "the cardinal device by which values become rationalized."[21] The total amount of funds collected at auctions often proves significant. A nonrandom sampling of nine auctions from 2006 to 2009 indicates that each collected on average close to seventy-eight thousand dollars, mostly via student bids.[22] The proceeds of the auction go to one or more charities chosen by the students. There was a wide range of donated items, from a weeklong holiday abroad for four (minimum bid, $3,250) to a short car drive from the School to Boston's Logan Airport ($20). The corollary of this valuation exercise is that, in this instance, one's ability to properly serve depends in part on one's ability to properly give back to the community.

As part of serving the School, and by extension its students, faculty members teaching first-year courses regularly donate items to these auctions. The sampling of auction results suggests that on average close to 80 percent of faculty members teaching any given section gave an item to be auctioned off. (Some faculty members also bid on donated items.) Many faculty members, particularly junior ones, put themselves up for auction in the guise of a dinner. More than 60 percent of faculty-donated items in the sampled auctions were dinners, ranging from $25 to $1,000, with a mean of $315 per auctioned-off dinner.[23] There were also a fair number of higher-priced faculty-donated items, for instance, a week at a Cape Cod beach house and a trip in a private jet. High-priced items are generally seen as a testimony to both the donor's and the bidder's wealth and generosity.

Commanding Proper Earnings

Since the late nineteenth century, US research universities have combined elements of many ideals, none of which include earning money as a core value. Central to their missions instead have been research, teaching, the appreciation of liberal and fine arts, and the use of practical knowledge to alleviate social problems.[24] There is thus, at the School, a tension between earning money and attaining other goals, resolved in part by the dichotomous pricing model adopted by many faculty members for external engagements. Faculty members taking on work outside the School are expected to command either high earnings or none.

I learned about these earnings dynamics early on and indirectly after fielding an unexpected call, one summer afternoon, in my office. A suave voice introduced herself on the phone and told me she was looking for someone to address a corporate gathering. Rapidly, however, she got to the point: she wanted to know my fees. Having been caught off guard (this was the first such inquiry I had received), I asked about her budget. She remained politely ambiguous. A conflict on dates brought the conversation to a rapid close. Upon hanging up, I wondered how to properly answer her question. The answer to setting a proper fee would become obvious a few months later.

Soon after this call, a senior colleague requested my help on a consulting project on a topic close to my area of expertise. The setting intrigued me, so I readily accepted. Given the work involved, a graduate student was also hired. His daily rate ($500) was set up front; mine was not. After completing the project, I was asked by my colleague to invoice my time. I assumed I might be "worth" six times the student's daily rate.[25] "This does not sound right. Do your homework: check with some other junior colleagues," she suggested. Inquiries with several colleagues indeed yielded a higher "proper" daily rate. "Anything lower than that would be selling short," I was repeatedly advised. Being seen as cheap was not an option.[26]

A faculty member's ability to command high earnings is not only a measure of his or her individual capabilities; it also signals and draws on the School's overall prestige. Commanding high earnings for speaking and consulting engagements upholds and reflects the value of the School's brand.[27] While the School benefits from the faculty's output in terms of research and teaching, faculty members also, to employ the sociologist C. Wright Mills's terminology, "borrow prestige" from the School.[28] Moreover, faculty members who teach graduate and executive students who then become successful leaders can, like sales staff in department stores that cater to prestigious customers, borrow from the expectations of their students' success. The School faculty, that is, collectively enacts a persona that commands high value since it trains those who go on to earn prestige.[29] Setting one's individual daily fee is thus implicitly a collective decision. Commanding high fees reflects and sustains the School's high-end position. In a way, it can be seen as properly serving the School.

For professors of management practice, many of whom occupied high positions in industry prior to joining the School, expectations that they will command high earnings are taken for granted. For many junior tenure-track faculty members, the expectation is more surprising. By academic standards, the average salary of a US business school professor is relatively high.[30] Yet at the School salaries represent only part of faculty earnings. The ability to charge high fees for speaking engagements and consulting services, thanks in part to School-associated prestige, can allow faculty members to increase their earnings and, in turn, to prove more generous on other occasions, such as during auctions.[31]

Not all faculty engagements, however, require payment. Another way to respond to external requests is to take them on for free. Some faculty members engage, for instance, in pro bono work for nonprofit and civic organizations, alongside their paid corporate engagements. These bodies, then, benefit, at no cost, from the faculty's expertise. The circumstances in which fees are waived is left to the faculty member's discretion. It is not so much what is done for nothing as the fact that something is done for nothing that proves important. As two senior School faculty members note, "Business is only useful as it serves [as] a means towards an end."[32] Choosing to work for free offers a glimpse of such ends. Such external engagements suggest that the individuals might be driven by something other than personal gain.

Once these norms around for-pay and gratis engagements are established, the handling of incoming requests like the phone call I received becomes much easier. The rule of thumb used by many junior faculty members is to turn down any requests that do not provide venues for exploring relevant research questions, offer adequate compensation, or involve a worthy cause.[33] Thus, for any engagements that are accepted, the fees will be either at the high end of the spectrum, reflecting the School's prestige, or zero. The midrange (i.e., several thousand dollars) is avoided. Also, School faculty members rarely seem to discuss openly the setting of engagement fees, perhaps suggesting that money matters are too important or too trivial to discuss.

Along with teaching and research, the activities described in this chapter keep faculty members quite busy. Within the School, expectations regarding the division of labor that supports such specialization are readily accepted. Off-campus, however, expectations are less easily enforced, as evidenced by my occasional missteps. "Could you buy multicolored Post-it notes," I recall asking my spouse by phone one day when I ran out of them. (The School stocks only yellow ones, and my assistant was out that day.) As I articulated the request, I heard a pause and suddenly felt bad. There was no reason I could not run the errand myself. The campus housed a convenience shop. The possibility of my walking there to purchase supplies had not, until then, crossed my mind. But such an act would con-

tradict two campus expectations. First, faculty members' circulation patterns rarely lead to the store (see chapter 1). Second, my assistant regularly
runs errands for me, picking up books at the library or getting supplies
for classes. Instead of running errands, I should certainly be doing other
things, such as patrolling community membership, serving the School, or
commanding proper earnings. My spouse was unconvinced.

* * *

We often ask what counts and what's expected in a given setting. As individuals, we regularly confront these questions and construct a variety of evolving answers. As members of collectives and organizations, we face similar
questions and often rely on cues and signs provided by other members to
reach informed conclusions.[34] For newcomers to the School, other staff
and faculty members help clarify expectations. In particular, by freeing up
faculty members' time to focus on particular activities, the School's administrative support system specifies what faculty members should ideally do.

Faculty members catch on quickly. On top of teaching and engaging
in research, they are expected to uphold the overall pursuit of the School.
Recognizing high-performing students (Baker Scholars) and identifying
those in need of more training (through forced temporary exits) allows faculty to meet these expectations by patrolling community membership. In
addition, making distinctions between students underscores individuals'
role in shaping their destinies, both at the School and in future corporate
life. Yet another way for faculty members to uphold the overall pursuit is
to adopt a dichotomous fee schedule for outside engagements, at times
waiving fees in support of causes they deem worthy. While the ends of the
School's enterprise remain amorphous (i.e., the cause), the presence of
such engagements proves important.

The extent of the division of labor on campus relies on and forces specialization.[35] While a strong division of labor tends to be associated with an
increasingly bureaucratic system, it also creates interdependency between
individuals occupying distinct social positions. School members now depend on one another to pursue their own tasks. Such dependency, in turn,
sets the foundation of communal life.[36] The communal life promoted at
the School is one in which order prevails: most individuals know what is
expected of them and what they can expect from others. Such an order is

not only practical—an efficient way to conduct activities—but instrumental, an effective way to achieve a broader goal. Cultural orders, including organizational ones, are not merely tools but also seeds for realizing cultural plans.[37] That the overarching ends remain indeterminate perhaps *constitutes* the broader goal.

Yet a key component of the organizational model remains in flux: variation still exists among the members of the faculty. Given the seeming amorphousness of the School's overarching goals and the uncertainty regarding faculty discretionary behaviors, up-front "quality control" is needed. Thus, selecting proper individuals, namely, those who are most likely to respond in a suitable manner to the numerous organizational signs, proves central to the pursuit. The next and last empirical chapter examines this selection process.

SIX

Selecting Faculty in the Proper Spirit

As their cities are composed of families, so their families are made
up of those that are nearly related to one another. . . . All the males,
both children and grand-children, live still in the same house, in
great obedience to their common parent.

THOMAS MORE, *Utopia*

For fortunate job candidates, landing a tenure-track academic position
often marks the end of a long search involving much travel and many face-
to-face meetings. It is customary for a job candidate to give a presentation
of his or her current research to the faculty of the prospective hiring department, and to meet most if not all of its members. My visit to the School
typified what any aspiring academic encounters at a major US university.
It included a job talk and many other rituals. As one foreign observer has
noted, US academic recruiting rituals usually include "breakfast, lunch
and dinner meetings with individuals or small groups, . . . short conversations with graduate students *en brochette*, . . . generous applause [after the
talk], and appointments for the candidate with deans and provosts."[1] My
experience at the School differed little from this summary. From breakfast
at the Charles Hotel to a conversation with the senior associate dean in
charge of faculty recruiting, the entire visit followed a predictable pattern.

Once I received the job offer by mail, however, the process veered somewhat from the well-worn path. I had known that the offer was arriving,
since the news had been delivered by telephone. The offer packet contained a flurry of documents, ranging from housing guidelines to descrip-

tions of health-insurance options. Despite the advance notice of its imminent arrival, I still felt relieved to finally be holding it in my hands. Eager
to formalize the end of my job search, I looked for a document to sign and
return confirming my acceptance. Unable to locate one among all the papers, I called the School's contact person to ask what I needed to sign. "Oh,
nothing," she replied. "Your word is enough." Sensing my confusion, she
added, "If you want to send me something, anything will do . . . even a
postcard! Congratulations again on joining our faculty."[2] I had imagined
signing a contract, but the implicit message was that applicants deemed
worthy of job offers from the School were de facto trustworthy enough to
keep their word. If they were not, how could they have been hired?

* * *

Many scripts shape teaching and research activities at the School, yet the
School's administration is still reliant on faculty member's discretion to
convey and enforce any normative views in the apparent organizational
void. Thus, selecting proper faculty members remains key to the successful
(moral) pursuit of the School. As dean Edwin F. Gay noted in 1908, when
probed about the School's position on teaching ethics, "The difficulty is to
find lecturers who can handle this theme in the proper spirit."[3] Thus the
organizational routines that dictate faculty members' entry into and exit
from the community are perhaps the most crucial to understand.[4] They
capture key rites of passage, namely admission to or exclusion from a collective.[5] Because rites of passage involve "dramatic representations," they
are important vehicles for affirming "shared meanings that constitute the
substance of a culture to its members."[6] Sometimes, an organizational
perspective can be entirely discerned in an institution's approach to member entry and exit.

As the brief description of my own hiring process suggests, joining
the School's faculty is treated as entering into a gentlemen's agreement,
not as a contractual relationship. The entry process affirms faithfulness
to a mission rather than an exchange of a service for a wage. It also seems
almost to assume prior intimacy between existing faculty members and
the new hire. Such an assumption is well founded, since historically new
hires have spent extensive periods of time at the School prior to their ap-

pointment. More recent hires, however, have increasingly diverged from this path. This shift has profound implications for the School's development and inner workings.

Faculty Composition: A Balancing Act

One spring when many of my students were graduating, several years after being hired, I decided to take part in the university-wide graduation ceremony. Doing so required crossing the Charles River and wearing appropriate academic attire. I did not own a cap and gown, or a hood, so my assistant placed a call to arrange a rental. I told her to mention my alma mater, New York University, since it is customary for the color of one's academic robes to signify that affiliation. The vendor, a longtime supplier to the School, asked who the robe was for. "For a faculty member," said my assistant. She identified me and my alma mater. The vendor's answer was prompt: "The robe will be crimson [Harvard University's color]." It seemed that crimson was the default color for all School faculty members requesting rentals.

My assistant repeated the name of the institution that had awarded my doctorate. "The issue will be pursued," replied the vendor in a professional manner. The next day my assistant received a call: the robe would be a generic black and the hood violet, in keeping with my alma mater's colors. "Such requests don't come too often," she was told. "Sorry for the confusion." Despite a growing number of external hires, most School faculty members, or at least those who attended graduation ceremonies, were still apparently trained at Harvard University.

Hiring graduates to teach in the department or university where they obtained their higher training is known in academia as *inbreeding*.[7] Though routinely deplored, inbreeding is commonplace and has long been documented in many academic settings. For instance, a 1938 study of all external faculty appointments at Indiana University between 1885 and 1937 found 43 percent to be Indiana alumni.[8] A recent study of law-school faculty hires at thirty-two universities found that an average of 20 percent of entry-level appointees had been trained at the hiring institution.[9] In the

Table 2. Distribution of highest degrees, HBS faculty, 2009

	Harvard PhD	HBS DBA	Other Harvard graduate degree	Non-Harvard degree	Total
Professor	23 (24%)	12 (10%)	1 (1%)	63 (65%)	99
with HBS MBA	8	6	1	2	17
Associate professor	8 (24%)	2 (6%)	—	23 (70%)	33
with HBS MBA	2	—	—	1	3
Assistant professor	7 (14%)	2 (4%)	—	40 (82%)	49
with HBS MBA	—	—	—	—	0
Professor of management practice	1 (7%)	2 (13%)	5 (34%)	7 (47%)	15
with HBS MBA	—	2	4	2	8
Totals	40 (20%)	16 (8%)	6 (3%)	135 (69%)	197
with HBS MBA	10	8	5	5	28

Note: The tabulation excludes (a) faculty members who left the School between June 2009, when the data was accessed, and December 2009, when the tabulation was calculated (three individuals); (b) those on leave (two individuals); and (c) visiting faculty (five individuals). Among those whose highest degree is not from Harvard University and who do not hold an HBS MBA, two individuals hold lesser degrees from Harvard University.
Source: HBS Faculty & Research website (http://www.hbs.edu/research/), accessed June 26, 2009.

latter study, Harvard and Yale Law Schools exhibited the highest proportions of appointment from within, with 81 and 73 percent of entry-level faculty hires respectively.

Of the 182 tenured and tenure-track faculty members at Harvard Business School in 2009, more than 30 percent had received their highest degrees from Harvard University. These degrees consisted mainly of PhDs conferred by the Faculty of Arts and Sciences (21 percent) and doctorates in business administration (DBAs) conferred by the School (close to 9 percent) (see table 2). The extent to which faculty members were recruited from the School's own ranks (those holding School DBAs) was deemed atypical even within the university, prompting occasional criticism of the School's incestuous practices.[10] Other observers, by contrast, interpret such inbreeding as a sign of strength, signifying that the School trains future faculty members properly. Bernard Berelson, who headed the Center for Advanced Study of the Behavioral Sciences at Stanford University, made a similar point about US graduate education in general, describing inbreeding at top universities as "naturally high since they have been the main producers: the oldest and best institutions always have more inbreeding than the others."[11] Inbreeding could therefore signify both social homophily and training quality.

Given the unique lens used to assess faculty members' performance at the School (see chapter 2), it is hardly surprising that successful candidates for recruitment and promotion often seem to be those groomed internally. These candidates tend to be seen as highly aligned with the School's expectations. They are also familiar with the quest for relevance and have usually mastered the School's inner workings. And a faculty member with a School MBA, as well as a School DBA, can tell first-year students at the initial meeting of a new class exactly where he or she sat when studying for the same degree. This overture reminds students of the timelessness of the institution and boosts the instructor's credibility, giving him or her a head start at demonstrating "good rapport" with the students.[12]

Yet even if inbreeding is viewed positively, maintaining an adequate level of external recruiting is equally important.[13] Even robust institutions require external inputs if they are to continue to flourish, and in this case striking a balance between Harvard-trained faculty members and external hires has enabled the School to grow.[14] Bringing select outsiders on board is a necessity, if only to replenish the teaching ranks. As early as the late 1950s and 1960s, a close observer of the School had already noted that "perhaps the most significant development" at the School was "the growth in faculty."[15] Between then and 2000, the faculty grew by close to eighty members.[16] Beginning in the 1950s, the School made a series of faculty appointments designed to strengthen its competence in quantitative fields and in the social sciences. This shift was contemporary with recommendations by the Ford and Carnegie Foundations that business schools should recruit from these disciplines.[17] Thus a purposeful recruitment of outsiders was pursued.

The outsiders' impact on the School was multifold. The growing, if still atypical, presence of colors other than crimson at graduation ceremonies was perhaps the most visible evidence of the shift. Weeklong summer training workshops to ensure the socialization of incoming faculty members also came into being, and in 2004 the School established a faculty teaching and learning center. The ultimate marker of proper socialization for non–Harvard-trained faculty members occurs, however, only upon being granted tenure at the School: those faculty members—and all other non–Harvard-trained faculty members who win tenure at the university— are traditionally awarded an honorary Harvard University degree upon their appointment. Such ex post facto recognition suggests full member-ship in the community and also symbolically validates, in a way, the appro-priateness of the appointment: in the absence of a Harvard upbringing, a proxy of purity is conferred. In recent years, the need to confer such a proxy seems to have increased.

A Changing Faculty Pipeline

The selection process for faculty positions at the School is labor-intensive. A subcommittee in each departmental unit pores over every detail in an applicant's job packet, which includes published and in-progress manu-scripts as well as letters of recommendation. Being hired by the School is internally considered an honor bestowed on only a select few. The School prides itself on conducting extensive due diligence on potential new fac-ulty members, and no detail is too trivial.[18] In the past, due diligence could often be performed over many years, thanks to the School's partial reli-ance on a unique recruitment pipeline: its pool of research associates. Re-cruitment subcommittees were privy to more extensive data on applicants drawn from this pool, a fact that facilitated faculty inbreeding.

Faculty members are allotted a certain amount of funds each year to hire research associates to help on various projects. These employees per-form tasks similar to those of the faculty, with the exception of classroom teaching. Their main duty, historically, was to write teaching cases, which were then edited by and copublished with faculty members. Still today, most associates write cases, but many also conduct field interviews, ana-lyze data, and draft sections of papers and books. A guide for associates published by the School in 1982 attributed the "extremely amorphous" nature of the job to "the characteristic of academic research," and encour-aged associates to acquire a "standard dictionary, a good business diction-ary, and a thesaurus."[19] The partial overlap between faculty members' work and that of associates is not incidental: associates used to be groomed to become faculty members. In other words, associates were often academ-ics in training and potential future faculty hires.[20] It is not surprising that faculty members and associates often develop strong relationships. (A de facto five-year limit on associates' appointments limits the duration of such relationships.)

By the time I joined the School in 2000, the typical profile of an associate was that of a talented undergraduate student, often recommended by someone known to the faculty member (e.g., a colleague at a university with a large undergraduate population). The applicants' backgrounds were truly impressive: academic star performers, speakers of multiple languages, and competitive athletes typically populated the set. With a few more years of appropriate work experience under their belts, they all seemed ideal candidates for the School's degree-granting programs. This had not always been the case. In the past, associates were mostly recent School MBA graduates who had been handpicked and encouraged by their instructors to become future faculty members. If I had been sifting through a set of applicants fifty years earlier, the probability of seeing the name of an MBA student I had taught would have been quite high.

This shift in the profile of associates is most evident in the nature of the information conveyed to new research associates. In a 1950 memorandum addressed to new research assistants (as they were then called), the assistants are urged to "please introduce yourself to professors, *even if you have had them in class*" (emphasis added). "There is a general desire to meet new men," the memo continues, "but occasional embarrassment at not remembering names."[21] The assumption is implicit that many of those hired would be current or former MBA students at the School. The implicit is made explicit when describing the use of library services: "If you have been a student here, you need not be reminded that the Library staff is extremely helpful." The option of earning a doctor of commercial science degree in conjunction with a research-assistant assignment was also clearly spelled out, in the hope that some assistants would equip themselves with appropriate experience for full-fledged faculty positions. Indeed, research assistants at that time were described as "apprentice teachers," despite an acknowledgment that their number was considerably larger than the number of future openings in the faculty ranks.[22]

In more recent memos and manuals addressed to new research associates, references to prior familiarity with the School and its faculty are absent, and the option to enroll in a concurrent doctoral program no longer exists. The reasons for this shift are multiple; two primary reasons are that the average age of MBA students has gradually increased since the 1950s and that external employers increasingly pay higher salaries than do universities.[23] By 2000 the contingent of School MBAs among the total population of associates had severely declined. And during the period from 2005 to 2009, when 632 research associates representing more than ninety universities were hired, fewer than 10 percent (58) held School MBAs. By contrast, 14 percent (88) came from Harvard College, the main provider of new recruits. (Wellesley College ranked third, with 5 percent [32] of all associates.) Even so, the 10 percent of associates with School MBAs would still be a large pool of potential future faculty members, if the traditional pipeline to a faculty appointment remained intact. But new faculty recruiting strategies have emerged.

A Generational Shift

In the absence of such a pipeline, where are new faculty members currently being trained? As two senior faculty members and their research-associate coauthor note in a recently published book, the typical new hire is increasingly likely to have trained outside the School, outside Harvard, and in a traditional academic discipline: "In 1980, 30 percent of the faculty held a Harvard MBA, and 36 percent held an HBS or Harvard University doctorate. By 1999, these figures had fallen to 20 percent and 30 percent respectively, and continued to fall thereafter. Increasing numbers of incoming faculty arrived from discipline-based Ph.D. programs."[24]

This recruiting pattern is in stark contrast to the School's past practices. "The record shows that young men developed in the School played an important part in shaping its progress," wrote Melvin T. Copland (who spent forty-five years on the faculty) after retiring in 1958.[25] "A complete list of the Faculty members who started out as research, instructional, or administrative assistants is too long to present here." Today, despite a few exemplars, only a very few research associates seem to enroll in the School's PhD program and then join its faculty. Instead, new junior faculty members are mostly "developed" outside the School.

This shift echoes a similar succession crisis that occurred in French universities in 1968, a year of intense social upheaval. At the time, many labeled the upheaval a generational crisis. But Pierre Bourdieu, a close observer of French academia, characterized it more specifically as a crisis between "academic generations."[26] That year in France, an academic establishment used to ensuring its own succession by producing new faculty members with similar social characteristics suddenly stalled. Suddenly, new members were coming from different social backgrounds. Many of the newcomers lacked their older colleagues' prestigious credentials, and their relative lack of identification with these colleagues led to a permanent change in the French academic system. The changes resulted in new, almost irrational hopes among intermediate-level academics (e.g., expectations of new careers within the "reformed" system). Meanwhile, nostalgia permeated the established academics' discourse. Confronted with a new generation's emergence, senior professors lamented a disappearing world.[27]

The demographic shift in the School's faculty was less radical than what happened in France. But the comparison nonetheless highlights the School's declining reliance on insiders to ensure faculty growth, and the increasing need today to socialize new faculty hires into the norms favored by the "elders." An apparently mundane episode captures the need to constantly restate established School norms. Every new faculty member is asked to schedule a photo shoot upon joining the School so that a picture can be posted on the School's website and used in promotional efforts. (Faculty members are also regularly invited to update their photos.) To avoid mix-ups, since many photos are taken on any given day, the photo shoot always begins with a shot of the faculty member holding a card bearing his or her name. The invitation to the session invariably reads, "Please wear professional dress," a reminder of School norms. The gentlemen's agreement that prevails during the hiring process translates into gentlemen's attire. Like most other new recruits, I followed the drill and arrived properly dressed in a jacket and tie.

Jackets and ties provide a veneer of continuity. But they obscure profound transformations in the profiles of their wearers. In terms of academic training, generational outlook, gender identity, and perhaps even "spirit," the School's faculty has gradually evolved. That jackets and ties, rather than blouses and skirts, are widely viewed as the default attire can-

not be overlooked. Gender dynamics at the School warrant an entire separate study. The perspective from which my methodological approach allows me to speak is not a female one. Other research designs are probably
better suited to exploring the School's gender dynamics.

"Russian Roulette"

A discussion of the faculty's evolution would be incomplete without consideration of faculty exits. Those faculty members who stay at the School
are not simply those selected to join; they are, by and large, those who are
not asked to leave. (Voluntary exits are not unknown, but they are fewer
in number.)

Like most US research universities, the School operates on an up-or-out
model. As the sociologists Theodor Caplow and Reece J. McGee reported
a half century ago in their study of the US academic labor market, "The
odds against the promotion of an assistant professor may be five or six to
one" at major research universities. Unsurprisingly, as Caplow and Mc-
Gee also observe, "There is a high level of both economic and emotional
insecurity during the early stages of the academic career before tenure has
been achieved."[28] At the School, the odds against promotion are probably
akin to those that Caplow and McGee found, as is the generalized sense of
insecurity shared by many untenured academics today.[29]

Insecurity is heightened at the School by its somewhat unique evaluative framework, which focuses on relevance (see chapter 2). For each
review in which a promotion is being considered, whether from assistant
to associate or from associate to full professor, the School's senior faculty
reads a summary of the candidate's case, described by an emeritus School
faculty member as a "twenty-page report written by a committee about the
candidate's achievements." The entire senior faculty then gathers in what
is known as the "Big Room" to discuss the individual's qualifications and
vote on the promotion. The emeritus professor recalls the process as having almost as profound an impact on the voting faculty members as it does
on the candidate: "No faculty member can sit through this process without
being reminded of the school standards, feeling humbled by the stan-

dards, evaluating one's own accomplishments, and recommitting to high performance in one's work."[30] After the vote, the School's dean makes the ultimate call, based on the recommendation of the faculty, on decisions not involving tenure. For tenure decisions, the university's president makes the final call, based on the dean's recommendation.[31]

The selective and routine involuntary exit of nontenured faculty members reinforces the exclusivity of the School's faculty. As in many elite educational settings, the notion of exclusion is integral to the creation of an elite status. As a recent study of an elite US boarding school points out, "Perhaps the most critical step in the creation of elite status is the rationalization of a method of exclusion that determines who gets a place inside the . . . bubble and who does not."[32] The School's approach to faculty hires and exits is a careful and lengthy process for selecting new members combined with an efficient and expedited exit process. Such a model is typical of tight-knit communities, which rely on high levels of trust among members to ensure that collective pursuits are carried out.

Any faculty member joining a major US research university is well aware of the up-or-out model. But the imagery routinely used at the School to depict faculty exits highlights what sets it apart from peer universities. "Do you like to play Russian roulette?" a colleague once asked me. I was unsure of her drift. "To be here," she explained, "you need to be a player. It's a bit like a game of Russian roulette. But while you usually have one chance out of six to get killed, the chances here are five out of six" (the same odds reported by Caplow and McGee). She smiled. Her vivid imagery was meant to be helpful. "Only one person out of six will make it to tenure, so consider yourself dead on arrival. That way, being here will seem like a liberating experience!"

While the roulette metaphor may contradict the trope linking purposeful individual action and outcomes that pervades School teaching notes, it accurately captures the insecurity that is typical among untenured faculty members at Harvard University and beyond. As an example, attrition rates for junior faculty members hired by Harvard University's Faculty of Arts and Sciences between 1998 and 2003 were 72 percent in the arts and humanities division and 85 percent in the social sciences.[33] By emphasizing situational rather than individual factors with respect to continued membership in the system, the roulette metaphor might help junior faculty members cope with their relative insecurity. But it also evokes the dispatch with which exits are handled at the School.

Once an individual is deemed unworthy of continued belonging, the speed with which evidence of his or her presence on campus vanishes is impressive. Professional moving specialists routinely and rapidly refurbish offices, erasing all traces of their past occupants. Their names may linger in the bylines of select teaching cases, and former students will occasionally ask about them. As at family reunions where uninvited family members go unmentioned, their very existence is invisible to newcomers even if their memory remains vivid among the old-timers.

Attrition is probably no lower at the School than at other peer institutions, but the subsequent career paths of exiting faculty members may partially explain the ignorance of their followers. Until recently, many exiting faculty members moved on to jobs in industry or at institutions more focused on teaching than on traditional academic research.[34] Their replacements on the faculty, increasingly trained in traditional graduate schools, have tended to be exposed more to the work of other scholars than to the activities of industry practitioners or master teachers.[35] Thus junior faculty members, increasingly trained outside the School, rarely recognize the names of their departed predecessors.

The year I rented a gown to attend Harvard's graduation ceremonies, three colleagues joined me for the celebration. As I write this sentence, two of them have left the School. The revolver took its toll. One colleague landed a position at another research university; the other joined a more teaching-oriented university. The memory of their passage is nonetheless engraved in my mind. Like outcast family members, their absence resonates as much as their presence did. Despite the efficiency with which their traces have been expunged, the recollection of our past interactions lingers on.

* * *

Several factors contribute to the consistency of an organization's perspective. Routines, in particular, are crucial elements of such constancy. When routines are properly adhered to, sets of tasks go forward without much intervention from above. In essence, routines allow the organization to reproduce itself almost endogenously.[36] For a given perspective to persist, however, disruptive external changes also need to be kept at bay. It is telling, for instance, that the School's administration takes pride in having almost never canceled classes.[37] (Even during the student protests of the late 1960s, the School, unlike other parts of the university, functioned, as the *Harvard Crimson* put it, "normally."[38]) The ability to function normally regardless of what is happening "outside" can be seen as a form of arrogance, but it also signals strong internal consistency.

Cultural reproduction, however, gets complicated when routines fail to specify overarching goals. In such instances, another key element in consistency of perspective is consistency in the School's membership profile. When external inputs cannot be ignored, it becomes necessary to incorporate them selectively into the internal pursuit. With respect to faculty, selecting hires in the proper spirit has become increasingly challenging from the School's perspective. In an academic labor market increasingly reliant on external hiring, less time can be devoted to observing potential new hires in action.

In the past, members of School recruiting committees could collect signs of "proper spirit" over an extended period (such as the combined duration of a candidate's appointment as a research associate and subsequent doctoral study). To assess candidates now, however, they must rely less on signs and more on signals: letters from faculty members at other universities, the purpose-written papers candidates include in their job packets. This change reflects both a generational shift in faculty composition and a shift in the hiring pipeline.

Any university devotes much effort to faculty selection. Bringing a new person on board, at the junior or the senior level, is consequential. A senior hire who joins a faculty with tenure might remain at the university for the remainder of his or her career. In the case of a junior hire, the hiring department typically invests many months in bringing the person up to speed in teaching and research, and helping him or her grow as a scholar.

In the context of the School, an added issue plays into the recruiting process: since morals remain mostly unscripted, the new hire will also be filling an apparent organizational void. In this respect, the shift from inbreeding to a more externally oriented recruiting model has created opportunities for both growth and slippage. The School needs new faculty members to replenish its ranks, and outside recruits have enabled it to do so. Meanwhile, however, the cumulative effect of new hires might affect the School's ability to sustain its particular perspective. Slippage can occur perhaps more frequently now than in the past, though its consequences remain to be seen.

CONCLUSION

Vocal Silence

I wouldn't like to live in a village but sometimes I would
I wouldn't like to live in a wigwam but sometimes I would
I'd love to live in Xanadu but not for ever
GEORGES PEREC, *On the Difficulty of Imagining an Ideal City*

The main contribution of this book has been to make our understanding of the interplay between routines and morals in organizational settings more complete and complex. At the most general level, the study has provided evidence that a more dynamic view of routines can enrich our comprehension of large-scale moral projects. By showing how individual discretion can exist within routines, the study highlights an attempt to write morals into an organizational script. In doing so, it uncovers the juxtaposition of relative freedom and constraint as a potential infrastructure for the making of morals.

By emphasizing the dissonant experience of performing routines apparently devoid of (direct) signals indicating how to behave but embedded in a context rich in (indirect) signs of proper behavior, the study identifies the potential for productive ambiguity in vocal silence.[1] Theoretically, multiple viewpoints can coexist in such silence.[2] The study's findings thus inject some humanity into the carrying out of large-scale moral projects. The "iron cage" of organizational life that Max Weber foresaw might prove, in a sense, less sturdy than it appears.[3] In its vocal silence, the cage might allow for the possibility of moral awakening, not merely the expected entrapment of its members.

* * *

Whereas the advancement of "better business standards" provides the setting for this study, the book's findings offer insights, more generally, into the organizational implementation of any moral pursuit. A project to moralize an entire field or occupation is in no way unique to business education. Many other fields and occupations have undertaken similar attempts at transformation. The creation of the British Broadcasting Corporation, for instance, was conceived as a way to achieve "good broadcasting" at a time when that field was deemed in need of revamping.[4] In the words of the historian Asa Briggs, paraphrasing the BBC's first managing director, good broadcasting meant that "the 'publics' are treated with respect not as nameless aggregates with statistical measurable preferences . . . but as living audiences capable of growth and development." The BBC's broadcasting would not be driven solely by ratings. The organization's mission was the "maintenance of high standards, the provision of the best and the rejection of the hurtful." Overall, its goal was to bring some sense of order to what was perceived as an unruly arena.

The emergence of training programs for professional naval officers in sixteenth- and seventeenth-century England offers another example of a moralizing project.[5] Ship commanders, originally a mix of gentleman-soldiers and skilled navigators from humbler origins, gradually became (after some training) "naval officers." For the more humble navigators, known as tarpaulins, this process entailed being trained to behave a bit more like gentlemen. The term *gentlemen*, according to Norbert Elias, distinguished the "upper and some portions of the middle class" from the rest of the populace.[6] Naval officers were increasingly asked to interact with foreign envoys and to represent the crown abroad; proper behavior was therefore expected. Thus training as a naval officer transformed tarpaulins into a semblance of gentlemen, and gentlemen into navigators. This process allowed for the expansion of the newly formed profession.

Such moralizing projects are not confined to the remote past. As Elias further explained in the 1950s, "Two groups with different social antecedents and different professional qualifications are sharing [today] with each other the management of state industries. People in charge of these industries are recruited partly from the middle classes and partly from men of working-class descent."[7] In a striking way, Elias foresaw the central challenge of elite university-based business education. His remarks capture a core feature of the mission it assigned itself, namely the dissemination of a shared perspective on proper business conduct. Thus, elite business schools are engaged not only in what the sociologists Pierre Bourdieu and Jean-Claude Passeron call "cultural reproduction" but also in cultural expansion.[8] Along with the sons (and, later, daughters) of businessmen, aspiring practitioners of the occupation needed to understand how to behave. Also, faculty members in these business schools were entrusted with upholding the moral pursuit. As such, elite business schools are intriguing settings in which to study moralizing projects. While the study's insights stem from the analysis of faculty socialization in one such school setting, they are likely to inform more broadly other moral organizational pursuits as well.

Routinizing Morals via Vocal Silence

Organizations and their inner workings play key roles with respect to morals. By constructing moral dilemmas as solely individual decision-making problems, we often forget that individuals operate in collective settings. Yet moral conduct rarely occurs ex cathedra or in context-free behavioral laboratories, as some scholarship might lead us to believe. Individuals make choices, but they do so as members of broader communities that partly shape their behavior. Like physicians making treatment decisions in hospitals or debt collectors working in collection agencies, other seemingly individual choices cannot be decoupled from their organizational context.[9] If we wish to discuss individuals' moral conduct, we need in particular to look into the organizational conditions that give rise to or hinder such conduct. Moreover, because large organizations rely on routines to operate, an examination of morals inevitably calls for an inquiry into the roles of routines in moral pursuits.

Inside organizations, the study highlights in particular the potential for leaders to manufacture members' morals via vocal silence. In an environment where many (if not all) organizational leaders clamor for the high moral ground, promoting even limited internal silence might appear to be a counterintuitive move. Yet relative organizational silence is perhaps precisely what allows morals to thrive. In the same way that enduring organizations might nurture dissonance rather than squash it, organizations with strong normative goals might promote vocal silence (and opportunities for contained dissent) rather than openly expressing normative views (and opportunities for repeated proselytizing). Vocal silence might provide the flexibility that past scholars have called for to produce moral conduct.[10]

The study also stresses the importance of scripting routines that couple collective guidance *and* individual latitude when socializing members into given morals.[11] Attempts to directly or indirectly shape members' behavior have long been noted in the organizational socialization literature; specifically, such shaping has been traced to a growing scholarly and managerial interest in members' psychological absorption of the organizational imperatives.[12] As Gideon Kunda notes, this collective shaping amounts to an attempt to "embed control 'inside' members."[13] By contrast, the simultaneous need to *refrain* from entering members' private worlds has received less attention.[14] (Scholars' recent use of the term *unobtrusive control* to depict less intrusive ways to manage a workforce hints at the power of such restraint.[15]) Yet members' somewhat routinized and contradictory experience of freedom and constraint might prove central to the organizational carrying out of moral pursuits.

To synthesize the main conclusions and broader implications of this study, it is appropriate to return to my introduction. I opened this book with three main questions, the answers to which can, I hope, be generalized to many organizations beyond the one analyzed here. First, I asked whether morals can be transmitted on a large scale via organizational scripts and routines. Second, I inquired whether the process of scripting morals might modify or even destroy them. Third, I questioned how morals might endure in organizations. The analysis of faculty members' socialization at the Harvard Business School provides tentative answers to these questions. Ethnographies rarely encourage smooth comparisons, but some possible generalizations can be drawn.

Can morals be transmitted on a large scale via organizational scripts and routines? The answer is probably more nuanced than past scholarship has suggested. There is no doubt that routinizing morals into more stable forms carries a risk of emphasizing process over substance. Since Max

Weber identified such a risk in the routinization of charismatic leadership, many other moral agendas have been shown to suffer a similar fate upon being scripted.[16] Recently, for instance, the sociologist Frank Dobbin documented comparable dynamics in the mainstreaming and routinization of affirmative-action policies in US corporations.[17] As corporate personnel experts formalized hiring and promotion practices in the 1970s to eradicate bias by managers, they also redefined discrimination more narrowly. Personnel experts, for instance, gradually promoted sexual-harassment training (a typical process) as a tool to discourage discrimination; in the process, they restricted its definition to sex-based discrimination. By the same token, in the School's context, specifying what "decent" conduct entails would redefine and probably restrict our understanding of decency.[18] When organizations try explicitly to write higher morals into their scripts, the internal translation process per se can create a significant hazard. The symbolic adherence to steps that allows an organization to claim that efforts are being made while minimal results are being achieved is hardly a success. In that sense, perhaps, morals cannot be written into scripts. What scripts can do, however, is allow for the prospect of morals to emerge.

Vocal silence recognizes the impossibility of overscripting morals but also the hope for progress. I have defined vocal silence as a routine that requires significant decision making on the part of those involved with little direct guidance from higher authorities in a context rich in normative signs. The School, I have argued, offers one instance of such vocal silence, but other organizations have also adopted this model. The German and Israeli military forces may best exemplify this approach. After World War II, both wanted to include organizational safeguards so that war atrocities would never be carried out unchallenged by the troops. The implicit goal was to moralize the military profession. In Germany, the safeguard took the form of promoting the concept of *Innere Führung* (literally, inner direction). In elaborating the concept in the 1950s, and recognizing that "the more inhuman the battle, the greater the need for a human spirit and decent manners," Count W. Baudissin explained that "the soldier will not give trustful obedience unless he feels that behind the order is a set of moral values which asks only what is fair in a given situation."[19] What constitutes fairness, human spirit, and decency was purposely left unspecified. By scripting silence into its routines, the German military tried to balance the claims of subordination against the demands of consciousness.[20] In a parallel move, the Israeli military promoted the concept of "purity of firearms," embodying the idea that servicemen and -women will "use their weapons and force only to the purpose of the mission, only to the necessary extent and will maintain their humanity even during combat."[21] Again, humanity was intentionally left undefined, but its contents could possibly be inferred from other soldiers' conduct.

These two approaches de facto create wide-reaching organizational silences. They also highlight other organizational efforts to script morals via vocal silence. I am not arguing that vocal silence is the proper way or the only way to script morals. Alternate models can also be imagined.[22] Yet relative silence as a means to undertake moral projects and scale them up has until now largely been ignored in the study of organizations. More often than not, silence is seen as a disabling organizational process. For example, silence has been shown to impede, change, or even destroy organizations.[23] Meanwhile the organizational benefits of silence have been overlooked. More specifically, the potential for silence to enhance moral pursuits requires closer consideration. Silent pursuits should not be seen exclusively as doomed ones. Under certain conditions, silence can perhaps prove generative.

The generative nature of silence lies primarily in its absorptive quality. This quality was well captured by James Bugental in his article "The Silence of the Sky," which used to be distributed to Harvard Business School students in a second-year elective course.[24] Bugental wrote, "We look upon the world with questing eyes that search for meaning, and we are turned back upon our questions with no answers. We seek in vain for the value, the virtue, the cause that is ultimate. . . . And still the sky is silent." A silent sky might trigger anxiety, but it can also create a nurturing void in which morals can perhaps emerge. Such a void might permit some transmission of morals, but it might also allow for the growth of different, less expected outcomes. Hence, silence might not be able to transmit a singular moral viewpoint; instead, silence might only allow multiple moral viewpoints to arise.

Can the scripting of morals modify or even destroy them? To answer this question with respect to scripting relative organizational silence, it is worth remembering that silence exists only in contrast to noise. While silence might surround some decisions, less silent cues invariably shape many, if not most, other decisions. Every silence theoretically allows for novel outcomes, yet in well-oiled settings any nested decision tends at least partially to fit the overall internal and external ethos. Control systems tend to build on, rather than replace, one another.[25] As Harrison White elegantly notes in the course of debunking economists' reliance on the concept of individual agency, agency is rarely a *problem*; more often it is a "neat kind of social plumbing" or a *solution* to attaining and maintaining control.[26] Agency might enhance autonomy in certain restricted cultural spheres, but it usually sharply increases control. Similarly, vocal silence might increase organizational control.

Consider the topic of social change. In everyday life, change comes in many flavors (e.g., gradual or radical) and encompasses many goals (encouraging the best talent or redistributing wealth). At the School, for instance, the typical understanding of change might prove narrower. The School's small-town atmosphere and stratified population point to a seamless communal coexistence (see chapter 1). Conflict avoidance is the norm; change is mostly viewed as gradual and consensual. In such a context, outcomes of silence are likely to echo the consensual ethos. For instance, labor unrest and strikes do not figure as regular occurrences at the School. Moreover, teaching cases that deal with labor unions' actions are hard to find in the School's curriculum. Thus, solutions found in relative silence that uphold an ethos of consensual decision making are probably easier to convey to other School members; alternate views of change (e.g., those embracing radical action) are likely to face more internal hurdles.

Alongside internal "noise," or signs that inform silence, external noise also infuses silence with meaning. Unless an organization operates in total isolation, external forces regularly impact internal activities. At the School, an insistence on relevance, in particular, acts as a constant antidote to excessive insularity, and also conveys outside noise in the organizational silence. Without relevance, the School's initial project of building "better business standards" might be confined to its campus.[27] By insisting on relevance, the goal is to ensure that the pursuit does not merely succeed locally but also finds an echo in the broader, external community.[28] To find an echo in the broader community, individual decisions need to resonate with at least some external audiences. In particular, alumni buy-in often proves crucial to internal success. Thus, an organizational model promoting vocal silences permits morals to be modified, but such modifications are heavily bound by internal and external dynamics.

That said, vocal silence can lead to gradual moral revision. Loosely tuned vocal silence can accommodate multiple shifting interpretations. To illustrate this point in the School's context, consider the potentially evolving work ethos. Historically, morals were seen as imbuing work per se with meaning. The early definition prevailing at the School, of business as an "activity of making things to sell at a profit—decently," signified the possibility of moral conduct *at* work.[29] This formulation can be traced to Max Weber's understanding of morals as a particular attitude toward one's work.[30] More recently, however, morals have sometimes been depicted as accompanying rather than informing work. An alumnus's story, published in the *HBS Alumni Bulletin*, exemplifies such a potential shift. The article explains that the alumnus "is the richest man in Turkey, and he's enjoying his wealth by giving lots of it away. . . . In addition to his support for public schools, he plans to spend $1 billion over the next 15 years to establish a private university."[31] The article conveys pride in his achievement, yet also introduces a subtle shift in ethos: the goal of decently selling at a profit is replaced by the goal of making a profit and then helping others. Put otherwise, the "decent" pursuit is situated outside of work itself and becomes sequential. Being decent suddenly gets disconnected from doing decent work. Though this alumnus might engage in decent work *and* philanthropy, the emphasis is on the latter. Repeated occurrences of such a shift in organizational voids can set the tone for broader changes. While internal changes might be contained, larger changes can occur over time due to the accumulation of apparently small shifts. Vocal silence is flexible, and morals can evolve without major organizational revision.[32]

The above remarks bear directly on the study's last question: *How, in a context of vocal silence, can morals endure?* Answers to this question rest on the assumptions we bring to the term *morals*. If morals are seen as shared understandings that need to be internalized and (re)discovered in order to prove enduring, then silence might be the only way for morals to endure. Vocal silence allows for individual reinvention and the plausibility of self-discovery. Because filling in the contents of silence can be experienced as an individual victory over one's subjectivity or an individual victory over the collective, the contents can seem self-constructed.[33] The confrontation, within vocal silence, between one's moral compass or inner direction and other drivers of action lays the groundwork for endurance; individuals are likely to develop greater commitment to morals they see as the result of their own efforts.[34] The (re)discovery of morals by every individual in a given cohort or generation of entrants forms the basis of continuity. In that sense, no moral pursuit can robustly endure *without* internal, individual friction; and vocal silence typically permits such friction.

If one subscribes to the above definition of morals, what might endure through relative organizational silence? I would argue that many shared understandings will endure, since the sources of morals are to be found not only in routines per se but also in the combination of routines with organizations' material structures, including the composition of their population.[35] As long as past members constitute an organization's majority, (past) morals are likely to endure. Despite vocal silence, much gets conveyed by other means in organizations. Strong cultures and strong morals go hand in hand.[36] The variety of cultural forms should not be underestimated. Apparently silent organizations tend to emit many cultural signs. Though some signs might appear missing (or silent) once filtered through the organizational perspective, they are nonetheless reconstituted by members. Thus, silence poses little threat to moral endurance in culturally rich and strong organizations.

By contrast, if morals are seen as external norms that need to be enforced, rather than shared meanings to be internalized and (re)discovered, then silence might appear quite threatening in the long term. Organizational solutions other than vocal silence are likely to sustain such morals. In such a context, for instance, rules and regulations are prime candidates for moral reproduction and persistence. The French social reformer Jean-Baptiste André Godin, who believed in a more external view of morals, relied on such regulatory mechanisms. For example, workers in the dwellings surrounding his factory who decided not to use the common facilities to wash their laundry were fined.[37] Here, silence on the issue would surely end in moral lapses.

Strategies for moral endurance are intrinsically linked to one's understanding of the nature of the moral project. The small semantic difference between a moral *order* (suggesting compliance) and a moral *pursuit* (suggesting rediscovery) might seem benign, yet it largely explains the adoption or not of vocal silence as a solution to a moralizing project. Whereas moral orders generally require voice, moral pursuits often rest on vocal silence. While moral orders favor command-and-control structures, moral pursuits build more readily on suggestion and leeway in internal regulatory structures. Thus, the endurance of distinct moral projects (orders versus pursuits) calls for the development of contrasting organizational plumbing.

Attributes of the Vocal Silence Model

Although my study is concerned, indirectly and in part, with a given organization's moral direction, I do not mean to suggest that the organization in question is badly in need of (moral) repair. The School's pursuit might displease some observers, particularly those who distrust corporate motives, but it still regularly concerns itself with a moral imperative.[38] To address this imperative, the School encourages its members to confront their values in the apparent organizational void. In doing so, it provides an attempt to scale up a moral pursuit. That such an organizational model has its shortcomings is undeniable. I have alluded to these shortcomings in previous chapters by noting the sometimes mixed emotions I have experienced as a faculty member.[39] Yet many such emotions can be traced, I believe, to four main attributes of a vocal-silence model, none distinctive to the School.

First, the promotion of vocal silence is a gradual approach to attaining higher morals. The model only sets the parameters for potential moral awakening and provides some guidelines (i.e., organizational signs) for expected outcomes but does not attempt to modify or strictly enforce given morals. In the School's context, a look at faculty members' perception of student socialization clarifies this point. (Though my study focused on faculty members, their discussion of student socialization echoes, I would argue, their own socialization process.)[40] Despite the School's grand objectives, faculty members are cautious about the extent of their imprinting. An analysis, based on a series of interviews with faculty members in the late 1980s, remarks, "Many [faculty members] believed that the goal was to 'change student behavior.' This view triggered the refrain that graduate business students are already adults and a school cannot expect and should not try to change their value systems." The report therefore adds, "Most faculty seemed more comfortable with the notion of encouraging students to be aware of the ethical implications of their business decisions, to recognize the significance of these implications, and to apply particular modes of reasoning to these decisions, as opposed to telling students what the 'good' or 'right' decision would be."[41] The holding up of a (moral) mirror is perhaps a better way to characterize part of the School's socialization model, and more broadly that of other organizations relying on vocal silence to drive their moral pursuits.

While the School is sometimes caricatured as an experiment in social engineering, most faculty members and administrators are aware of the limits of the experiment.[42] A debate that occurred some ninety years ago on whether to include labor relations, and particularly labor's point of view, in the School's instruction illustrates such awareness. In 1921 several manufacturers had voiced their discontent that a leader of the International Association of Machinists union was lecturing at the School. In reply to an inquiry by a member of the School's Visiting Committee, dean Wallace Donham explained, "I have not the slightest fear that these men [students] will be thrown off their feet by the type of instruction that we are giving. . . . We are not ex cathedra laying down the laws about business and the way it must be done; we are not trying to put these men in leading strings and control their opinions; we are not endeavoring to prevent them from thinking and to keep them from having a basis on which to think for themselves." He concluded, "On the contrary . . . , we are trying to give them the basis for sane thought and independent thought."[43]

In other words, though administrators and many faculty members appear to invest high hopes in the endeavor, they are also quick to recognize the limits of the organizational effort. Linda Hill, a senior faculty member, may have captured this tension most acutely. "If we expect managers to exercise moral agency and courage," she wrote in 2006, "then our first task as their educators is to keep in mind who management students really are and offer them a preview of what managerial life will really be like." To do so, "our next responsibility is to provide them with the tools they need to live consistently with their values while at the same time raising their aspirations for how business can be a positive societal force."[44] Thus, the goal of changing students' values, deemed possibly too utopian, is replaced by the more attainable and gradual goal of raising their aspirations. The notion of raising aspirations echoes a warning articulated by Donham in 1929 regarding the School's inability to create moral fiber from scratch. In his words, "Although moral fiber can scarcely be created in the student, the more common ethical dilemmas of business can be presented to him."[45] Despite a limited capacity to change adult students in just two years, more pragmatic hopes are set forth for raising aspirations and helping sustain, if not create, moral fiber.

Other organizations using vocal silence must also be patient about seeing their goals realized. When engaged in moral pursuits of revisiting collective aspirations or redefining overarching goals, patience is needed. But not all morally informed organizational projects are moral *pursuits*. Some projects, such as those addressing outright financial misconduct, require more direct and immediate intervention from higher authorities. These projects require the implementation of moral *order*. (The backdating of transactions or the fraudulent setting of interbank lending rates will not be fixed by vocal silence.) Vocal silence cannot always be a solution.

Second, a model of vocal silence remains highly reliant on the composition of the organization's membership to enact morals. Despite the many organizational routines that can guide thought and action, ultimately a majority of members need to endorse and enact morals in the organizational void. When a large majority does not exist, difficulties can arise. I will again shift my focus from faculty members to students to illustrate my argument. Consider the students' reception of the notion of an "MBA oath."[46] Shortly after the 2008 financial crisis, the idea of an oath articulating the School's moral pursuit was floated. The fact that the idea of an oath was first voiced by two faculty members suggests ongoing interest, perhaps even concern, about the direction of business education.[47] But its mixed reception among students also highlights the School's dependence on its membership to achieve its goals. In reaction to a student initiative promoting an oath stating (among other clauses) "I will act with utmost integrity and pursue my work in an ethical manner," other students rebelled. The means toward the end were first open to debate. As a student critic of the oath noted, "If you really care about those who need electricity or those who are jobless, then pursue your own ambitions aggressively, for the profit motive is the true engine of prosperity."[48] But beyond a discussion of means, some students challenged the idea that signing an oath would be a proper mechanism to attain the stated goals. A nonrandom poll of 362 School students indicated mixed support for an MBA oath (52.8 percent favorable versus 47.2 percent unfavorable).[49] Students may have resisted stabilizing in writing the School's implicit collective goals and, in doing so, may also have indirectly upheld a model of vocal silence. Regardless of its eventual resolution, the episode underlines the need for broad membership support in enacting morals in silent organizations.

At the School, the evolving composition of the student body and alumni is commonly seen as either an enabling or a disabling factor in the pursuit of higher morals.[50] While faculty members might appear to occupy influential positions at the School, their discretion is also constrained by other constituencies. For example, two senior faculty members recently expressed their belief that the identity of managers has fundamentally mutated and that such a change might explain moral drift in business.[51]

Besides students and alumni, other organizational members also need to be considered. Relatively silent organizations depend on the discretion of all members. In the School's setting, the identity of faculty members in particular might also have changed over time. Relatively silent organizations, particularly those with older established positions like the School, navigate a fine line between conservatism and innovation. Too little innovation and the organization might lose its relative attractiveness to members; too much change and it might lose its members' support. In this context, a silent moral project cannot alienate its past and current members. Like professionals who aim to integrate established orders, not to subvert them, relatively silent organizations mostly work from within.[52] This means that they depend on their members' continued endorsement to perform. The endorsement of the majority, however, is sufficient for organizational performance, which leads to my next point.

Third, minority members will probably feel more conflicted in organizations that promote vocal silence than in those reliant on more direct control. By organizations reliant on direct control, I mean those reliant mostly on scripts that permit little decision making on the part of those involved. In such organizations, members need only to follow the scripts or dissent. The insurance and fast-food industries provide many examples of such organizations.[53] Dissent is a clear expression of conflict, rather than an indication of a conflicted state of mind. In organizations that promote vocal silence, the process of "self-discovery" can easily pinpoint gaps between individual subjectivity and the broader organizational ethos (conveyed via internal and external noises). For organizational minorities, the size of the gap probably makes such a confrontation more daunting. In organizations that promote vocal silence, minority members are likely to carry an excess burden of adjustment. They will experience more friction than members more aligned with the organizational ethos. Such friction in turn might lead to a more conflicted state of mind, and perhaps even to more covert conflict.[54] At the same time, friction may be the most important means to gradually foster organizational change.

Some survey data suggest that friction might be at play in the setting I studied. A 2008 Harvard University–wide survey documented a significant difference between male and female School faculty members' satisfaction levels. Though the overall mean for the School was the second highest among the nine surveyed Harvard faculties, male School faculty members, with an average satisfaction level of 4.53 (on a 5-point scale), seemed to drive the results. Female faculty members reported a significantly lower 3.83 on the same scale.[55] (The level of female faculty satisfaction was higher for the School than for three other Harvard faculties, but the School was one of only two faculties exhibiting a significant male/female gap in satisfaction levels.) There are probably multiple explanations for this gap.[56] My hypothesis is that the prevailing model of vocal silence heightens differences among members' experiences. Varied experiences easily grow on a petri dish of relative silence. Because such experiences also, by definition, remain silent, they might take longer to accumulate and inform broader organizational dynamics. Each member can easily believe that she or he is going through a "unique" experience before a collective awareness threshold is reached.

This hypothesis implies that relatively silent organizations need to do more than others to ease the entry of nontraditional members into their ranks if the goal is to retain them. Perhaps the most significant fact about new moral pursuits is that they are often rooted in old beliefs. The project (here, moralizing business) might be innovative in its design (section-based case-method teaching), and its physical setting (a residential campus) might be new, but its underpinnings are firmly grounded in the past (maintaining standards). As Herbert J. Gans notes in his study of suburbia, new towns are ultimately old communities on new land.[57] Similarly, moral pursuits often represent old hopes in new dress. This scenario implies costs for new entrants and, at best, a delay in the incorporation of their new hopes into the pursuit. This observation also informs my final point.

Fourth, organizations reliant on vocal silence to promote higher morals will always seem immature. By acknowledging the role of silence, this organizational model implies that more can always be imagined and achieved. The School and other mission-driven organizations are inherently works in progress. Until the entire field in which the organization operates is transformed, the organization needs to persevere. Transformation of the field remains a perpetual hope, and thus the target may make the venture seem less successful than it is. As Tom Burns concluded in his 1997 study of the BBC fifty years after its founding: "The BBC is even now, I believe, comparatively immature and unformed."[58] That immaturity, I would argue, is inherent to mission-driven organizations, but even more salient in those adopting a model of organizational silence. The silence is a constant reminder of what is not yet stabilized. It allows for hope and aspirations to grow almost unchecked. Such immaturity is both the relatively silent organization's optimism and its shortcoming.

The unfulfilled aspect of the pursuit is ultimately the raison d'être of organizations reliant on vocal silence to promote higher morals. Remarks made by Harvard University's president Drew G. Faust during the School's centennial made this point quite salient. Hundreds of people, including faculty members, students, and alumni, had gathered under a white tent covering the lawn in front of the School library. The sheer size of the gathering signaled the glory of the occasion. When President Faust took her turn to speak, she told the story of three stonecutters who are asked why they work. The first one answers that he cuts stones to make a living. The second says he cuts the most exquisite stones to do the best job of stonecutting in the entire county. And the third says he cuts stones to build a cathedral.[59] "Leadership," she added, "needs a purpose." The stonecutters of the third kind, she explained, are those "we need to educate." Her remarks drew applause but also created some unease. The tent suddenly felt a bit heavier than it had before. Her remarks captured silent organizations' main limitation, namely the perpetual immaturity of their pursuit. They also captured these organizations' main hope, namely the possibility of constantly re-imagining their purpose.

Scripting relative immaturity might seem like an unsatisfactory solution to a complex problem. The solution nonetheless accommodates the contemporary tensions between morals and individual subjectivity. In Durkheim's writings, individuals play no specific role in reaching moral judgment. The limited agency accorded to individuals is evident in the following statement: "Should we say that a society's highest self-consciousness is only attained by and through an individual's mind?" Clearly not, Durkheim answers.[60] In his view, the highest consciousness is reached collectively, almost impersonally.[61] Thus, morals transcend any individual.

By contrast, in contemporary Western societies that tend to favor individuality over collectivism, individuals are sometimes seen as the guarantors of proper conduct. While George Homans could claim in 1950 that, at the level of a small (collective) group, society could always cohere, the same claim might today prove more problematic.[62] In an era that praises individual subjectivity and responsibility, adhering to collective norms lacks appeal.[63] Any positive attributes of shared norms quickly get recast as negative attributes of sameness (or even imposition). Many norms previously seen as enabling communal life become limiting factors in modern society.

The individual (re)discovery of a shared understanding in vocal silence might prove to be a way to reunite these contradictory views of morals. As Georges Davy notes in his introduction to Durkheim's work, collective thought can be seen as an individual's victory over his or her own subjectivity.[64] The rediscovery of the collective understanding can be framed as a pursuit within oneself, one more in harmony with the expectations of contemporary individualistic Western societies. The hope is that individuals rediscover who they are collectively and in the process become moral beings. Put otherwise, routinizing morals via vocal silence is a probabilistic bet on a sufficient number of individuals choosing the correct path.

Implications

The book's findings aim to help specify a fairly universal model of vocal silence, but they also carry context-specific implications. Though the study's theoretical puzzle revolves primarily around the possibility (or not) of coupling routines and morals, the findings might also speak to audiences intrigued by other puzzles. In particular, I will discuss here some of the book's implications for the functioning of higher education and the making of corporate morals.

While the book focuses on the socialization of Harvard Business School faculty members, its findings also showcase the "plumbing" of a type of educational pursuit. The monolithic nature of higher education is increasingly being challenged. Not all business schools operate like the one described here. Similarly, law and medical schools exhibit much more variation than their belonging to a common field might suggest. Only recently have the varied organizational underpinnings of higher-educational pursuits begun to be examined.[65] This study adds to this stream of research by making clear that organizational context matters. Despite strong external institutional pressures, higher-educational settings exhibit a wide-ranging cultural diversity. Much more needs to be done, however, to document the variety of models present within any given higher-education field. We need to better understand the specific way a given school or university "thinks" in order to assess its broader role in society.[66] Examining its organizational DNA is a way to start answering that question.

Given the scope of the educational pursuit and the expressed ideal of promoting better business standards, Harvard Business School administrators faced the difficult question of routinizing morals early on. Organizational design choices needed to be made. Such choices and their subsequent adjustments formed the basis for a model of socialization.[67] Over decades, the School fine-tuned a model that I have described as one of vocal silence to reach the goal of "moralizing" its faculty members, possibly its students, and, ideally and more broadly, the conduct of business. Whether the described solution to the routinization of morals is effective—whether, that is, the socialization of faculty members achieves its goals and in turn encourages students to develop "higher" morals—is beyond the scope of my study. What the study does document, however, is the organizational attempt to carry out such a moralizing project.

Institutions of higher education come in many flavors, but the one described here stands at a particular crossroad of major institutions. As the sociologist Mitchell Stevens and his coauthors note, universities are "hubs" connecting modern societies' major institutions while remaining "officially independent and intermittently critical of them."[68] How business schools try to educate, train, and socialize future managerial elites for the world that they are about to enter or return to is rarely examined.[69] How the Harvard Business School in particular does so is often poorly understood. Because the School produces leaders who go on to occupy key positions in a wide array of institutions (not limited to the corporate world), it is crucial to understand how students are educated in this setting and what culture gets produced. By unveiling part of the School's inner workings, this study hopefully provides a clearer view of its socializing efforts of its faculty members, but also indirectly its students.[70] At a minimum, it offers an analysis that can serve as a mirror or contrast for further inquiries into similar or alternative educational models.

The book's findings can also provide a window into the making of corporate morals. Corporations tend to be led by a small number of individuals trained at a few schools, including the one I studied.[71] Despite the preeminence of the corporate form in modern economies, it remains poorly understood how a perspective supportive of its development, activities, and goals is promoted. If it is true, as Charles Perrow asserts, that organizations, particularly corporations, increasingly "make our culture," it seems only right to pay attention to the training of their leaders.[72] Corporate morals have long intrigued scholars and practitioners alike, but the need to better specify what they entail—including their anchors and variations—has gained more urgency in light of the repeated financial crises of the early twenty-first century.[73] How corporate leaders and their morals are "made" requires closer study. By treating business schools, or at least the subset with a moral trope, as institutions, the study of the making of corporate morals becomes in part a study of the inner workings of those institutions.

What is currently known about corporate morals? Scholars have repeatedly tried to specify their contents. Melville Dalton's (1959) seminal book *Men Who Manage* provided a nuanced view of managerial elites, and more contemporary scholars have made further strides on this front.[74] The sociologist Robert Jackall's work, in particular, clearly suggests the existence of some shared ways in which managers think about their world.[75] Jackall skillfully shows, for instance, that managers typically look to their superiors within the hierarchy for guidance on issues of right and wrong, and often operate on timelines dictated by their own promotion schedules (e.g., investing only in projects likely to yield results before their next promotion review). Subsequent research has uncovered other corporate norms, such as executives' characteristic ways of working outside of conventional work hours and their preference for nonconfrontational conflict management.[76] Some executives' sense that negotiating crises and uncertainties is a natural condition of employment might also prove to be a widespread corporate belief.[77] As a classic (and still relevant) study of US business education noted a half century ago, "No one would argue that there is a clear and precise code of conduct applicable to business . . . , but the norms within which employees operate are nonetheless real."[78] Such norms are what the sociologist Calvin Morrill labels "the rules of the game" among executives and the keys to understanding, for example, issues of accountability and career dynamics in corporations.[79] Today, Emile Durkheim's late-1890s claim that individuals involved in commerce and industry obey no morals of any kind proves difficult to defend.[80]

This book adds to our understanding of corporate morals by highlighting some likely anchors of these morals. As an example, by stressing individual action in the School's classrooms as a potentially central explanation for success or failure, preexisting social differences become partly naturalized.[81] The role and importance of social context, including one's upbringing, in explaining outcomes are likely to be deemphasized in the process. Individuals are mostly depicted as being in charge of their destiny.[82] In addition, the warlike terminology permeating descriptions of business decisions in teaching notes coexists with a tamed and stratified "small-town" campus setting. The resulting juxtaposition of an individual's agitated private realm and a harmonious collective context might echo or foreshadow corporate norms—such as an overall preference for covert conflict. These hypotheses, obviously, require deeper probing.

Manufacturing Morals nonetheless makes clear the difficulty of specifying corporate morals. It may be that apparent *underspecification* is a key attribute of corporate morals. The apparent restraint from endorsing any given set of morals might be the study's key implication with respect to corporate morals. Senior faculty members' recent description of the School's first-year required ethics course as one that does not endorse any particular point of view seems to supports such an interpretation.[83] They note that "students must feel that the classroom is a safe, protected environment in which they can openly explore and question one another's deeply held beliefs without the need to parrot back a prescribed philosophy or point of view." Thus the difficulty of specifying corporate morals may not be the result of a lack of morals, but an artifact of the content of corporate morals, namely a desire to keep in play *multiple* viewpoints within the broader boundaries of what is deemed acceptable.

Such an aspiration to accommodate multiple viewpoints within limits has been apparent throughout the School's history. For example, Charles Gragg, a faculty member who authored the 1940 teaching note "Because Wisdom Can't Be Told," explained that "the principal object of professional education is to accelerate a student's ability to act in a mature fashion under conditions of responsibility."[84] What constituted a mature fashion was purposely left unspecified. Gragg added that "each student is free to present and hold to his own views." The more recent introduction into the School's curriculum of materials on managers' legal duties (e.g., their fiduciary duty) qualifies such a statement. Yet with respect to moral decision making, faculty members involved in the School's formal ethics course offerings seem to agree with Gragg: they note that managers' actions need to "be guided and consistent with relevant ethical standards" or to meet "relevant" ethical "requirements," but steer clear of specifying what those standards or requirements are.[85] Put otherwise, moral thinking is essentially viewed as a process that can accommodate (within limits) multiple moral viewpoints. That such apparent freedom is granted in a setting that simultaneously contains an abundance of normative cues is probably what permits such underspecification. For all corporate managers to coalesce under a tent, its size needs to be sufficiently large and its poles sufficiently solid. To paraphrase and qualify Durkheim's statement, those involved in commerce and industry might obey multiple morals rather than no morals at all.[86] Thus, in the corporate world, being relatively silent about endorsing any unique moral perspective might be a form of morality after all.

Postscript

At the end of a November day in 2009, my cell phone rang while I was still in my office. I was a candidate, that fall, for promotion to untenured associate professor. "Please hold. The dean wants to talk to you," I was instructed. Recently promoted colleagues had told me that the dean calls each candidate individually to convey promotion decisions, regardless of the outcome. The moment of uncertainty before the decision is conveyed must be the longest experienced by faculty members at the School. The dean quickly told me I had been promoted. Upon arriving home that evening, I found a bottle of champagne waiting at the front door. A note of congratulation from the dean was attached.

I soon learned that there had been much discussion and some unease among senior faculty members about my conducting a study at the School. My promotion packet had included a description of this project. Though the dean's office had been cooperative about providing access to staff and archives, I knew the context had just changed. The fact that close to eighty senior colleagues had discussed this project's outline as part of my review process had tainted my field in ways I had naively not foreseen. Some School members strongly urged me to redirect my efforts toward other projects.[1] As a way to exorcise the pressure, I stowed the bottle of champagne at the back of a kitchen cabinet; this seemed like a vain act of defiance. I did not show up at my office for the next few days, until scheduled appointments forced me to do so. The reassurance of close friends, some at the School, failed to comfort me. I initially agreed that suspending the study for a while was the only path forward. Some colleagues even suggested that the study's design was so compromised that I would have to abandon it entirely.

After several weeks, I returned to the first entries in my field journal. They captured a feeling of out-of-placeness that a fair number of other new School faculty members seemed to share. My field notes and journal entries described faculty members learning to operate within a new perspective. I could relate to Bronislaw Malinowski's experience of abruptly feeling "quite alone" when embarking on his journey to the Trobriand Islands.[2] In retrospect, I think this project was my way of coping with what I perceived as the School's strangeness or the friction I experienced in the face of relative organizational silence. The desire to tame my unease provided a partial impetus for the study. My hope for this ethnography was to properly capture and analyze that experience of unease. Relatively silent organizations are well equipped to absorb and contain members' experiential variations in organizational voids. Yet the experience of vocal silence, as I suggested earlier, can differ starkly depending on where one comes from and where one stands. By explaining the socialization dynamics, this study hopes to make such apparent silence less lonesome, particularly for organizational minorities. Rereading my journal entries convinced me that I should pursue this project. Writing this book is also my attempt to accompany other new entrants into organizations reliant on vocal silence.

Acknowledgments

I am deeply indebted to the many people whose direct and indirect support made this book possible. First I want to thank the students in my Harvard Business School MBA classes with whom I enacted in the moment—and often understood only much later—what the School might be about. The students taught me more than they probably ever imagined. I am very grateful for their patience and collective wisdom.

I also thank the deans who oversaw the School during the writing of this study for putting up with my persistence in completing this project. Few institutions want to see their inner workings publicly discussed; the School is no exception. Yet both dean Jay Light and dean Nitin Nohria respected my decision to pursue this study. Without endorsing it, they made sure I could proceed as long as I did not use proprietary School data or breach other faculty members' privacy.

My great indebtedness extends as well to many colleagues who have generously shared their time and thoughts. The initial impetus for the book grew out of conversations with Amy Wrzesniewski and Harrison White. Amy understood, perhaps better than I did, what might be in the making when she gave me a book titled *Harvard Works Because We Do* upon my arrival at the School. This book, by Greg Halpern, is a collection of portraits of and short texts by Harvard University staff members (e.g., custodians and security guards), but it leaves untouched faculty members. In a way, that book is a necessary companion to the one you hold. I cannot thank Amy enough for believing in this project. As for Harrison, his enthusiastic reaction to the project's premise, at a time when I seriously doubted that there was a project, proved crucial. Ever since I attended his Columbia University graduate seminar in the early 2000s, his capacity to continuously marvel at human behavior has hugely inspired me. This book is a much delayed token of gratitude. More recently, Jack Gabarro's nurturing insights on early draft chapters proved instrumental in polishing the project's scope and contents. At that time, few understood better than Jack my eagerness to comprehend the School's inner workings, and his openness to such an inquiry was very liberating. During the project's more intensive writing stage, John Van Maanen, above all, proved an attentive reader and confidant. His unwavering support and sharp critical eye, particularly when the road seemed rocky, were what most book writers can only dream of. His line-by-line comments, including some delivered in a roadside coffee shop near Boston's Logan Airport, helped sharpen my argument immensely.

Many other colleagues and individuals also helped along the way. I thank in particular Julie Battilana, Robin Ely, Herminia Ibarra, Kate Kellogg, Rakesh Khurana, Jay Lorsch, Joshua Margolis, Leslie Perlow, and Mike Tushman for their detailed feedback on the manuscript or parts of it. I thank as well Joe Badaracco, Mike Beer, Paul Carlile, Jane Dutton, Martha Feldman, Victoria Johnson, Lynn Paine, Siobhán O'Mahony, Lakshmi Ramarajan, Mitchell Stevens, Sandra Sucher, Catherine Turco, and Tieying Yu for their clarifying questions and reactions to my framing efforts; Catherine Paradeise and Christine Musselin for reminding me of the international dynamics of higher education; and Paul Healy for helping me ensure that I did not use proprietary School data or breach other faculty members' privacy.

At the University of Chicago Press, Doug Mitchell artfully shepherded the project into print while offering sharp insights on improving the manuscript. Tim McGovern's resourcefulness made the editorial journey almost a breeze. And Joel Score proved a miracle worker when expertly editing the book. Finally, the Press's anonymous readers provided vital feedback on the manuscript. I wish I could thank them by name.

Even books with only one author are generally products of collective efforts. Over the years Kelly Baker, Barbara Cleary, Sarah Johnson, and Erin McFee provided much needed research assistance. Steven Shafer and Ann Goodsell offered extremely constructive feedback on the entire manuscript. Ayn Cavicchi capably helped me code and analyze the case teaching notes discussed in chapter 4. Catherine Hammond's and Han Lei's artistic eyes wonderfully enriched the book. And Lisa Riva's expert support allowed me to juggle the project with many other demands. I am indebted to the Harvard Business School's Division of Research and Faculty Development for funding all of these efforts. I also thank the friendly staff of Diesel Café in Somerville, where many initial chapter outlines first saw the light of day.

Finally, I thank my family for their support of my work. My parents' and my sister's gentle inquiries about the project's progress expressed not just concern about its development but also trust in my ability to complete it. My aunt's and uncle's repeated requests to read the book when it was still unwritten reminded me that I had to move forward so as not to disappoint these avid readers. Most importantly, my spouse, Patrick, has been my strongest supporter. When a senior colleague once told me that attempting to complete this study would be like walking a tightrope between two skyscrapers with lit dynamite in my hands, I recounted the exchange to Patrick. The next day an illustrated postcard awaited me at breakfast. Patrick had found a card that portrayed a man on a tightrope, walking somewhat miraculously from a rooftop toward the moon: he held the loose end of the rope in his hand as he proceeded upward. Even if I never reach the moon, I am deeply grateful to Patrick for accompanying me on such journeys.

APPENDIX

Data and Methods

Examining the process of composing a book can seem like a navel-gazing exercise. Drafts and rewrites, small breakthroughs and missed turns, surprises and mistakes all typically combine to form a book. Why bother pulling back the curtain on this process? I would argue that doing so reveals a lot about the study's content and findings. Consider, for example, "servant novels"—novels written by maids during the nineteenth century. The context of their composition is rarely remembered. Yet how they were crafted and peddled on the streets, and how they reached other servants' hands, helps explain their tone and content.[1] Restricting one's angle of vision on servant novels to the end product, without taking their making into account, misses much of what the form was about. Similarly, the findings of this study on organizational socialization cannot be confined to the finished product you now hold in your hands. They encompass the product *and* its composition. A study's content depends on how it is carried out, and how it is carried out in turn conditions its content.

How did this study of faculty members' socialization at the Harvard Business School come about, and what does it entail? This appendix discusses the study's context and data sources. Inductive qualitative research designs sometimes elicit elaborate post hoc rationalizations of conscious but also somewhat haphazard decisions. If I were to rationalize, I would say that I have always been curious about, and slightly frightened by, organizations that claim to transform their members. The US higher-education system is a context in which the notion of "reinvention" is particularly powerful.[2] With the proper combination of abilities, perseverance, and financial resources, many students of all ages embark on academic journeys to become who they aspire to be. Particularly in professional schools, like business, law, and medical schools, the transformation narrative is frequently implicit.[3] The corollary to notions of individual reinvention is the argument that academic settings shape members' trajectories. (The leap from shaping trajectories to shaping individuals is one that most institutions are careful not to make.) How this shaping occurs puzzled me—thus, my rationale for joining and studying the Harvard Business School.

The previous paragraph does not, of course, capture the way the study was conceived. An intersection of preexisting interests, curiosity, and timely encounters gave rise to the project. As Kai Erikson once remarked, scholars "live careers in which they occasionally become patients, occasionally take jobs as steel workers or taxi drivers, and frequently find themselves in social settings where their trained eye begins to look for data even though their presence in the situation was not engineered for that purpose."[4] My situation fits that description. Like *Boys in White*, a study of a medical school conducted by Howard S. Becker and colleagues in the 1950s, my study has, in a sense, "no design"—that is, like Becker, I had "no well-worked-out set of hypotheses to be tested, no data-gathering instruments purposely designed to secure information relevant to these hypotheses, no set of analytical procedures specified in advance."[5] But if the term *design* is understood in a broader sense as an attempt to understand what Becker called "those elements of order," a design did gradually emerge. What began as a diary of my experiences at the School slowly became a more structured and encompassing endeavor.

Initially, the diary was meant only as a record of my personal recollections. It is difficult to pinpoint the precise moment when its function changed, but two events precipitated the decision to expand the project. First, one day in 2007 a sentence by Michael Taussig made me pause: "Anthropology is blind to how much its practice relies on the art of telling other people's stories—badly."[6] Though I did not go so far as to reject my past research (on "other people") as an utter failure, his words resonated strongly: Why not try telling your own story? When Harrison White, who had helped me shape my dissertation, asked me the same year what I was up to, I described the amorphous idea of studying the School's socialization of its faculty. White, as a former member of Harvard University's sociology faculty, was familiar with the context. He asked what data I would use; I mentioned my notes. In his unique way, he said it would be "criminal" not to pursue the idea; his words convinced me to launch the project.

Field Notes

Four years intervened between the day I was interviewed for a faculty position at the School and the moment I formally ended my field-note taking (January 2005 to January 2009). During this period, I entered field notes in my journal whenever events dictated and/or time permitted, leading to approximately four hundred single-spaced pages of typed notes. For researchers inclined toward the ethnographic approach, the length of time spent in the field working or living with other field-participants (generally over a year), is what counts most in collecting valid data.[7] Witnessing what happens in a field over extended or repeated periods of time is the most accepted way of generating legitimate insight.[8] The assumption is that a trained ethnographer will gradually, through analyses of his or her field notes, come to understand the participants' thoughts and behaviors.

My notes range from bare descriptions of routine activities—"At noon, I went to eat at Baker Commons with X. Picked tilapia fish in spicy sauce from the buffet as well as cooked asparagus. We sat down with Y, who needed to run to catch a plane to New York to meet alumni"—to more subjective feelings experienced on or off campus: "Tomorrow is the first teaching day of the semester. It's already late, but I have a hard time falling asleep. There's a transition in the teaching plan that does not feel right. I need to figure it out before class." These notes formed the basis of the data used in this book. They were usually recorded at the end of the day, sometimes early in the morning, at home. During the day, I sometimes scribbled sentences on any handy piece of paper to remind myself later what had happened or how I had felt; I transcribed the sentences into my journal verbatim without any conscious self-censoring.

On several occasions I tried to shift the note-taking activity to my office, which seemed more efficient: I could witness something and immediately record it. In practice, this approach rarely worked. Taking notes about the School at the School proved difficult. When, for instance, two years into my journal, I decided (once again) to try taking notes at my office, the frequency and quality of my field notes notably declined. I simply could not do it there. Here is an excerpt from my journal during this attempt: "September 24, 2007: I stare at my open Word file and realize I have gone a week without taking notes. I thought I was 'stronger' in a way, that I could segment my activities and that the writing would progress easily." The note taking did not go easily; I decided to transfer it back off site, where it remained until the study's end.

Whereas my initial note-taking activity was without clear purpose, it slowly evolved over the years to focus on what I considered the most enduring elements of the community I lived in. Gradually, the main questions I tried to answer through observation and the iterative analysis of these notes came to resemble those posed by urban sociologists: What were the School's main social groups? How could the relative permanence and stability of the School's populations be characterized? What did the School take for granted? What undertakings capture the greatest amount of attention?[9] I attempted first to answer these questions from my own standpoint. When I could not find clear answers, I figured out the types of data (including archival data) that might help me answer them, and purposely went about trying to collect them. Certain archives I could access (e.g., students' auction data); others were off-limits (students' ratings of the faculty). When possible, I opted for public sources like annual reports and public Internet pages to enrich my notes. My first two years were the most productive in terms of note taking; by the end of the second year, only exceptional moments made it into my notes. In retrospect, I wish I had continued more steadily to take exhaustive notes about all of my experiences. Instead, I rationalized my reduced note-taking activity by convincing myself that my learning curve had "flattened out."[10] Put otherwise, my note taking ended when I reached relative saturation in my perceived understanding of the School.

Specifying the data excluded from this study is as important as spelling out what data were included. All data deemed confidential by Harvard University's Committee on the Use of Human Subjects were excluded. In particular, the content of discussions at School-wide faculty meetings as well as at departmental meetings, and of discussions related to specific hiring, promotion, or firing decisions were excluded. Similarly, any exchanges with colleagues and others affiliated with the School that clearly identified the protagonists or the events in question were excluded. (While it would be illusory to claim that the excluded data did not cognitively inform the book's writing, I made sure to keep out any off-limits data from the book's pages.) The identities of informants were also disguised to ensure the anonymity of data sources. Moreover, because pseudonyms are not always sufficient to guarantee anonymity for readers familiar with the people involved, personal identifiers have sometimes intentionally been modified.[11] Like Gaye Tuchman, who conducted an ethnography of the corporatization of a US university, my constant goal in writing up the findings was not to harm anyone.[12]

The methodological choices supporting the study entail several assumptions, some of which are also limitations. Most importantly perhaps, a premium is placed on everyday life. As John Van Maanen and Deborah Kolb note, "Like the carving out of a shoreline by the incessant slapping of a sea, ethnographers assume everyday life in organizations has more to do with shaping the behavior of the membership and the nature of the organization itself than the prescribed table of organization, the so-called external environment, or the dramatic . . . high-level decision making."[13] This orientation means, for instance, that I probably paid too little attention to exceptional events such as the School's centennial celebrations in 2008 and the appointment of a new dean in 2010. I also did not spend much time on broad trends in higher education and academic labor markets facing the School.[14] Omitting a discussion of the environment may be even more limiting in a study of an academic setting than in studies of other settings. Indeed, from an ecological perspective, academic settings fit into a distinct category of organizations, those generally "lacking in a specific economic base."[15] Despite the fact that many universities have become quite adept at monetizing knowledge, this relative ecological characteristic might suggest a lesser need to focus on the environment, but Roderick McKenzie corrects that misperception by noting that academic settings are "much more subject to the vicissitudes of human fancies and decrees than are the basic types of human communities [such as towns or firms]."[16] In other words, academic settings largely depend on their environment for survival and growth. This study examines the School's attempts to shape or react to its environment but leaves many external forces unspecified. Prior research on the development of US business schools can provide that context.[17]

Experiential Data Sources

Unlike contextual data, experiential data intentionally abound in the book's narrative. Personal interactions between a researcher and his field are inherent to field research and crucial to illuminate findings. Living in a field is not without personal consequences, and those consequences can enhance as well as derail the research pursuit.[18] This process explains why a researcher's personal history needs to be considered when assessing field-research outputs. In particular, the researcher's prior experience in another culture is often considered crucial (alongside length of stay) when assessing ethnographic work.[19] Interactions that can be compared and contrasted with past experiences yield the best insight. Prior experience is not acquired solely via distant travel; close settings can also provide for it.[20] For example, the experience of being different from the dominant group in any setting offers good training for field research. Properly disclosing one's history in a field qualifies one's findings and is fairly standard in much ethnographic writing.

Treating personal interactions as an integral part of the research pursuit and as relevant data points for analysis is, however, less common: "The information obtained, rather than the experience lived, remains the focus of most field-based studies," as Robert A. George and Michael O. Jones observe.[21] Only in rare instances are the experiences involved in data gathering openly discussed and deemed relevant to the inquiry.[22] Yet the researcher can legitimately be seen as an "instrument" or "device" of his craft, to employ Peggy R. Sanday's terms, using her own reactions to capture observations that might otherwise go unnoticed.[23] In that sense, lived experiences can become actual data points for analysis.[24] This assumption has profound implications for how data are collected and analyzed, suggesting in particular a need for more reflexive (or introspective) approaches to analyzing field settings.

Only in the past few decades has such a reflexive approach to ethnography been initiated. Kenneth E. Read, one of the first anthropologists to experiment openly with a reflexive approach and to expose the limitations of conventional treatment of field data, did so to gain insight into clan rituals. *The High Valley*, a first-person account of his time in New Guinea, was published in 1965. As Read later explained, the book was not meant as conventional ethnography. Instead, it is the "record of a dialectic between one kind of person and other kinds of persons."[25] He added that he could not view the individuals he had lived with only as "objects of clinical concern" and "repositories of needed information"; thus he chose a first-person (reflexive) account.[26] For Read, the methodological shift was a felt necessity.

Reflexive accounts of field experiences have since become more widespread in the social sciences.[27] No longer do their authors need to adopt pen names to publish such work. In 1954, when the anthropologist Laura Bohannan, still a junior faculty member, first published a reflexive account of her fieldwork with the Tiv tribe of southern Nigeria, she called it "an anthropological novel" and used a pen name.[28] She thus inadvertently introduced a new genre that would gain wider acceptance. Read was the first to openly embrace the genre, but many others also followed.[29] Using reflexive approaches, Jeanne Favret-Saada, Kay Kaufman Shelemay, and Loïc Wacquant respectively studied witchcraft in rural French communities, expatriates' lives in Ethiopia, and Chicago boxers' code of conduct.[30] Similarly, Carolyn Ellis relied on the reflexive genre to study issues of dependency in families with chronically ill members.[31] Thanks in part to the reflexive approach, all of these works yielded novel insights into largely neglected realms of inquiry.

Reflexive ethnographic approaches call for closer attention to the instrument (the self) that analyzes the data than do other types of ethnographic writing. Unlike "confessional" ethnographers, whose primary interest is the writing form itself (the confessional tale), reflexive scholars tend to consider their experiences of the field to be most critical to the genre. Reflexive ethnographies (sometimes labeled "experimental") thus go beyond confessional tales because they typically "represent fieldwork experiences as vital techniques for structuring their narratives of description and analysis."[32] What counts is how the lived experience contributes to the analysis, almost regardless of the writing form. The reflexive genre also allows unique (and possibly previously unheard) voices to emerge from the field; the depiction of reflexive ethnography as a feminist methodological form—well suited to conveying women's experiences in a male-dominated world—illustrates this potential of the genre.[33] Subjectivity, far from being avoided, is openly embraced.

I also relied heavily on my field experiences to structure the narratives and analyses in this book. Following Wacquant's recommendation, I played the game to know the game. In his words, I put my "own organism, sensibility, and incarnate intelligence at the epicenter" of the field context that I intended to dissect.[34] Often I did not fully understand an event or interaction until months or years later; regularly, I let myself be guided by the field. I favored rich communication modes (rather than surveys or formal interviews), and I sought out field density.[35] When something felt strange, I took it as a sign to pay close attention. Similarly, when something felt right, I treated it as an opportunity to pinpoint what had triggered the feeling. In short, I relied on my emotions and feelings to guide my inquiry and analysis.

The limitations of reflexive ethnographies should, however, be made clear. Gary Alan Fine warns strongly against the temptation to transform "the intensive labor of field research into the armchair pleasures of 'me-search.'"[36] I hope not to have fallen into that trap; it is up to the reader to judge. Also, issues of personal bias are inherent in all ethnographic data-collection processes, particularly reflexive ones. When in doubt about the representativeness of particular data, I took solace in E. E. Evans-Pritchard's words: "If allowances are made for the personality of the writer, and if we consider that in the entire range of anthropological studies the effects of these personal differences tend to correct each other, I do not think that we need worry unduly over this problem [personal bias]."[37] The solution is therefore to generate more ethnographies to build a better shared understanding of a given context. I look forward to reading complementary accounts of the School, as well as reflexive accounts of other mission-driven settings.

Position in the Field

The ethnographic literature contains many variations on authors' positions in the field. The "research-participant" position is perhaps the most common. Many researchers adopt the position of trainee: typically, other field participants explicitly know that the researcher will later exit the field. Such designs cast the researcher first as a scholar and secondarily as a participant (though the boundaries can blur); thus the term *research-*

participant.[38] (The less precise term "participant observer" generally means the same thing.) Sallie Westwood's research on a British hosiery factory and Peter Moskos's account of his stint as a newly minted police officer in Baltimore exemplify such designs.[39] Westwood, with management's approval, spent a year on the shop floor, working alongside other employees at jobs like stitching stockings and socks. All of them knew who she was and that she would leave. Similarly, Moskos's colleagues were aware that he was a graduate student; they taught him the tricks of the trade but were aware that he would move on. They sometimes made his temporary status explicit, saying, "Oh, that's right, you're not a cop. You're just here to get your PhD."[40] Projects reliant on the research-participant position have yielded penetrating insights into numerous communities.

The research-participant position is typically contrasted with that of the "total participant," which calls for the researcher to be first and foremost a participant and only occasionally (at best) a researcher. Rachel Sherman's work as a paid employee at luxury hotels and Matthew Desmond's time as a firefighter are examples of such field positions. In both cases, their fellow workers considered them colleagues first.[41] Though role conflicts can occur (if, for instance, the participant is recast as an observer or vice versa), the balance usually tilts to the side of the total participant.[42] This was my position at the School. To other School members, I was primarily a faculty member and secondarily an ethnographer. I was also a trainee, but one who, if all went well, might remain in the field. Though my possible exit from the field probably crossed the minds of some colleagues, I do not believe that it defined my position any more than it did that of other untenured junior faculty members.

For some academics, the total-participant position is fraught with methodological hazards and is therefore best avoided. Essentially, the risk of developing too much intimacy with a field or a setting is viewed as a potential distraction from "scientific" inquiry. (By intimacy, I mean deep involvement with others in the field.) This critique explains why many researchers deeply involved with other field participants choose not to highlight such intimacy. Consider Nels Anderson's research on homeless men.[43] Only a revised introduction to his study, written nearly forty years later, acknowledges that he was "an intimate participant observer of the life of the hobo on the road." Likewise, Michèle Lamont's study of how professors on funding panels assess the work of their colleagues hardly mentions her own participation in funding discussions. Though she seems familiar with such panels, she steers clear of introducing data on her own experiences.[44] Only rarely do researchers overtly showcase their intimacy with the field.[45] Others, like Anderson, disclose it years later once their scholarship has gained legitimacy.[46] Intimacy is oftentimes seen as a double-edged sword, quite dangerous to manipulate: it sharpens the analysis, but also potentially taints the results.[47]

When studying in particular one's own environment, the intricacies of the study often lead scholars to recommend staying clear of such pursuits. Yet the prohibition should not be conflated with potential methodological issues. As Cara Richards observes, anthropologists have long noted the special problems involved in studying their own culture. The norm in the field of anthropology is to take on such a project, at best, only as a second field study.[48] Richardson points out, however, the peculiar exception that both American and English universities, when training foreign-born anthropologists, often encourage them to study their own cultures. She then poses the obvious question: "Why allow foreign anthropologists to do something most American and English anthropologists are forbidden to do?"[49] Transforming a methodological concern into an outright prohibition is an easy way to tangle different issues.[50] Methodological concerns cannot be dismissed, but they should be addressed as such, not as a stand-in for a sweeping prohibition.

The methodological caution voiced by critics of intimacy should be taken seriously. I tried to address their concern by, for example, enrolling the help of two senior colleagues—a School insider and an outsider—to act as "clinical supervisors" while I conducted this research. (I approached them regularly with working hypotheses and asked them to push back with alternate hypotheses.) I believe, however, that focusing only on a researcher's level of intimacy with a field distracts from a potentially more decisive issue, namely a researcher's degree of freedom in the field. Put otherwise, I would posit that intimacy is a justified risk to take as long as the researcher does not feel excessively constrained by the field. Thus the question of intimacy often masks a question of autonomy.[51]

While full autonomy is ideal for the conduct of research, few field researchers really attain it. Like ideal informants, ideal field researchers often occupy insider/outsider positions in the contexts they study.[52] They are deeply familiar with the context but not fully bound by its traditions. They can partly escape the group's social control without fear of exclusion because they are already at the margins. Consider, for instance, the informants whom Paul Rabinow relied on to conduct fieldwork in Morocco.[53] All of his informants—whether the French expatriate café owner who had failed financially or the descendant of a Moroccan saint who ran a prostitution ring—spoke with clarity about what they knew because they viewed it simultaneously from up close and from afar. (The café owner vividly evoked the expatriate life he had once been part of but could no longer afford, and the saint's descendant described with precision the community he had grown up in but would never fully return to, given his occupation.) Most researchers intimate with a field face serious challenges, but some of them can find the relative freedom necessary to speak from within.[54]

My untenured position put me, however, in a de facto insider/outsider role. I was an insider because I participated in the School's educational pursuit. As a faculty member, I had to learn the insider's tricks of the trade. But, given the probability of obtaining tenure at the School, I was also a potential outsider. This in-between status gave me a relative freedom I would not have enjoyed if I had been tenured at the School when conducting the study. (The employment security that accompanies tenure technically offers increased freedom, but it also increases social dependence on the collective because very few tenured faculty members at the School move to other universities.) In addition, pursuing this project confused some of my colleagues. For a junior faculty member to talk openly about the School's inner workings is somewhat taboo.[55] This confusion, when it was conveyed to me, in turn sometimes made me feel even more of an outsider, paradoxically creating greater autonomy for me in the field. Overall, such autonomy proved helpful to the analysis, though it occasionally restricted my access to data.

Relations with Other School Members

The proper handling of my relations with others at the School, particularly colleagues, was a crucial methodological and ethical concern throughout the project. John Van Maanen's warning that the relation between the "knower and the known" is "most problematic," and anything but "independent," forced me to revisit the question regularly.[56] Early on, for instance, an attentive colleague saw me taking profuse notes during a meeting (as I often do, mostly by habit) and remarked, "I wonder if you're taking notes about us. Perhaps you'll write a study of us one of these days?" At the time, I did not know I would, but his reaction highlighted the potential challenges of doing so.

My colleagues' reactions to this study varied. A few strongly encouraged me in the pursuit, most cooperated when approached with specific questions, and some repeatedly expressed reticence. The warnings of earlier researchers had prepared me for this spectrum of reactions. When Theodore Caplow and Reece J. McGee studied the academic labor market in the early 1950s, for instance, some colleagues "expressed grave doubts" about the ability of what they called "natives" of the academy to "tolerate the explorer in spite of his close identification with themselves."[57] (Thankfully, many other of their colleagues proved more cooperative.) On a practical basis, when a few of my colleagues told me that for a multitude of reasons the project could not proceed, I followed Howard S. Becker's advice to fieldworkers: act as though all you can hear is yes or maybe.[58] I also made every effort to inform as many people as possible about my pursuit, organizing early on a seminar in my department, spelling out the project in my research statement (distributed to all tenured faculty members), and freely answering all questions. I did not want to work undercover, nor would the Institutional Review Board allow me to do so.

Yet the question of whether I was an impostor, and whether I was revealing the School's tricks, continued to trouble me. The idea that "at its core, fieldwork must be regarded as something of a traitorous activity" lingered.[59] Everett Hughes's use of terms like "spy," "double agent," and "betrayal" to describe fieldworkers and fieldwork captures both the potential stigma attached to the endeavor and the possibility that others might feel violated.[60] Pierre Bourdieu also articulates this dilemma in his study of French academics. Despite the most careful efforts, he notes, "one will never completely escape the suspicion of performing an act of denunciation."[61] When doubting my status as a member of the community, I reassured myself by thinking of my project as what Irving Goldman calls the "skilled revelation of a skilled concealment." Even when a shaman reveals the tricks behind the magic, its power does not diminish; quite the contrary. Using the example of Kwakiutl Indian ceremonies in which "secret matters are always hidden and can be experienced, therefore, only in simulated form," Goldman remarks that even seeing an obvious simulation does not render the ceremonies any less potent.[62]

From my viewpoint, there is no betrayal in mere depiction; betrayal lies in wrongful depiction of a setting, its practices, and its inhabitants. Rather than trying to find something insiders would not know, the ethnographic approach makes salient what most insiders already know. The main aim of this book is thus to describe what insiders consider obvious, and the strongest test for this book is whether insiders consider its depictions "true." If so, this account of a moment in time might prove beneficial as the School evolves. To ensure that my descriptions were accurate, I shared drafts write-ups of the study with select insiders and former insiders. (The former insiders were sought to ensure that insiders' suggestions were not intended solely to sanitize the findings.) Their comments helped further qualify the book's data and argument. While the argument remains my own, these readers' input helped ensure that the depictions were not too idiosyncratic. My hope is that the book convinces without betraying and that it reveals the obvious.

Why?

A few colleagues asked me repeatedly during the course of this study why I was pursuing it. They were hoping, I am guessing, to find keys or pointers to the as yet not fully shaped findings in my own mind. They wanted perhaps to preempt any revelations in the findings. As a process researcher, I tend to ask *how* questions rather than *why* questions: motives can easily be invented on the spot, but processes are harder to reconstruct and therefore less prone to post hoc rationalization. Despite our best attempts at introspection, we often remain somewhat blind to our own intentions; thus, a direct answer to a why question needs to be treated skeptically.

Even so, why questions are legitimate, and the tentative answers of other fellow travelers can perhaps start to provide an incomplete key to the study's motivations. "Like building a watch," writes Michael Taussig, ethnographic research can provide the "sense of security" that arises from having "a system" and then "a schedule."[63] This holds, of course, particularly true when the system being described appears novel and risky (as the School initially appeared to me). The watchmaker analogy speaks to me, and it seems plausible that conducting this project provided a sense of relative security to a newcomer to the School. The desire to better "know" my environment by conducting this ethnography is a plausible motivation. But the daily environment at the School is fairly routinized, not chaotic. What came my way was mostly expected; thus, engaging in this project could also be seen as a reaction to a sense of being overly protected. Ethnographic fieldwork is sometimes seen as a dilettante's pursuit, one that partly transgresses systems of control.[64] In that spirit, I cannot help but wonder if pursuing the project might also have been a way of creating security through insecurity, namely by slipping out of the sphere of perceived control. Imagining oneself outside a system—at least conceptually, to study it—while physically in its midst might generate a sense of (relative) freedom from organizational pressures. Relatively disrupting the system and its schedule can therefore be seen as a possible alternative goal.

Finally, another reason to pursue the project might have been my relative solitude in the field. Anthropologists have long noted the loneliness of the fieldworker's pursuit, yet it is often presented as the inevitable outcome of a unique position in the field. A common assumption is that field research results in solitude.[65] I would argue that the directionality of the link might be misunderstood: perhaps some classes of scholars become field researchers. Thus the imagined "outcome" of the field might simply be an artifact of the fieldworker prior to entry into the field. For instance, Peter Moskos has suggested that introverted scholars might be good at conducting fieldwork.[66] Though introversion does not equate with solitude, it might result in relative solitude in the field. This question is an open-ended one, but it might have informed my pursuit of this project. Despite the caveat I expressed about why questions, these questions are justified. A better understanding of a researcher's motivations can qualify findings. When studying in particular one's own setting, a heightened need to qualify is expected. It helped, nonetheless, that many past researchers, including academics, have turned their attention to their own settings.

Academic Insiders' Writing

Universities, colleges, and other educational settings have long been the focus of research by academic insiders. (By insiders, I mean individuals intimately familiar with given settings, not solely faculty members.) What Talcott Parsons and Gerald M. Platt called a "self-conscious understanding" of the US educational system in their own study of academia is not uncharted terrain.[67] As early as 1938, Frances D. Donovan published an account of school teaching, that she referred to as "largely a testimony of one who has spent nineteen years as a teacher in several different schools."[68] More recent examples of the genre include studies of the shifting financial realities of higher education, the peer funding-review process, and college admission, all written by academic insiders.[69] The criticism that academics turned their attention to everything but their own employers probably held true in the 1950s, but it seems less warranted today.[70] Many studies have since been published on academia by insiders.

A closer examination of these productions reveals that academic insiders' writing consists of three main subgenres: (1) authorized accounts of named academic settings; (2) authorized accounts of unnamed academic settings; and (3) unauthorized accounts of named academic settings.[71] The choice of subgenre probably reflects authors' personal preferences and degrees of comfort with disclosure, as well as differing requirements from institutional review boards and shifting interpretations of what constitutes academic freedom of expression.

Authorized accounts of named academic settings are quite abundant. As illustrations, studies on medical schools were conducted by Howard S. Becker et al. (1961) and Robert Merton et al. (1957) at Cornell University, the University of Kansas, the University of Pennsylvania, and Western Reserve University. In these accounts the setting is transparent, the findings are contextualized, and material from named archival sources often complements the collected data. More recent examples include Byron Good's description of physician's training at Harvard Medical School, Henry Rosovsky's account of the inner working of Harvard University's Faculty of Arts and Sciences, Atul Gawande's book on a surgical residency at a Harvard University teaching hospital, Shamus Rahman Khan's work on adolescent socialization at St. Paul's elite boarding school, and Jacques Siracusa's book on teaching sociology at the French universities of Paris-8-Saint-Denis and Paris-10-Nanterre.[72] There are numerous such authorized accounts of Harvard Business School.[73] The most popular one is perhaps Jeffrey Cruik-shank's history of the School.[74] The memoirs of former faculty members like Melvin Copeland and Fritz Roethlisberger represent other versions of the subgenre.[75] Charles Orth's study of student life offers yet another window into the School's operations. As an assistant professor at the School, Orth relied on data from two sections he taught during the 1959–1960 academic year to write his findings.[76] (The key difference between his study and mine is his focus on students and mine on faculty.) Taken together, these works provide a very rich depiction of the School.

The second subgenre, authorized accounts of unnamed academic settings, includes Melvin Konner's account of the socialization process in medical school, as well as Melvin D. William's ethnography of an anthropology department, focusing mainly on its politics.[77] More recently, studies of boarding schools and the corporatization of a university also fit the subgenre,[78] as do studies on how campuses shape students' political beliefs or career trajectories.[79] Disciplinary traditions and legal considerations can lead to decisions to disguise a setting. (In practice, however, brief Internet searches easily identify such settings.) I am not familiar with any such studies of the Harvard Business School.

Lastly, most prominent universities will, at some point, become the subject of unauthorized accounts that name their settings. A book on Harvard Law School typifies this subgenre.[80] Nor is the Harvard Business School immune to such projects.[81] As an illustration, John Van Maanen compared classroom experiences at the School and at MIT's Sloan School of Management.[82] He sat in on a class at Harvard Business School but did not intend to study it—a typical example of what Jeffrey W. Riemer calls "opportunistic research."[83] Recently a former student and journalist also wrote an account of his two years at Harvard Business School.[84] Another such account concentrates on the place of women in business.[85] Some of these studies offer unique views of the School from the writer's perspective, but others prove less convincing.[86] The authors' personal agendas sometimes cast doubt on their findings. For instance, a former research associate's account of the School links the US trade deficit to the School's supposed decline.[87]

I chose to write an account of the School authorized by Harvard University's Institutional Review Board. While I informed the School's administration of the study's design and regular progress as part of my annual activity reporting to the dean's office, I did not consider explicit authorization (beyond that of the Institutional Review Board) necessary to pursue the project. Though I sometimes wished for fuller cooperation, particularly to interview other faculty members and gain access to archives, an explicit endorsement might have constrained me more than I would want. The path I chose yielded intimacy, relative freedom, and partial access to institutional data (full access to all routine activities, limited access to some archives), which I considered an acceptable compromise given the methodological issues discussed here.

Notes

Preface

1. Calvin Morrill and David A. Snow, "The Study of Personal Relations in Public Places," in *Together Alone: Personal Relationships in Public Spaces*, ed. Calvin Morrill, David A. Snow, and Cindy H. White (Berkeley: University of California Press, 2005).
2. Bronislaw Malinowski, *Argonauts of the Western Pacific: An Account of the Native Enterprise and Adventure in the Archipelagoes of Melanesian New Guinea* (Long Grove, IL: Waveland Press, 1984).

Introduction

1. Louis B. Barnes, C. Roland Christensen, and Abby J. Hansen, *Teaching and the Case Method* (Boston: Harvard Business School Press, 1994); C. Roland Christensen, David A. Garvin, and Ann Sweet, eds., *Education for Judgment: The Artistry of Discussion Leadership* (Boston: Harvard Business School Press, 1991).
2. Building on George H. Mead's work, socialization is here viewed as the internalization of the generalized other through social interactions. See Mead, *Mind, Self and Society from the Standpoint of a Social Behaviorist* (Chicago: University of Chicago Press, 1934). Through vocal silence, however, socialization is temporally kept at bay.
3. For a sociological discussion of morality, see Steven Hitlin and Stephen Vaisey, "Back to the Future," in *Handbook of the Sociology of Morality*, ed. Hitlin and Vaisey (New York: Springer, 2010).
4. Stephen Vaisey, "Motivation and Justification: A Dual-Process Model of Culture in Action," *American Journal of Sociology* 114, no. 6 (2009).
5. Emile Durkheim, *Emile Durkheim on Morality and Society*, ed. Robert N. Bellah (Chicago: University of Chicago Press, 1973). For a similar use of morality, see Marcel Mauss: "Morality is the art of living communally as evidenced by the presence of the notion of right." Mauss, *Manuel d'éthnographie* (Paris: Editions Payot, 1967), 279 (author's translation).

6. John Van Maanen, "Observations on the Making of Policemen," *Human Organization* 32, no. 4 (1973).

7. For a rich discussion of the interplay of culture and morals, see Viviana A. Zelizer, *Economic Lives: How Culture Shapes the Economy* (Princeton, NJ: Princeton University Press, 2010).

8. Mitchell Duneier, *Slim's Table: Race, Respectability, and Masculinity* (Chicago: University of Chicago Press, 1992); Duneier, *Sidewalk* (New York: Farrar, Straus and Giroux, 1999); William F. Whyte, *Street Corner Society: The Social Structure of an Italian Slum* (Chicago: University of Chicago Press, 1943).

9. For an overview of morals in organizations, see Robert Jackall, "Morality in Organizations," in Hitlin and Vaisey, *Handbook*. Life insurance companies and direct sales organizations provide convincing cases of work organizations shaping and reflecting morals. See Viviana A. Zelizer, *Morals and Markets: The Development of Life Insurance in the United States* (New York: Columbia University Press, 1979); Michael G. Pratt, "The Good, the Bad, and the Ambivalent: Managing Identification among Amway Distributors," *Administrative Science Quarterly* 45, no. 3 (2000); Nicole Woolsey Biggart, *Charismatic Capitalism: Direct Selling Organizations in America* (Chicago: University of Chicago Press, 1989); Cheris Shun-ching Chan, "Invigorating the Content in Social Embeddedness: An Ethnography of Life Insurance Transactions in China," *American Journal of Sociology* 115, no. 3 (2009).

10. Galit Sarfaty, *Values in Translation: Human Rights and the Culture of the World Bank* (Stanford, CA: Stanford University Press, 2012); Victoria Johnson, *Backstage at the Revolution: How the Royal Paris Opera Survived the End of the Old Regime* (Chicago: University of Chicago Press, 2008).

11. For examples of shared moral views among organizational members, see Diane Vaughan, *The Challenger Launch Decision: Risky Technology, Culture, and Deviance at NASA* (Chicago: University of Chicago Press, 1996); Steven Peter Vallas, "Workers, Firms, and the Dominant Ideology: Hegemony and Consciousness in the Monopoly Core," *Sociological Quarterly* 32 (1991).

12. The process of promoting a perspective should not be confused with the "coercive persuasion" described by Edgar H. Schein and his coauthors in their study of American prisoners in China. In coercive persuasion, individuals are "subject to unusually intense and prolonged persuasion in a situation from which they cannot escape." This obviously does not apply to HBS faculty members. See Edgar H. Schein, Inge Shneier, and Curtis H. Barker, *Coercive Persuasion: A Socio-Psychological Analysis of the "Brainwashing" of American Civilian Prisoners by the Chinese Communists* (New York: W. W. Norton, 1961), 18.

13. Howard S. Becker et al., *Boys in White: Student Culture in Medical School* (Chicago: University of Chicago Press, 1961), 36. Whereas values transcend contexts, a perspective need not apply elsewhere. I use *perspective* instead of *value* because a perspective is situationally specific—describing thought and actions in a single context—as are the data for this book. In many organizations, the prevailing hope is that members will retain what they learn even after they leave the organization, but such spillover does not necessarily occur. If a given perspective is imported into a new setting (such as another school), it can safely be seen as a more deeply held value. Another way to distinguish a perspective from a value is to adopt Pierre Bourdieu's terminology and designate a per-

spective as a *specific habitus* and a value as a *general habitus*. A general habitus
is a system of dispositions developed early in life (and implicitly assumed to
persist); a specific habitus is acquired later via education, training, and control
within given organizational settings. See Bourdieu, *Méditations Pascaliennes*
(Paris: Editions du Seuil, 1997), 120–21; Matthew Desmond, *On the Fireline:
Living and Dying with Wildland Firefighters* (Chicago: University of Chicago
Press, 2007), 12–13.

14. John Van Maanen, "Golden Passports: Managerial Socialization and Graduate
Education," *Review of Higher Education* 6, no. 4 (1983): 436. For a broader discussion of culture in organizations, see Calvin Morrill, "Culture and Organization Theory," *Annals of the American Academy of Political and Social Science* 619,
no. 1 (2008); John Weeks, *Unpopular Culture: The Ritual of Complaint in a British Bank* (Chicago: University of Chicago Press, 2004), 31–56; Charles O'Reilly
and Jennifer Chatman, "Culture as Social Control: Corporations, Cults, and
Commitment," in *Research in Organizational Behavior*, ed. B. Staw and L. Cummings (Greenwich, CT: JAI Press, 1996); Harrison M. Trice and Janice M.
Beyer, *The Cultures of Work Organizations* (Englewoods Cliffs, NJ: Prentice Hall,
1993).

15. Gideon Kunda, *Engineering Culture: Control and Commitment in High-Tech Corporation* (Philadelphia: Temple University Press, 1992), 11.

16. Michael F. D. Young, ed. *Knowledge and Control: New Directions for the Sociology
of Education* (London: Collier-Macmillan, 1971).

17. Culture is defined here as an emerging construct that builds, for instance,
on linguistic schema, formal categorization, role distinctions, and routines
in organizations. For a discussion of culture, see Susan S. Silbey, "Taming
Prometheus: Talk of Safety and Culture," *Annual Review of Sociology* 35 (2009):
355–58. For examples of organizations intent on building their members'
moral commitment, see Rosabeth Moss Kanter, *Commitment and Community:
Communes and Utopias in Sociological Perspective* (Cambridge, MA: Harvard
University Press, 1972), 73–74.

18. Robin Leidner, *Fast Food, Fast Talk: Service Work and the Routinization of Everyday Life* (Berkeley: University of California Press, 1993), 231.

19. Ibid., 28; Arthur L. Stinchcombe, *Information and Organizations* (Berkeley:
University of California Press, 1990), 32–72. For an inquiry into the role of
routines in organizations, see Diane Vaughan, "The Dark Side of Organiza-
tions: Mistake, Misconduct, and Disaster," *Annual Review of Sociology* 25 (1999);
Vaughan, "Autonomy, Interdependence, and Social Control: NASA and the
Space Shuttle Challenger," *Administrative Science Quarterly* 35, no. 2 (1990);
Vaughan, *Challenger Launch Decision*; Vaughan, "Theorizing Disaster: Analogy,
Historical Ethnography, and the *Challenger* Accident," *Ethnography* 5 (2004).

20. To routines, Weber contrasts not morals but charisma. Yet his definition of
charisma contains many moral undertones. He defines charismatic authority
as resting "on devotion to the specific and exceptional sanctity, heroism or the
exemplary character of an individual person, and of the normative patterns or
order revealed or ordained by him." See Weber, *The Theory of Social and Economic Organization*, ed. Talcott Parsons (New York: Free Press, 1947), 328. For a
discussion of the opposition between charisma and routines, see ibid., 71–72.

21. Leidner, *Fast Food*, 231. For a broader discussion of such routinization, also see

George Ritzer, *The McDonaldization of Society: An Investigation into the Changing Character of Contemporary Social Life* (Newbury Park, CA: Pine Forge Press, 1993).

22. Leidner, *Fast Food*, 216.

23. Carol A. Heimer, "The Unstable Alliance of Law and Morality," in Hitlin and Vaisey, *Handbook*, 195.

24. Jackall, "Morality in Organizations," 206.

25. Tim Hallett and Marc J. Ventresca, "Inhabited Institutions: Social Interactions and Organizational Forms in Gouldner's Patterns of Industrial Bureaucracy," *Theory and Society* 35, no. 2 (2006); Stephen R. Barley and Gideon Kunda, "Bringing Work Back In," *Organization Science* 12, no. 1 (2001).

26. Higher-status professions tend to be harder to study because of access limitations. Yet even with less access, studying higher-status professions is crucial to the elaboration of theory. As Everett C. Hughes notes, "Until we can find a point of view and concepts which will enable us to make comparisons between the junk peddler and the professor without intent to debunk the one and patronize the other, we cannot do our best work in the field." See Hughes, "Work and Self," in *The Sociological Eye: Selected Papers* (Chicago: Aldine-Atherton, 1971), 342.

27. Close to half of HBS faculty members are untenured.

28. Becker et al., *Boys in White*, 36–37.

29. A key implication of this methodological choice is that the book does not explicitly discuss the content of formal ethics course offerings at the School. Two main explanations justify the absence of such a discussion: (1) the study deals primarily with the socialization of faculty members. not of students, and (2) only a small subset of untenured faculty members is socialized to teach these courses. Two courses with an explicit moral focus that are not discussed in this book are the first-year MBA requirement "Leadership and Corporate Accountability" and the second-year MBA elective "The Moral Leader." The latter course was introduced in the 1980s and relies on an exploration of literature to approach moral dilemmas. The former was established in 2004 as the first required full-length ethics course in the School's history. Its roots, however, go back to the late 1980s, when a module titled "Leadership, Values, and Decision Making" was offered at the beginning of the first-year MBA curriculum. For details on these courses, see Sandra J. Sucher, *Teaching the Moral Leader: A Literature-Based Leadership Course* (New York: Routledge, 2007), 11–16; Thomas R. Piper, Mary C. Gentile, and Sharon Daloz Parks, *Can Ethics Be Taught? Perspectives, Challenges, and Approaches at Harvard Business School* (Boston: Harvard Business School, 1993); Lynn Sharp Paine, *Instructor's Guide to Leadership and Corporate Accountability (LCA)* (HBSP Note 5-307-032) (Cambridge, MA: President and Fellows of Harvard College, 2006); John S. Rosenberg, "An Education in Ethics: Teaching Business Students Life Lessons in Leadership," *Harvard Magazine* 109, no. 1 (2006).

30. The study does not focus much on how the School's faculty differs from those at other business schools or on how the School positions itself outside. The fact that the School is often viewed as elite and sometimes prides itself on its uniqueness might seem to make it an extreme case of business education. Indeed, nonreplicability is a common organizational survival strategy.

Nevertheless, the School's faculty plays an important role in business education worldwide. Each year, hundreds of faculty members from other business
schools enroll in intensive programs taught by the School's faculty to learn
case-method teaching. Moreover, the School has served as a model for many
other programs worldwide. (In the 1960s it helped launch MBA programs at
the Indian Institute of Management in Ahmedabad, India, and at the IESE
Business School in Spain.) If Harvard Business School is an extreme case, it
might illustrate with particular intensity what is also attempted elsewhere in
academia or in other settings. For comparative data on business schools, see
Srikant M. Datar, David A. Garvin, and Patrick Cullen, *Rethinking the MBA:
Business Education at a Crossroads* (Boston: Harvard Business Press, 2010);
Rakesh Khurana, *From Higher Aims to Hired Hands: The Social Transformation of
American Business Schools and the Unfulfilled Promise of Management as a Profes-
sion* (Princeton, NJ: Princeton University Press, 2007).

31. Norbert Elias, *The Court Society* (New York: Pantheon Books, 1983), 35.

32. For links between culture and practices, see William Hamilton Sewell, *Logics of
     History: Social Theory and Social Transformation* (Chicago: University of Chicago
     Press, 2005), 162–65. For more discussion of practice theories, see Mar-
     tha S. Feldman and Wanda J. Orlikowski, "Practicing Theory and Theorizing
     Practice," *Organization Science* 22, no. 5 (2011); Silbey, "Taming Prometheus."
     For empirical examples on the interplay between culture and practices, see
     Stephen R. Barley, "Technology as an Occasion for Structuring: Evidence from
     Observation of CT Scanners and the Social Order of Radiology Departments,"
     Administrative Science Quarterly 31, no. 1 (1986); Beth Bechky, "Object Lessons:
     Workplace Artifacts as Representations of Occupational Jurisdiction," *American
     Journal of Sociology* 109, no. 3 (2003).

33. An alternative hypothesis is that (past) shared moral order creates community.
     Here, faculty members' moral stand prior to joining business schools might
     form the basis of the schools' morals; thus, schools are merely artifacts of prior
     socialization. For an operationalization of such a logic in urban settings, see
     Stephen Vaisey, "Structure, Culture, and Community: The Search for Belong-
     ing in 50 Urban Communes," *American Sociological Review* 72, no. 6 (2007).

34. Jack Katz, "On the Rhetoric and Politics of Ethnographic Methodology," *Annals
     of the American Academy of Political and Social Science* 595 (2004): 286–88.

35. In the School's context, I write this sentence with hope but also with humility,
     since I am well aware that many individuals other than faculty members also
     contribute to the socialization of students. Successful alumni, enthusiastic
     students, nurturing administrators, and attentive career counselors all play
     nontrivial roles in the complex educational endeavor. Likewise, the behavior
     of custodians and other support staff members contributes to creating unique
     learning environments. Yet despite the multiplicity of influences, and even
     though few business students aspire to become professors, faculty members
     hopefully play an important part in the students' education.

36. As Robin Leidner notes in describing interactive settings, "The workers work
     on the people who are their raw materials . . . and the organizations work on
     their employees." See Leidner, *Fast Food*, 2.

37. Students also play a key role in socializing students. As a close observer of
     students' experience at the School concluded in 1963, "We are now convinced

that the major lesson *many* students learn during their first year at the School is how to get along in the social milieu of a section while maintaining a level of academic performance sufficient to ensure their passage from the first to the second year." Getting along in a socially constructive way in the section's milieu was among the School's goals, and faculty members played their part in this process. See Charles D. Orth, *Social Structure and Learning Climate: The First Year at the Harvard Business School* (Boston: Division of Research, Graduate School of Business Administration, Harvard University, 1963), 188.

38. Faculty members are prime beneficiaries of what Arthur Stinchcombe calls an organization's "attention structure," the arrangement within an organization of attention-controlling structural elements that characterize a system of activities. For instance, the ways tasks are divided and time is allocated contribute to such a structure. This structure, in turn, helps select "officials" increase their influence on the actions of other members. See Stinchcombe, *Constructing Social Theories* (New York: Harcourt, Brace & World, 1968), 235–36.

39. Among the more than forty-three thousand living School MBA alumni in 2011, 36 percent hold jobs in traditional corporate settings, such as the energy, consumer-goods, manufacturing, retail, technology, and transportation sectors. Another 25 percent work in the financial sector, and 16 percent work in consulting or professional-services firms; even one step removed from more traditional corporations, these alumni can strongly influence business norms. The high proportion of recent graduates joining the finance and consulting sectors directly out of School (44.4 percent and 21.1 percent, respectively, of the class of 2007) may even enlarge the School's role in corporate America, since their work spans multiple firms. See Bulletin Staff, "Hi-Ho, Hi-Ho: Class of 2007 Goes to Work," *HBS Alumni Bulletin*, 2007.

40. While School students are not a random sample of corporate executives, they do occupy influential positions in corporate America; their morals might foreshadow broader corporate morals.

41. Neil J. Smelser describes assistant professors at the University of California as second-class citizens laboring "under the shadow of not yet having received tenure and living under chronic anxiety in approaching the tenure decision." See Smelser, *Reflections on the University of California: From the Free Speech Movement to the Global University* (Berkeley: University of California Press, 2010), 207.

42. Pierre Bourdieu, *Homo Academicus* (Paris: Editions de Minuit, 1984), 11 (author's translation).

43. An objection I heard several times when I told colleagues about this project was that I do not belong to "the Big Room"—a term for the room where the School's tenured faculty meets and, by extension, for the tenured faculty itself. My goal is only to offer a particular view of the School, that of an untenured faculty member.

44. For the most illuminating analysis of students' experiences at the School, see Orth, *Social Structure*. For other students' accounts of life at the School see, for instance, Robert Reid, *Year One: An Intimate Look inside Harvard Business School* (New York: Avon, 1994); Fran Worden Henry, *Toughing It Out at Harvard: The Making of a Woman MBA* (New York: G. P. Putnam's Sons, 1983).

45. In unveiling a university's inner workings, the study also answers a recent call for more organizational emphasis in scholarship on higher education.

See Mitchell L. Stevens, Elizabeth A. Armstrong, and Richard Arum, "Sieve, Incubator, Temple, Hub: Empirical and Theoretical Advances in the Sociology of Higher Education," *Annual Review of Sociology* 34 (2008): 129.

46. Those most likely to benefit from reading the book may be readers intrigued by organizational socialization issues but only somewhat familiar with Harvard Business School. The School's critics will lament the absence of accounts that confirm their critiques, even as its supporters fault me for not putting more emphasis on the accomplishments of the School and its alumni. For examples of other publications focusing on the School, see J. Paul Mark, *The Empire Builders: Inside the Harvard Business School* (New York: William Morrow, 1987); Peter Cohen, *The Gospel According to the Harvard Business School: The Education of America's Managerial Elite* (Baltimore: Penguin, 1973); David W. Ewing, *Inside the Harvard Business School: Strategies and Lessons of America's Leading Business School* (New York: Times, 1990).

47. For examples of scholarship on the generative nature of routines, see Terry L. Amburgey, Dawn Kelly, and William P. Barnett, "The Dynamics of Organizational Change and Failure," *Administrative Science Quarterly* 38 (1993); Michael D. Cohen and Paul Bacdayan, "Organizational Routines Are Stored as Procedural Memory: Evidence from a Laboratory Study," *Organization Science* 5, no. 4 (1994); Martha S. Feldman, "Organizational Routines as a Source of Continuous Change," *Organization Science* 11, no. 6 (2000).

48. Martha S. Feldman and Brian T. Pentland, "Reconceptualizing Organizational Routines as a Source of Flexibility and Change," *Administrative Science Quarterly* 48 (2003). The authors define routines as "repetitive, recognizable patterns of interdependent actions, carried out by multiple actors" within an organization (95).

49. John Van Maanen and Brian T. Pentland, "Cops and Auditors," in *The Legalistic Organization*, ed. S. Sitkin and R. Bies (Beverly Hills, CA: Sage, 1994).

50. For a similar argument on the potentially dynamic nature of bureaucracy, see Paul S. Adler and Bryan Borys, "Two Types of Bureaucracy: Enabling and Coercive," *Administrative Science Quarterly* 41, no. 1 (1996).

51. My definition of silence concerns the organizational withholding of direct guidance on given topics, not individual members' withholding of their opinions on such topics. For a discussion of silence from members' perspective, see Elizabeth Wolfe Morrison and Frances J. Milliken, "Organizational Silence: A Barrier to Change and Development in a Pluralistic World," *Academy of Management Review* 25, no. 4 (2000).

52. See, for instance, Kunda, *Engineering Culture*.

53. For a discussion of signs and signals, see Diego Gambetta, *Codes of the Underworld: How Criminals Communicate* (Princeton, NJ: Princeton University Press, 2009); James A. Densley, "Street Gang Recruitment: Signaling, Screening, and Selection," *Social Problems* 59, no. 3 (2011).

54. Signs are "dormant potential signals" and are not conspicuously displayed. See Diego Gambetta and Heather Hamill, *Streetwise: How Taxi Drivers Establish Their Customers' Trustworthiness* (New York: Russell Sage Foundation, 2005), 13.

55. Joanne Martin, *Cultures in Organizations: Three Perspectives* (New York: Oxford University Press, 1992), 138–41.

56. Members' participation is central to promoting any given culture or building commitment. See O'Reilly and Chatman, "Culture as Social Control," 172; Ger-

ald R. Salancik, "Commitment Is Too Easy!" *Organizational Dynamics* 6, no. 1 (1977): 68–70.

57. By dissonance, I mean the ability to keep multiple evaluative principles in play. See David Stark, *The Sense of Dissonance: Accounts of Worth in Economic Life* (Princeton, NJ: Princeton University Press, 2009), 17.

58. Harrison C. White, "Agency as Control," in *Principals and Agents: The Structure of Business*, ed. John W. Pratt and Richard J. Zeckhauser (Boston: Harvard Business School Press, 1985), 188.

59. Khurana, *From Higher Aims to Hired Hands*.

60. For a discussion of identity work in business schools, see Gianpiero Petriglieri and Jennifer Louise Petriglieri, "Identity Workspaces: The Case of Business Schools," *Academy of Management Learning and Education* 9, no. 1 (2010). Moral projects are also salient in law schools. As a study of the Harvard Law School puts it, "Law school education is deeply infused with ideological assumptions regarding the nature of everyday social life." Robert Granfield, *Making Elite Lawyers: Visions of Law at Harvard and Beyond* (London: Routledge, 1992), 2.

61. Debra J. Schleef, *Managing Elites: Professional Socialization in Law and Business Schools* (Lantham, MD: Rowman & Littlefield, 2006), 15.

62. As Arthur L. Stinchcombe has argued, most universities and, by extension, most business schools engage in "monopolistic competition"—a competition in which each participant tries to deliver a unique product or dominate a unique territory. Stinchcombe also argues that it is a set of routines that "run more or less automatically" that enables an organization to engage in such competition. In other words, the development of routines equips some organizations to do what other cannot, and schools promote different routines. See Stinchcombe, "Monopolistic Competition as a Mechanism," in *Social Mechanisms: An Analytical Approach to Social Theory*, ed. Peter Hedström and Richard Swedberg (Cambridge, UK: Cambridge University Press, 1998), 268.

63. For instance, the goals of the first university-based business school, at the University of Louisiana, were quite prosaic: promotion of "scientific management" and advancement of graduates' careers. As Martin Ruef has pointed out, the Louisiana school's founder edited a review that published numerous articles on the management of slaves. Changing the prevailing perspective on how business ought to be conducted hardly registered on that school's agenda. See Ruef, "From Higher Aims to Hired Hands: The Social Transformation of American Business Schools and the Unfulfilled Promise of Management as a Profession (Review)," *Administrative Science Quarterly* 53 (2008): 747.

64. For a review of such organizations, see Marya Hill-Popper Besharov, "Mission Goes Corporate: Understanding Employee Behavior in a Mission-Driven Business," doctoral dissertation, Harvard University, 2008.

65. Daniel J. Boorstin, *The Americans: The Colonial Experience* (New York: Random House, 1958), 178–79.

66. Norbert Elias, *The Civilizing Process: Sociogenetic and Psychogenetic Investigations* (Oxford, UK: Blackwell, 2000); Elias, *Court Society*.

67. Charles Perrow, *Organizing America: Wealth, Power, and the Origins of Corporate Capitalism* (Princeton, NJ: Princeton University Press, 2002), 220.

68. Khurana, *From Higher Aims to Hired Hands*, 98.

69. As an illustration, the founding dean of Northwestern's School of Commerce

(now the Kellogg School of Management) expressed a normative trope in his 1913 assertion that business education would "go far toward removing the conflict between business and ethics. Ibid., 99. For other examples, see Gabriel Abend, "The Origins of Business Ethics in American Universities, 1902–1936." *Business Ethics Quarterly* 23, no. 2 (2013): 171–205.

70. Elite business schools' moral goals ran counter, at the time, to prevailing views in other parts of the university. Indeed, as business school administrators embraced the moral pursuit, many other university administrators were increasingly deemphasizing curricular forms of moral guidance in their faculties and relegating "character development" to extracurricular activities. See Julie A. Reuben, *The Making of the Modern University: Intellectual Transformation and the Marginalization of Morality* (Chicago: University of Chicago Press, 1996), 7.

71. Jeffrey Cruikshank, *A Delicate Experience: The Harvard Business School, 1908–1945* (Boston: Harvard Business School Press, 1987), 44.

72. The dean, Wallace B. Donham, further explained, "The socialization of industry from within on a higher ethical plane, not socialism nor communism, not government operation nor the exercise of the police power, but rather the development from within the business group of effective social control . . . is greatly needed." See Herbert Gintis and Rakesh Khurana, "Corporate Honesty and Business Education: A Behavioral Model," in *Moral Markets: The Critical Role of Values in the Economy*, ed. Paul J. Zak (Princeton, NJ: Princeton University Press, 2008), 324.

73. Khurana, *From Higher Aims to Hired Hands*, 114. For a discussion of calling, see Max Weber, *The Protestant Ethic and the Spirit of Capitalism* (San Francisco: Jossey-Bass, 1958).

74. Amy Wrzesniewski, "Finding Positive Meaning in Work," in *Positive Organizational Scholarship: Foundations of a New Discipline*, ed. K. S. Cameron, J. E. Dutton, and R. E. Quinn (San Francisco: Berrett-Koehler, 2003).

75. Khurana, *From Higher Aims to Hired Hands*, 118.

76. Cruikshank, *A Delicate Experience*, 106.

77. George F. Baker, cited by Wallace B. Donham, "Report of the President and Treasurer of Harvard College 1924–25," *Official Register of Harvard University* 23, no. 2 (1926): 122.

78. The other qualities of a good administrator were flexibility, courage, imagination, initiative, and perseverance. See Orth, *Social Structure*, 48. Those characteristics could easily be attributed to the Boston Brahmins—the merchant families that migrated to the city from Beverly, Portsmouth, Salem, and other commercial ports between 1790 and 1830—whose history was intertwined with that of Harvard University.

79. These citations are from dean John McArthur's foreword to a book on ethics published by the School. The book's first chapter, by Thomas R. Piper, also reiterates the School's moral imperative. See Piper, Gentile, and Parks, *Can Ethics Be Taught?*, x–xiii. A few years earlier, in 1985, McArthur also wrote that School faculty members were "committed to pursuing research on the way business actually *does* function, as well as theoretical explorations of how it perhaps *should* function." See McArthur, "Foreword," in *Principals and Agents: The Structure of Business*, ed. John W. Pratt and Richard J. Zeckhauser (Boston: Harvard Business School Press, 1985), vii.

80. It is also perhaps worth noting that when morals were disconnected from

managerial practice, the student body did not seem to react favorably to the experience. The initial "ethics" courses taught at the School were led by a faculty member with a doctorate in philosophy, and their introduction in the 1930s did not gain sufficient student support. Only after World War II did the School resume its efforts to address ethical issues in business, and those efforts were targeted at more practical ethical considerations. See Piper, Gentile, and Parks, *Can Ethics Be Taught?*, 152–53.

81. Alfred D. Chandler, *The Visible Hand: The Managerial Revolution in American Business* (Cambridge, MA: Harvard University Press, 1977), 467.

82. As an example, an observer of the School charged bluntly in 1979 that "the 'soulful corporation' no longer driven by the profit motives but directed by technicians was widely promulgated to nullify the growing antagonism of workers and lower professionals toward the powerful monopoly corporations." See Andrew L. Barlow, "Coordination and Control: The Rise of Harvard University 1825–1910," doctoral dissertation, Harvard University, 1979.

83. Abraham Flexner, *Universities: American, English, German* (New York: Oxford University Press, 1930).

84. Talcott Parsons and Gerald M. Platt, *The American University* (Cambridge, MA: Harvard University Press, 1973), 255.

85. Each new crop of workers (here, faculty members) brings its own experiences to the table, making the model highly reactive to sudden demographic shifts.

86. As an example, the teaching notes that faculty members use to prepare their courses help ensure some teaching consistency and provide frames and anchors. See Robert D. Benford and David A. Snow, "Framing Processes and Social Movements: An Overview and Assessment," *American Sociological Review* 26 (2000); Amin Ghaziani and Delia Baldassarri, "Cultural Anchors and the Organization of Differences: A Multi-Method Analysis of LGBT Marches on Washington," *American Sociological Review* 76, no. 2 (2011).

87. Interesting parallels can be drawn between "moral" and "safety" pursuits. As Ruthann Huising and Susan S. Silbey note, safety culture might be enhanced by "macromagement," or what they define as "the opposite of the negatively valenced concept of micromanagement where supervisors closely monitor and control subordinates." Macromanagement and partial silence might be linked. See Huising and Silbey, "Governing the Gap: Forging Safe Science through Relational Regulation," *Regulation and Governance* 5, no. 1 (2011): 35.

88. For another example of moving beyond the structure and agency dichotomy, see Carol A. Heimer and Lisa R. Staffen, *For the Sake of the Children: The Social Organization of Responsibility in the Hospital and the Home* (Chicago: Chicago University Press, 1998).

Chapter One

1. "Beautiful" and "impressive" are direct quotes from the 1996 campus master plan. Dober Lidsky Craig and Associates, "Harvard University, Graduate School of Business Administration: Campus Master Plan" (1996), 11.

2. Charles W. Killam, "Harvard Graduate School of Business Administration," *Architectural Forum* 47, no. 4 (1927): 310.

3. Melvin T. Copeland, *And Mark an Era: The Story of the Harvard Business School* (New York: Little, Brown, 1958), 71.

4. Mauro F. Guillén, "Scientific Management's Lost Aesthetic: Architecture, Organization, and the Taylorized Beauty of the Mechanical," *Administrative Science Quarterly* 42, no. 4 (1997); Guillén, *The Taylorized Beauty of the Mechanical: Scientific Management and the Rise of Modernist Architecture* (Princeton, NJ: Princeton University Press, 2006), 3.

5. Guillén, "Scientific Management's Lost Aesthetic," 710.

6. Harvard Business School, "Harvard Business School Annual Report," (Cambridge, MA: President and Fellows of Harvard College, 2007), 25.

7. Dober Lidsky Craig, "Campus Master Plan," 19.

8. The banning of most traffic from the campus goes back to the deanship of John McArthur, who headed the School from 1980 to 1999. See Jeffrey Cruikshank, "A Force for Good," *HBS Alumni Bulletin*, December 2008, 34.

9. Dober Lidsky Craig, "Campus Master Plan," 31.

10. The idea of a residential campus was conceived by a task force convened by dean Wallace B. Donham at his summer home at Chatham on Cape Cod. Copeland, *And Mark an Era*, 71–72.

11. Another 275 students from other Harvard departments also moved on campus in 1926, bringing the total student population that year to 796. Jeffrey Cruikshank, *A Delicate Experience: The Harvard Business School, 1908–1945* (Boston: Harvard Business School Press, 1987), 125.

12. By 1964, two years after Gans ended his study, "Levittown" had grown to 6,200 households, totaling 25,000 residents. See Herbert Gans, *The Levittowners: Ways of Life and Politics in a New Suburban Community* (New York: Vantage, 1967), 22.

13. Mario Luis Small, *Villa Victoria: The Transformation of Social Capital in a Boston Barrio* (Chicago: University of Chicago Press, 2004).

14. Only in 2009 did a map of campus appear outside at one entrance.

15. Dober Lidsky Craig, "Campus Master Plan," 29.

16. "Sherman Hall History," Archives Resource Files (Facilities), Baker Library Historical Collections, 2008.

17. From 1908 to 1926 the School occupied space in Harvard Yard, the historical home of Harvard College.

18. The difficulty for faculty of remembering students' names is common in professional schools and other academic settings with large class sizes. For evidence in a medical school, see Howard S. Becker et al., *Boys in White: Student Culture in Medical School* (Chicago: University of Chicago Press, 1961), 89.

19. Halvorson Company, "The Original Landscape Design of the Harvard Business School, 1925–1927" (2000), 24.

20. The bell rang only on joyous occasions, such as during graduation exercises or to mark somber events, such as the 1968 assassination of Martin Luther King Jr. See, Steve Bradt, "After 78 Years at Harvard, Danilov Bells Will Return to Russia," *Harvard University Gazette*, May 29, 2008.

21. Copeland, *And Mark an Era*, 312.

22. In 1930 Abraham Flexner suggested renaming Harvard's Graduate School of Business the Boston School of Business. See Clark Kerr, *The Uses of the University*, 5th ed. (Cambridge, MA: Harvard University Press, 2001), 4.

23. For more details, see Victoria Kabak, "HBS Rings in New Russian Bell," *Harvard Crimson*, October 2, 2007; Harvard Magazine staff, "Baker Re-Belled," *Harvard Magazine* 108, no. 2 (2007): 79.

24. Halvorson Company, "Original Landscape Design," 6–7.

25. Ibid., 13.

26. Jamil Khan, "On-Campus Interview Series: A Spangler Squirrel," *Harbus*, May 10, 2004.

27. For a discussion of humor and jokes at work, see Jacqueline Frisch-Gauthier, "Le rire dans les relations de travail," *Revue française de sociologie* 2 (1961); Renée C. Fox, *Experiment Perilous: Physicians and Patients Facing the Unknown* (Glencoe, IL: Free Press, 1959), 76–82; Philip Bradney, "The Joking Relationship in Industry," *Human Relations* 10, no. 2 (1957). For a recent example of reliance on jokes to gain insight into contexts, see Matthew Desmond, *On the Fireline: Living and Dying with Wildland Firefighters* (Chicago: University of Chicago Press, 2007), 94–100.

28. The presence on campus of more unruly wild turkeys also provides material for laughter. I suspect the turkeys wake up later, since I rarely spotted them in the morning. But during the day, their presence, even if limited, hardly goes unnoticed: they often run after walkers. (A count put their number at the School at two in 2008, and in 2009 the only remaining one was removed due to aggressive behavior.) Again, School members found ways to incorporate them into the campus's life. The turkeys' behaviors, for instance, served as parables for students' experiences. A turkey supposed to have attacked a student going for a job interview with a consulting firm is said to have provided a "heavenly" intervention, saving the student from a "wretched" life. Even the most unruly animal on campus acts with a purpose. For details, see V. Primus, "Tough Turkeys," *Harvard Magazine* 110, no. 4 (2008): 76. Alex Godden, "Feathered Friends," *Harbus*, November 5, 2007, 8. For another example of a turkey story, see Patrick Bateman, "Two Parables of the Wild Turkey," *Harbus*, November 16, 2007.

29. The fact that I noticed it is as much a reflection on me as on the School. See Peter Moskos, "In Defense of Doing Nothing: The Methodological Utility of Introversion," in *New Directions in Sociology: Essays on Theory and Methodology in the 21st Century*, ed. Ieva Zake and Michael DeCesare (Jefferson, NC: McFarland, 2011).

30. There was some disagreement among informants as to whether locks prevent only theft or also movement.

31. The 1930s reconstruction of colonial Williamsburg and the current Dartmouth College campus are noted examples of neo-Georgian architecture.

32. Joan Wickersham, "What Gets Built at Harvard, What Doesn't, and Why?" *Harvard Magazine* 110, no. 1 (2007): 56.

33. Dober Lidsky Craig, "Campus Master Plan," 24–25.

34. The only exception is the building housing both the main library and some faculty offices, which enjoys a fairly constant flow of students, often occupying the chairs and tables on the ground floor. (Faculty offices are on the second and third floors.)

35. Harbus staff, "This Month from Baker: Tips and Tidbits from Baker Staff," *Harbus*, April 2, 2007.

36. Newer offices in Baker Library were slightly smaller, only 220 square feet.

37. Seniority within a unit, not faculty rank, commonly determines office allocation.

38. I sometimes stayed in my office beyond 7 pm (the start time of the cleaning crew's shift), but my office was not first in line to be cleaned; thus I never saw the cleaning crew.

39. Unlike the book's numerous other pictures, these three are the only ones with indications of hours when they were taken. Greg Halpern, *Harvard Works Because We Do* (New York: Quantuck Lane Press, 2003), 112–17.

40. See chapter 3 for more details on end-of-semester gifting practices.

41. I recall thinking, when I arrived, how easily my passage could also be erased.

42. From 2003 to 2008, on average forty-three existing faculty members changed offices each year. Adjusting for the move of an entire area in 2005, the average drops to approximately thirty-five.

43. In 2006–2007, a typical faculty teaching load at the school involved two classes, often taught the same semester, and some other more limited teaching. The arrangement made it possible to concentrate one's main teaching duties during one semester—a practice referred to as "stacking."

44. The tunnels are also occasionally referred to as "utilidors" in architectural plans. See Beyer Blinder Belle (Architects & Planners LLP), "Campus Plan Executive Report" (2007), 11.

45. These dining rooms have since been consolidated. Copeland, *And Mark an Era*, 73.

46. When called to a rare meeting in a part of campus not usually used by faculty, orientation in the tunnels can become problematic. During one such trek, I tried to reach a meeting room located on the student side of campus. After almost five minutes of seemingly erratic underground movement, I decided that if I did not surface immediately I would be late. I surfaced and saw nearby the building I had started from. Walking above ground, and asking students for directions, I rapidly reached the desired location, five minutes late—a notable breach of School etiquette.

47. In 2005, for instance, there were three known notary publics among the School's staff.

48. Copeland, *And Mark an Era*, 283.

49. For a discussion of complete institutions, see Arthur L. Stinchcombe, "Social Structure and Organizations," in *Handbook of Organizations*, ed. James G. March (Chicago: Rand McNally, 1965).

50. In 2009 the faculty club and the dean's summer dining options were closed to reduce operating costs.

51. Some high-level administrators and a limited number of other categories of residents also have access to faculty dining facilities.

52. The sculpture, titled *Presence*, was made by Mary Frank.

53. Unlike other Harvard athletic facilities, access to the School's facilities was restricted to School affiliates. A law student or an undergraduate student could not use them, thus fueling the School's reputation for insularity vis-à-vis other faculties. One of the campus master plan's goals was to create a consolidated "community" athletic facility; see Moshe Safdie and Associates, "Harvard Business School Master Plan: Preliminary Design Decisions" (1984).

54. I thank Claudine Madras for the description of the weight room.

55. The chapel's seating capacity is limited to seventy people. I arrived for one such concert a few minutes prior to the performance and found that, despite my two years on campus, I recognized no one in the audience. No other member of the faculty seemed present, nor did many students. (Multiple faculty-wide meetings had by then exposed me to my colleagues, or at least their faces. And I had taught close to 270 students who were still on campus.) At last, I spotted a familiar face: a faculty assistant I knew. She smiled and approached me. We exchanged a few words and she told me most other attendees were staff members. The attendance patterns I observed at several other chapel events were similar to the one described here.

56. Most students with cars opted for yearly parking in another facility, not daily parking.

57. The link between architectural and social distinctions has long been noted. See, for instance, Walter Benjamin's comments on the French utopian Charles Fourier's idea of establishing apartments in street galleries with "twenty different categories of rental, priced from 50 to 1,000 francs." Walter Benjamin, *The Arcades Project*, trans. H. Eiland and K. McLaughlin (Cambridge, MA: Harvard University Press, 1999).

58. School administrators are well aware of these difficulties and have spearheaded initiatives to increase social interactions among campus members. Initiatives aimed at bridging categorical divides have included small group dinners mixing faculty and students and faculty-led case discussions with staff members. Also, many residents, regardless of category, have been invited to large School events.

59. John Van Maanen, "Displacing Disney: Some Notes on the Flow of Culture," *Qualitative Sociology* 15, no. 1 (1992).

60. Chandra Mukerji, *Territorial Ambitions and the Gardens of Versailles* (Cambridge, UK: Cambridge University Press, 1997).

61. For the link between housing and community, see Robert S. Lynd and Helen Merrell Lynd, *Middletown: A Study in Modern American Culture* (New York: Harcourt Brace, 1929). In another example, Nicole Marwell observes that Brooklyn's entrepreneurial Hasidic community (which favors mixed-use buildings) could not thrive in the neighborhoods favored by Hispanic communities (dominated by low residential buildings), and vice versa. See Marwell, *Bargaining for Brooklyn: Community Organizations in the Entrepreneurial City* (Chicago: University of Chicago Press, 2007).

62. Robert E. Park and Ernest W. Burgess, *The City: Suggestions for Investigation of Human Behavior in the Urban Environment* (Chicago: University of Chicago Press, 1984).

63. Ibid., 156.

64. Ibid., 1.

65. For an example of an incident, see Abby Fung, "Crime Drops in Cambridge," *Harvard Crimson*, June 5, 1997.

66. Since its inception, the bridge was designed only for foot traffic. (See "Proposed Foot Bridge across the Charles, Named for Weeks, to Link Harvard Groups," *New York Times*, November 9, 1925.) The footbridge, intentionally built to bring steam pipes from Cambridge to the campus, provides a shorter walk between

the School and the eastern part of Harvard Yard where a number of academic buildings housing disciplinary departments in the Faculty of Arts and Sciences are located. (See Copeland, *And Mark an Era*, 74; Killam, "Harvard Graduate School," 311.)

Chapter Two

1. All names have been changed to preserve anonymity.
2. The review process is increasingly being conducted electronically.
3. My definition of professional purity is broader than the one offered by Andrew Abbott. While he defines purity as "the ability to exclude nonprofessional issues or irrelevant professional issues from practice," I also see it as encompassing an ability to include (new) issues in practice. See Abbott, "Status and Status Strain in the Professions," *American Journal of Sociology* 86, no. 4 (1981): 823.
4. Theodore Caplow and Reece J. McGee, *The Academic Marketplace* (New York: Basic Books, 1958), 83.
5. The University of California system provides a nice illustration of this evaluative frame. See Neil J. Smelser, *Reflections on the University of California: From the Free Speech Movement to the Global University* (Berkeley: University of California Press, 2010), 182.
6. Edward Bellamy, *Looking Backward, 2000–1887* (New York: Grosset and Dunlap, 1888), xix.
7. Mary Douglas, *Purity and Danger: An Analysis of Concepts of Pollution and Taboo* (New York: Routledge Classics, 2002), 5. Classifications and distinctions have long been posited to underline moral order. See also Emile Durkheim and Marcel Mauss, "De quelques formes primitives de classification: Contribution à l'étude des représentations collectives," *Année sociologique* 6 (1903); Rodney Needham, *Right and Left: Essays on Dual Classification* (Chicago: University of Chicago Press, 1973); Mary Douglas, *How Institutions Think* (Syracuse, NY: Syracuse University Press, 1986).
8. Most US universities adhere to a model whereby an assistant professor is reviewed for a position as a tenured associate professor within five or six years. Some research universities also offer appointments as associate professor without tenure; these individuals are typically reviewed for tenure within two years of their appointments (extending the tenure clock to seven years). Harvard University's nine-year clock is atypical even within the subset of research universities with longer clocks.
9. Past scholarship has shown that person-organization "fit" upon entry predicts many important outcomes, including job satisfaction and actual length of employment. See Jennifer Chatman, "Matching People and Organizations: Selection and Socialization in Public Accounting Firms," *Administrative Science Quarterly* 36, nos. 459–484 (1991).
10. Catherine Paradeise et al., "Practical Relevance and Academic Excellence: Four Business Schools in Context," in *The Transformation of Higher Education Institutions and Business Schools*, ed. Andrew Pettigrew (Oxford: Oxford University Press, forthcoming).
11. Jean M. Bartunek and Sara L. Rynes, "The Construction and Contributions

of 'Implications for Practice': What's in Them and What Might They Offer?" *Academy of Management Learning and Education* 9, no. 1 (2010).

12. The course, created in 1946, dealt with issues of individual motivation, productivity, and satisfaction. Fritz J. Roethlisberger, *The Elusive Phenomena: An Autobiographical Account of My Work in the Field of Organizational Behavior at the Harvard Business School*, ed. George F. F. Lombard (Boston: Harvard University Press, 1977), 113.

13. Jeffrey T. Polzer et al., "Crossing Boundaries to Increase Relevance in Organizational Research," *Journal of Management Inquiry* 18, no. 4 (2009): x. For a broader discussion of relevance in business education, see Mie Augier and James G. March, *The Roots, Rituals, and Rhetorics of Change: North American Business Schools after the Second World War* (Stanford, CA: Stanford University Press, 2011), 215–39.

14. For a discussion on the plasticity of relevance, see Alexander Nicolai and David Seidl, "That's Relevant! Different Forms of Practical Relevance in Management Science," *Organization Studies* 31 (2010).

15. The political arena offers perhaps a similarly flexible usage of the notion of relevance. In politics, the term *policy relevant* is an indirect way of demanding that certain priorities be followed. See Jack Katz, "On the Rhetoric and Politics of Ethnographic Methodology," *Annals of the American Academy of Political and Social Science* 595 (2004): 281.

16. Caplow and McGee, *Academic Marketplace*, 61.

17. Douglas, *Purity and Danger*.

18. *California Management Review* and *Sloan Management Review* are other examples of management-oriented outlets.

19. *Harvard Business Review* is published by Harvard Business School Publishing, an integral part of the School's organizational structure. Dean Wallace Donham initiated in 1921 a plan to create the *Review* as an outlet to make a substantial contribution to business education. See Melvin T. Copeland, *And Mark an Era: The Story of the Harvard Business School* (New York: Little, Brown, 1958), 331.

20. For a typical overview of doctoral training, see Patricia Adler and Peter Adler, "The Identity Career of the Graduate Student: Professional Socialization to Academic Sociology," *American Sociologist* 36, no. 2 (2005).

21. High student ratings suggest local relevance. Because many students end up in managerial positions, local relevance is often interpreted as a proxy for managerial relevance.

22. School junior faculty members can teach in executive-education programs as part of their teaching requirement. This is not the case at some other business schools (e.g., MIT Sloan School of Management).

23. Faculty members are assigned to one of ten distinct units (known also as areas), such as marketing or accounting, and all areas are typically represented. Between 2003 and 2009, there was one exception to the full-representation norm, when only nine units were represented.

24. In 2003, 46 percent of presenters at the Faculty Research Symposium were untenured; in 2004, 55 percent; in 2005, 60 percent; in 2006, 20 percent; in 2007, 70 percent; and in 2009, 42 percent. (No symposium was held in 2008.) After 2010, the symposium's format was modified.

25. Such media attention is typical of many elite universities. Arthur Stinchcombe

calls this phenomenon the "column inches in the *New York Times*" premium
commanded by such institutions. See Stinchcombe, "Monopolistic Competition as a Mechanism," ed. Peter Hedström and Richard Swedberg (Cambridge,
UK: Cambridge University Press, 1998), 275.

26. Frederick G. Bailey, *Morality and Expediency: The Folklore of Academic Politics*
(Chicago: Aldine, 1977), 124.

27. See, for instance, the discussion of a public sociology by Michael Burawoy, "For
Public Sociology," *American Sociological Review* 70 (2005).

28. Bailey, *Morality and Expediency*, 21.

29. The main exceptions are teaching cases, which will be discussed later.

30. Diana Crane, *Invisible Colleges: Diffusion of Knowledge in Scientific Communities*
(Chicago: University of Chicago Press, 1972). Crane's work expands on long-
noted tensions between administrators and faculty members. See Thorstein
Veblen, *The Higher Learning in America: A Memorandum on the Conduct of
Universities by Businessmen* (New York: B. W. Huebsch, 1918).

31. For a discussion of the subcaste's dominance, see Harrison C. White, "Innovation in Style" (paper presented at the Instituting and Institutions Conference,
University of California, Santa Barbara, March 7, 2003), 7.

32. Jeffrey Cruikshank, *A Delicate Experience: The Harvard Business School, 1908–
1945* (Boston: Harvard Business School Press, 1987), 256.

33. Increasingly, journals publish lists of accepted and upcoming articles in an
effort to yield influence even prior to actual publication. For a critique of this
method and, more broadly, the "audit culture," see James P. Walsh, "Embracing
the Sacred in Our Secular Scholarly World," *Academy of Management Journal*
36, no. 2 (2011).

34. Discussions of research quality in French academia illustrate well the new
academic dynamics. See Christine Musselin, *The Market for Academics* (New
York: Routledge, 2009); Christine Musselin and Catherine Paradeise, "France:
From Incremental Transition to Institutional Change," in *University Gover-
nance: Western European Comparative Perspectives*, ed. Catherine Paradeise et al.
(Dordrecht: Springer, 2009).

35. Jeffrey Pfeffer, "A Modest Proposal: How We Might Change the Process and
Product of Managerial Research," *Academy of Management Journal* 50, no. 6
(2007).

36. Crane identified four further categories of subcaste membership, alongside the
"high-producers," in her study of the academic subfield of rural sociology—all
based on the number of publications in the field within a given time period.
Crane, *Invisible Colleges*.

37. David Riesman, *Constraint and Variety in American Education* (Lincoln: University of Nebraska Press, 1956), 104.

38. Stinchcombe, "Monopolistic Competition."

39. More precisely, 46 percent of full professors (46 out of 99), 42 percent of associate professors (14 out of 33), and 41 percent of assistant professors (20 out of
49) had been trained in a discipline. (These figures include joint degree holders
with a doctorate in a discipline.)

40. Locals and cosmopolitans have opposing orientations toward organizational
loyalty, commitment to specialized skills, and outside reference groups. Alvin
Gouldner first used the terminology *locals* and *cosmopolitans* in 1957. See Roeth-

lisberger, *Elusive Phenomena*, 257–72; Alvin W. Gouldner, "Cosmopolitans and Locals: Toward an Analysis of Latent Social Rules," *Administrative Science Quarterly* 2 (1957).

41. Harvard Business School, "Harvard Business School Annual Report," (Cambridge, MA: President and Fellows of Harvard College, 2007), 35.

42. For details on the inner workings of funding panels, see Michèle Lamont, *How Professors Think: Inside the Curious World of Academic Judgment* (Cambridge, MA: Harvard University Press, 2009).

43. Historically, training for the professions, such as law or medicine, formed the core of the European university. With time, however, the core became the periphery. See Talcott Parsons and Gerald M. Platt, *The American University* (Cambridge, MA: Harvard University Press, 1973), 225.

44. Jay O. Light, "Harvard and HBS: The Next 100 Years," in *Centennial Global Business Summit, October 12–14 2008: Executive Summaries* (Boston: President and Fellows of Harvard College, 2009).

45. Bailey, *Morality and Expediency*, 28; Smelser, *Reflections*, 240.

46. Copeland, *And Mark an Era*, 74.

47. Roethlisberger, *Elusive Phenomena*, 258.

48. Even for business-school-trained faculty members without disciplinary backgrounds, the divide between micro and macro researchers disappeared to allow for a new overarching identity.

49. This percentage was calculated by examining the cards that faculty members posted on their office doors in 2009. The cards were faculty members' standard business cards (except for those in two areas at the School). Once faculty members with endowed chairs, professors of management practice, and members of areas with standard tags were eliminated, seventy-two faculty members remained. Of these, only twenty-one included "of business administration" on their cards.

50. Cruikshank, *A Delicate Experience*, 213.

51. The two races are also sometimes referred to as two cultures. See Srikant M. Datar, David A. Garvin, and Patrick Cullen, *Rethinking the MBA: Business Education at a Crossroads* (Boston: Harvard Business Press, 2010), 76–80.

52. See Crane, *Invisible Colleges*.

53. White, "Innovation in Style," 12.

54. Caplow and McGee, *Academic Marketplace*, 221.

55. The quest for relevance is not unique to the School; many other academic settings, including disciplinary departments, face similar pressures. Speaking of the humanities, Louis Menand remarked that doctoral students are trained as experts in a subfield and then asked "to perform tasks for which they have no training whatsoever: to teach their field to non-specialists, to connect what they teach to issues that students are likely to confront in the world outside the university, to be interdisciplinary, to write for a general audience, to justify their work to people outside their discipline and outside the academy." At the School, the perceived pressure to take on all of these tasks seems stronger than it does elsewhere in the academy. See Menand, "The Ph.D. Problem: On the Professionalization of Faculty Life, Doctoral Training, and the Academy's Self-Renewal," *Harvard Magazine* 111, no. 2 (2009): 91.

56. Joseph C. Hermanowicz, *Lives in Science: How Institutions Affect Academic Careers* (Chicago: University of Chicago Press, 2009).

57. White, "Innovation in Style," 7.

Chapter Three

1. Executive education and doctoral education are the other two main teaching venues at the School.

2. Readers seeking advice on case-method teaching might refer to Louis B. Barnes, C. Roland Christensen, and Abby J. Hansen, *Teaching and the Case Method* (Boston: Harvard Business School Press, 1994); C. Roland Christensen, David A. Garvin, and Ann Sweet, eds., *Education for Judgment: The Artistry of Discussion Leadership* (Boston: Harvard Business School Press, 1991).

3. These tensions reflect the widely held view that uniformity in human interactions is incompatible with high-quality service. See Robin Leidner, *Fast Food, Fast Talk: Service Work and the Routinization of Everyday Life* (Berkeley: University of California Press, 1993), 30.

4. A similar meeting is held for the faculty members who deliver second-year elective courses.

5. Community values include "respect for the rights, differences, and dignity of others," "honesty and integrity in dealing with all members of the community," and "accountability for personal behavior." Harvard Business School, "Community Values, Spring Report" (Boston: Harvard Business School, 2007).

6. For more on faculty support for case writing, see chapter 5.

7. A similar form of regulation prevails in direct-sales organizations, whose agents are strongly encouraged (though not forced) to follow the company's scripts. See Nicole Woolsey Biggart, *Charismatic Capitalism: Direct Selling Organizations in America* (Chicago: University of Chicago Press, 1989), 147.

8. In the classroom, the dexterity with which an instructor prepares boards and juggles other teaching materials is often a good indicator of tenure in the system.

9. Once a teaching plan is stabilized, it is published as a signed teaching note. The teaching groups often rely on more recently updated plans, even for cases with published teaching notes.

10. A slightly dated study of the spending habits of ninety-six Berkeley faculty members refers to a "class ideal that cares little about fashion even when income permits some emphasis in this direction." Jessica B. Peixotto, *Getting and Spending at the Professional Standard of Living: A Study of the Costs of Living an Academic Life* (New York: Macmillan, 1927), 156.

11. Rachel Sherman, *Class Acts: Service and Inequality in Luxury Hotels* (Berkeley: University of California Press, 2007), 243; Michael Taussig, *What Color Is the Sacred?* (Chicago: University of Chicago Press, 2009), 81.

12. The clothier's calls were made in 2005, apparently only to male faculty members.

13. For a discussion of color preferences and social classes, see Pierre Bourdieu,

186 Notes to Pages 57–66

"Remarques provisoires sur la perception sociale du corps," *Actes de la recherche en sciences sociales* 14, no. 1 (1977).

14. Beginning in 2008, custom software was made available to produce calling charts. Prior to that, seating charts were hand-marked.

15. A strong teaching plan is a plan that engages students, covers every salient aspect of a case, delivers a conceptual payoff, and is easy to memorize.

16. Female faculty members usually keep their jackets on.

17. One such classroom, used in the 1970s, was located in a hotel (Le Mirador) in Switzerland. A more recent classroom opened in an office building in China. For more details on the latter opening, see Stephanie Mitchell, "Harvard Center Shanghai," *Harvard Magazine* 112, no. 5 (2010).

18. Lavanya Manohar, "Getting It Right!," *Harbus*, September 29, 2009.

19. For a discussion of war stories in another occupational setting, see Julian E. Orr, *Talking about Machines: An Ethnography of a Modern Job* (Ithaca, NY: Cornell University Press, 1996), 125–43.

20. In effect, students are encouraged to construct "provisional selves" by watching former counterparts in action. See Herminia Ibarra, "Provisional Selves: Experimenting with Image and Identity in Professional Adaptation," *Administrative Science Quarterly* 44, no. 4 (1999).

21. Not all student sections welcome applause. At the beginning of the year, section members agree on some (section-specific) norms of conduct. For more detail on student sections, see Charles D. Orth, *Social Structure and Learning Climate: The First Year at the Harvard Business School* (Boston: Division of Research, Graduate School of Business Administration, Harvard University, 1963).

22. For the importance of war stories in another context, See Orr, *Talking about Machines*, 134.

23. Five minutes past the class's scheduled start time, the section's educational representative contacted the instructor's department. When a faculty assistant realized what had happened, the department immediately dispatched a back-up instructor.

24. Ending a class a few minutes early was never an issue, but twenty minutes early was.

25. For instance, my educational representative did not notice anything amiss the day of my "failure."

26. As Nicole W. Biggart writes, "Self-control does not feel controlling." See Biggart, *Charismatic Capitalism*, 164–65.

27. Deviations from the norm always help highlight the expected. See Howard S. Becker, *Outsiders: Studies in the Sociology of Deviance* (London: Free Press, 1963). Harold Garfinkel, *Studies in Ethnomethodology* (Englewood Cliffs, NJ: Prentice Hall, 1967). John Heritage, *Garfinkel and Ethnomethodology* (Cambridge, UK: Polity Press, 1984).

28. The term prevails despite the fact that exchanges occurring outside a session's time boundaries are not graded.

29. Most faculty members' office doors are kept partly open during student meetings to avoid potentially uncomfortable situations.

30. Orth, *Social Structure*, 42.

31. Appointments with faculty are not perceived by students as completely risk-free. As one student recalled, "When I told a student in my dorm about my plan

to see professors, she cautioned me not to show any of my weaknesses when I met with them." Fran Worden Henry, *Toughing It Out at Harvard: The Making of a Woman MBA* (New York: G. P. Putnam's Sons, 1983), 78.

32. Harvard University Graduate School of Business Administration, "Information for Research Assistants" (Baker Library, E75B.42, 1931), 2.

33. The support available to perfect the art of teaching is, by any measure, extremely generous. Many faculty members benefit from the assistance of the C. Roland Christensen Center for Teaching and Learning, established in 2004 to promote and support teaching at the School.

34. Teaching routines exemplify the coexistence of freedom and guidance in the school's educational pursuit.

35. Jeffrey Cruikshank, *A Delicate Experience: The Harvard Business School, 1908–1945* (Boston: Harvard Business School Press, 1987), 84.

36. Sharon Daloz Parks, "Young Adults and the Formation of Professional Ethics," in *Can Ethics Be Taught? Perspectives, Challenges, and Approaches at Harvard Business School*, ed. Thomas R. Piper, Mary C. Gentile, and Sharon Daloz Parks (Boston: Harvard Business School, 1993), 62.

37. Preaching in silence also means that the shared message is not made explicit. This approach allows for multiple (silent) preachers to coexist within the same community and for their audiences to argue the pros and cons while projecting their own interpretations on the preachers' messages. In the same manner that Cosimo de Medici built an extended patronage network by remaining mostly silent when receiving visitors, relatively silent preaching accommodates the broadest audience. John Padgett and Ansell Christopher, "Robust Action and the Rise of the Medici, 1400–1434," *American Journal of Sociology* 98, no. 6 (1993).

Chapter Four

1. Paul R. Carlile, "Using Artifacts to Interpret and Negotiate Knowledge across Domains," in *Artifacts and Organizations*, ed. Anat Rafaeli and Michael Pratt (Mahwah, NJ: Lawrence Erlbaum, 2004).

2. Luc Boltanski and Eve Chiapello, *Le nouvel esprit du capitalisme* (Paris: Gallimard, 1999); Anne Both, *Les managers et leurs discours: Anthropology de la rhethorique manageriale* (Bordeaux: Presses Universitaires de Bordeaux, 2008).

3. The reliance on teaching notes or plans to structure the classroom experience is increasingly common in other academic settings. For examples, see Dennis Hayes and Robin Wynyard, *The McDonaldization of Higher Education* (Westport, CT: Bergin & Garvey, 2002).

4. Clayton M. Christensen, "If Harvard Business School Were a Religion, It Could Be Mormonism," http://www.washingtonpost.com/national/on-leadership/if-harvard-business-school-were-a-religion-it-could-be-mormonism/2012/05/11/gIQA04biIU_story.html (accessed July 30, 2012).

5. Because notes are available only to School instructors and other registered educators, the case contexts in these and other illustrations of typical case material have been disguised.

6. One-third of all the notes available for each of the ten traditional required first-year MBA courses offered during the 2007–2008 academic year (fall 2007

and spring 2008) were randomly selected, for a total of sixty-one notes. (One short-lived negotiation course was omitted from the analysis.) The sampled notes were coded in accordance with grounded theory guidelines. For details on this procedure, see Barney Glaser and Anselm L. Strauss, *The Discovery of Grounded Theory* (Chicago: Aldine, 1967). The author and an independent coder performed the coding. Discrepancies were resolved through discussion. Only the most common codes are reported here.

7.   For a discussion of how medical education constructs its objects, see Byron J. Good, *Medicine, Rationality and Experience: An Anthropological Perspective* (Cambridge, UK: Cambridge University Press, 1994).

8.   The small sample dealing with emotions (seven notes across four courses) is not large enough, however, to reach robust conclusions.

9.   Karen Ho, *Liquidated: An Ethnography of Wall Street* (Durham, NC: Duke University Press, 2009).

10. For examples of corporations promoting a view of managers as agents of change, see Vicky Smith, *Managing in the Corporate Interest: Control and Resistance in an American Bank* (Berkeley: University of California Press, 1990), 82; Nicole Woolsey Biggart, *Charismatic Capitalism: Direct Selling Organizations in America* (Chicago: University of Chicago Press, 1989), 105–6.

11. Katherine S. Newman, *Falling from Grace: Downward Mobility in the Age of Affluence* (Berkeley: University of California Press, 1988), 75.

12. Max Weber, *The Protestant Ethic and the Spirit of Capitalism* (San Francisco: Jossey-Bass, 1958). For a discussion of Weber's formulation of the secularization of the Protestant ethic, see R. N. Bellah et al., *Habits of the Heart: Individualism and Commitment in American Life* (New York: Harper and Row, 1985); Newman, *Falling from Grace*, 274.

13. Martin Ruef, *The Entrepreneurial Group: Social Identities, Relations, and Collective Action* (Princeton, NJ: Princeton University Press, 2010).

14. In a sense, silence calls for noise.

15. This analysis also holds for the ethical decisions in the "Leadership and Corporate Accountability" course. Some LCA teaching notes do, however, clearly spell out managers' legal responsibilities. For a discussion of managers' economic, legal, and ethical responsibilities, see Paine, *Instructor's Guide*.

16. Some faculty members share their "personal perspective" more frequently, often at the end of a class session and after students have debated a variety of options. For an example of such an instance, see John S. Rosenberg, "An Education in Ethics: Teaching Business Students Life Lessons in Leadership," *Harvard Magazine* 109, no. 1 (2006): 48.

17. Daisy Wademan, *Remember Who You Are: Life Stories That Inspire the Heart and Mind* (Boston: Harvard Business School Press, 2004), 2–3.

18. Ibid., 3.

19. Wademan, *Remember Who You Are*, 34, 74, 149, 172.

20. Brent D. Rosso, Kathryn H. Dekas, and Amy Wrzesniewski, "On the Meaning of Work: A Theoretical Integration and Review," *Research in Organizational Behavior* 30 (2010): 91–127.

21. These remarks were made in one of my classes. Many colleagues receive such praise, however, so such remarks should not be read as evidence of "good" teaching skills.

22. For a discussion of education as a form of social control, see Michael F. D. Young, ed. *Knowledge and Control: New Directions for the Sociology of Education* (London: Collier-Macmillan, 1971), 1–7.

23. Benford and Snow, "Framing Processes"; Amin Ghaziani and Delia Baldassarri, "Cultural Anchors and the Organization of Differences: A Multi-Method Analysis of LGBT Marches on Washington," *American Sociological Review* 76, no. 2 (2011).

24. For a discussion of a question-driven as opposed to answer-driven approach to teaching, see Charles I. Gragg, *Because Wisdom Can't Be Told* (HBSP Case 9-451-005) (Cambridge, MA: President and Fellows of Harvard College, 1940).

25. Sumantra Ghoshal, "Bad Management Theories Are Destroying Good Management Practices," *Academy of Management Learning & Education* 4, no. 1 (2005).

26. Michèle Lamont, *The Dignity of Working Men: Moralities and the Boundaries of Race, Class, and Immigration* (New York: Russell Sage Foundation, 2000), 247.

27. Newman, *Falling from Grace.*

Chapter Five

1. For a discussion on the division of labor and morals, see Emile Durkheim, *The Division of Labor in Society* (Glencoe, IL: Free Press, 1964), 11–29. For a more contemporary discussion, see Everett C. Hughes, *Men and Their Work* (London, UK: Collier-Macmillan, 1958), 78–80.

2. Robert E. Park and Ernest W. Burgess, *The City: Suggestions for Investigation of Human Behavior in the Urban Environment* (Chicago: University of Chicago Press, 1984), 14.

3. Andrew Abbott, *The System of Professions: An Essay on the Division of Expert Labor* (Chicago: University of Chicago Press, 1988); Beth Bechky, "Object Lessons: Workplace Artifacts as Representations of Occupational Jurisdiction," *American Journal of Sociology* 109, no. 3 (2003).

4. The practice, long discontinued, has now been resurrected.

5. Basic concierge assistance was free, with charges for some more targeted assistance. This assistance was, however, discontinued in 2009 following the financial crisis. For details on such assistance, see Rachel Sherman, "'Time Is Our Commodity': Gender and the Struggle for Occupational Legitimacy among Personal Concierges," *Work and Occupations* 37, no. 1 (2010).

6. Professional and occupational mandates are always constructed in contrast to competing mandates; see Abbott, *System of Professions.*

7. Arthur L. Stinchcombe, "Social Structure and Organizations," in *Handbook of Organizations*, ed. James G. March (Chicago: Rand McNally, 1965).

8. With tenure and seniority, faculty members increasingly take on committee assignments, the direction of educational programs, or the leadership of ad hoc projects.

9. John Van Maanen also noted the pervasiveness of shame (versus guilt) when comparing HBS and MIT Sloan classroom environments; see Van Maanen, "Golden Passports: Managerial Socialization and Graduate Education," *Review of Higher Education* 6, no. 4 (1983).

10. Not being a member of the committee overseeing these cases, I can only report

the experience of how a non–committee member perceives the criteria for continuation.

11. For a discussion on the creation of organizational records, see Eliot Freidson, *Professional Powers: A Study in the Institutionalization of Formal Knowledge* (Chicago: University of Chicago Press, 1986), 175–76.

12. Grades take the form of I (highest), II, or III (lowest). Technically a lower grade, IV, exists, but it is rarely used.

13. This quote is taken from an article addressing depression at the School titled "Letter to a young RC [Required Curriculum]," *Harbus*, September 10, 2007, 6.

14. Variations in grade-disclosure policies, though heavily debated within the School, has played relatively little role in my grading experience. Grade disclosure to external employers, with the student's consent, has historically been the norm. To allow students to experiment with a wider range of course offerings (in which they might or might not earn lower grades) and act less competitively in the classroom, a brief experiment of grade nondisclosure was pursued. By 2006, however, it was abandoned.

15. Caren Kelleher, "Do Grades Matter at HBS?" *Harbus*, September 14, 2009.

16. A (nonrandom) poll of 270 first-year MBA students in 2009 found that only 59 percent thought grades mattered, while 41 percent did not (ibid.). Students at Harvard Law School also believe some class grades are random; see Robert Granfield, *Making Elite Lawyers: Visions of Law at Harvard and Beyond* (London: Routledge, 1992), 132.

17. Jeffrey Cruikshank, *A Delicate Experience: The Harvard Business School, 1908–1945* (Boston: Harvard Business School Press, 1987), 211.

18. For a discussion of the prevalence of self-praise and self-blame in the United States, see Ofer Sharone, "Chemistry or Specs: Comparing Job Search Games and Subjective Responses to Unemployment" (paper presented at the International Sociological Association Annual Conference, Gothenburg, Sweden, July 16, 2010).

19. Harvard University Office of the Senior Vice Provost, "Faculty Development and Diversity, Annual Report 2009" (Cambridge, MA: Presidents and Fellows of Harvard College, 2009).

20. The self-interested rational actor model is best exemplified by an agency theory view of the firm; see Michael C. Jensen and William H. Meckling, "Theory of the Firm: Managerial Behavior, Agency Costs and Ownership Structure," *Journal of Financial Economics* 3, no. 4 (1976).

21. Park and Burgess, *City*, 16.

22. The sampling was conducted by collecting bid sheets from nine auctions over four years. While the sampling was not random, I suspect the sheets were fairly representative.

23. Of 177 faculty items donated in the sampled auctions, 111 were dinners.

24. Nannerl O. Keohane, *Higher Ground: Ethics and Leadership in the Modern University* (Durham, NC: Duke University Press, 2006). Also, see Gaye Tuchman, *Wannabe U: Inside the Corporate University* (Chicago: University of Chicago Press, 2009), 173.

25. Commensuration is a common way to gauge value. See Wendy Nelson Espeland and Mitchell L. Stevens, "Commensuration as a Social Process," *Annual Review of Sociology* 24 (1998).

26. For similar reaction to price "busting" among professional magicians, see Graham M. Jones, *Trade of the Tricks: Inside the Magician's Craft* (Berkeley: University of California Press, 2011), 184.

27. For a discussion of academic brands, see Tuchman, *Wannabe U.*

28. C. Wright Mills, *White Collar: The American Middle Classes* (New York: Oxford University Press, 1951), 173.

29. Members of dominant groups tend to forge their own legitimation for their high status, and faculty members are not exempt from such temptations. See Paul Willis, *Learning to Labor: How Working Class Kids Get Working Class Jobs* (New York: Columbia University Press, 1977), 123.

30. The average salary for a US business school professor (all ranks combined) was, in 2010, $110,000 per year. See AACSB, "Average Faculty Salaries at U.S. AACSB International Member Schools," http://www.aacsb.edu/dataandresearch/salaries.asp (accessed April 14, 2011).

31. A more detailed analysis of faculty members' earnings and giving is needed to confirm this proposition. Financial contributions can also be an alternative to volunteering.

32. Jay Lorsch and Rakesh Khurana, "The Pay Problem," *Harvard Magazine* 112, no. 5 (2010): 35.

33. Experienced external requestors are quick to understand the priorities and provide perks to lure hesitant faculty members (e.g., a teaching engagement in an attractive location with travel for the spouse). But few junior faculty members have time to devote to such engagements.

34. For a more detailed discussion of worth, see David Stark, *The Sense of Dissonance: Accounts of Worth in Economic Life* (Princeton, NJ: Princeton University Press, 2009).

35. As early as 1776, Adam Smith wrote about the links between the division of labor and specialization. Smith, *An Inquiry into the Nature and Causes of the Wealth of Nations* (Dublin: Whitestone, 1776). Max Weber later reinforced that point. Weber, *Economy and Society: An Outline of Interpretative Sociology* (Berkeley: University of California Press, 1978).

36. Serge Paugam, "Introduction," in *De la division du travail social* (Paris: Presses Universitaires de France, 2007).

37. Orlando Patterson, "Taking Culture Seriously: A Framework and an Afro-American Illustration," in *Culture Matters: How Values Shape Human Progress*, ed. Lawrence E. Harrison and Samuel P. Huntington (New York: Basic Books, 2001).

Chapter Six

1. Sanjay Subrahmanyam, "One for the Money, Two for the Show," *L'homme* 187–188 (2008): 93–94.

2. I trust that my confirmation postcard can still be found in the School's archives.

3. Jeffrey Cruikshank, *A Delicate Experience: The Harvard Business School, 1908–1945* (Boston: Harvard Business School Press, 1987), 84.

4. Though nonfaculty staff members are integral to the School's operations, my data do not allow for analysis of their entry and exit. Moreover, I did not col-

lect data on specific hiring, promotion, and tenure decisions or participate in promotion and tenure discussions; the chapter therefore provides a faculty view from below (see appendix).

5. Arnold Van Gennep, *The Rites of Passage* (Chicago: University of Chicago Press, 1960). The term *rites of passage* as used here also includes rites of degradation (e.g., firing). For a discussion of the variety of organizational rites, see Janice M. Beyer and Harrison M. Trice, "The Communication of Power Relations in Organizations through Cultural Rites," in *Inside Organizations: Understanding the Human Dimension,* ed. Michael Owen Jones, Michael Dane Moore, and Richard Christopher Snyder (Newbury Park, CA: Sage, 1988).

6. Ibid., "The Communication of Power Relations in Organizations through Cultural Rites," 142.

7. Theodore Caplow and Reece J. McGee, *The Academic Marketplace* (New York: Basic Books, 1958), 49.

8. A. B. Hollingshead, "Ingroup Membership and Academic Selection," *American Sociological Review* 3, no. 6 (1938).

9. Theodore Eisenberg and Martin T. Wells, "Inbreeding in Law School Hiring: Assessing the Performance of Faculty Hired from Within," *Journal of Legal Studies* 29, no. 1 (2000).

10. Jeffrey Cruikshank, "A Force for Good," *HBS Alumni Bulletin,* December 2008, 33.

11. Bernard Berelson, *Graduate Education in the United States* (New York: McGraw-Hill, 1960), 116.

12. Faculty might be selected because of prior *habitus,* not because of what they learned as doctoral students at the School or elsewhere. Habitus is a system of dispositions and ways of thinking about and acting in the world that is formed early in life. The socialization promoted by the School might therefore prove negligible in light of prior experiences. See Pierre Bourdieu, *Méditations Pascaliennes* (Paris: Editions du Seuil, 1997). A discussion of this concept in a recent setting can be found in Matthew Desmond, *On the Fireline: Living and Dying with Wildland Firefighters* (Chicago: University of Chicago Press, 2007).

13. *Inbreeding* has multiple definitions. In its strictest form, it means hiring the School's doctoral students (and sometimes MBA graduates) as professors of management practice. More loosely, inbreeding also encompasses hiring any Harvard-trained faculty—including, for instance, doctoral students from Harvard's Graduate School of Arts and Sciences. A Harvard-trained economist might therefore qualify as in- or out-bred depending on one's definition.

14. The benefit of outsiders is best described by Harrison White, who notes that institutions reproduce themselves via "some peculiar balancing of interpenetrations by values across network and locality." See White, "Innovation in Style" (paper presented at the Instituting and Institutions Conference, University of California, Santa Barbara, March 7 2003), 8.

15. Cruikshank, *A Delicate Experience,* 283.

16. For the 1958 data, see Melvin T. Copeland, *And Mark an Era: The Story of the Harvard Business School* (New York: Little, Brown, 1958), 343–68.

17. Rakesh Khurana, *From Higher Aims to Hired Hands: The Social Transformation of American Business Schools and the Unfulfilled Promise of Management as a Profession* (Princeton, NJ: Princeton University Press, 2007), 233–90.

18. A telephone call received by one job candidate illustrates such attention to detail: a faculty assistant called to ask if she wanted to revise her curriculum vitae because he had noticed a discrepancy between the title of a submitted work in progress and its listing on her vitae.

19. Harvard University Graduate School of Business Administration, "Nuts and Bolts: A Guide to HBS Services for Research Assistants" (Baker Library Historical Collections, E75B.62, 1982), 2–3, 12.

20. I thank Mikell Hyman for helping me better understand research associates' position at the School.

21. Harvard University Graduate School of Business Administration, "Information for Research Assistants" (Baker Library, E75B.42, 1950), 5–6.

22. Ibid., 8.

23. Nancy O. Perry, "A Job with a Future," *HBS Bulletin* (1990).

24. Srikant M. Datar, David A. Garvin, and Patrick Cullen, *Rethinking the MBA: Business Education at a Crossroads* (Boston: Harvard Business Press, 2010), 253.

25. Copeland, *And Mark an Era*, 187.

26. Pierre Bourdieu, *Homo Academicus* (Paris: Editions de Minuit, 1984), 192.

27. Ibid., 237.

28. Caplow and McGee, *Academic Marketplace*, 223.

29. For current examples of such dynamics, see the work of the sociologist Neil J. Smelser and the anthropologist Arthur Kleinman. Smelser, *Reflections on the University of California: From the Free Speech Movement to the Global University* (Berkeley: University of California Press, 2010), 207. Kleinman, *Writing at the Margin: Discourse between Anthropology and Medicine* (Berkeley: University of California Press, 1997), 130–33.

30. Michael Beer, *High Commitment, High Performance: How to Build a Resilient Organization for Sustained Advantage* (San Francisco: Jossey-Bass, 2009), 275.

31. The promotion process is quite similar to the one described by Melvin T. Copeland almost fifty years earlier. See Copeland, *And Mark an Era*, 189–93.

32. Ruben Gaztambide-Fernandez, *The Best of the Best: Becoming Elite at an American Boarding School* (Cambridge, MA: Harvard University Press, 2009), 198.

33. "Where the Women Are—and Aren't," *Harvard Magazine* 113, no. 3 (2011).

34. A public-source survey of nonretiring faculty members who left the School during the period from 1991 to 1994 suggests that 20 percent entered industry, 40 percent joined universities mainly focused on teaching, and 40 percent moved to universities mainly focused on research.

35. In 2007 the School alumni bulletin began publishing "occasional articles . . . catching up with former HBS faculty members." The initial article was a portrait of Leonard Schlesinger, who had gone on to leadership positions in the retail industry. See Bulletin Staff, "Where Are They Now?" *HBS Alumni Bulletin*, 2007.

36. Martha S. Feldman and Brian T. Pentland, "Reconceptualizing Organizational Routines as a Source of Flexibility and Change," *Administrative Science Quarterly* 48 (2003).

37. Regular instruction at the School was suspended in 1943 during the Second World War and resumed in 1945. (See "Timeline," Harvard Business School Institutional Memory website, http://institutionalmemory.hbs.edu/timeline/1943/h063sc/navy_supply_corps_midshipmen-officers_school_launched.html.)

38. William R. Galeota, "Class Attendance Falls Drastically as Harvard Observes Moratorium," *Harvard Crimson*, October 16, 1969.

Conclusion

1. Joanne Martin makes clear that ambiguity can be experienced as liberating or debilitating—that is, as freedom from unhelpful constraints or as a source of confusion and even paralysis. See Martin, *Cultures in Organizations: Three Perspectives* (New York: Oxford University Press, 1992), 138.
2. Vocal silence might encourage a certain type of "social knowledge." Social knowledge often encompasses "normative statements that draw on descriptive information to recommend or condemn a certain course of human conduct." See Charles Camic, Neil Gross, and Michèle Lamont, *Social Knowledge in the Making* (Chicago: University of Chicago Press, 2011), 3. Yet the social knowledge produced via vocal silence almost deliberately tries to exclude overt normative statements.
3. Max Weber, *The Protestant Ethic and the Spirit of Capitalism* (San Francisco: Jossey-Bass, 1958).
4. Tom Burns, *The BBC: Public Institution and Private World* (London: MacMillan Press, 1977), 35–36.
5. Norbert Elias, *The Genesis of the Naval Profession*, ed. René Moelker and Stephen Mennell (Dublin: University College Dublin Press, 2007).
6. Ibid., 31.
7. Ibid., 49.
8. Pierre Bourdieu and Jean-Claude Passeron, *Reproduction in Education, Society, and Culture* (London: Sage, 1990).
9. Joshua D. Margolis, "Responsibility in Organizational Context," *Business Ethics Quarterly* 11, no. 4 (2001).
10. Carol Heimer and Lisa Staffen have suggested that flexibility might be a key feature of organizations that aim to produce individual responsibility. They do not specify, however, how flexible organizations are designed. See Heimer and Staffen, *For the Sake of the Children: The Social Organization of Responsibility in the Hospital and the Home* (Chicago: University of Chicago Press), 354–55.
11. Vocal silence allows organizations to simultaneously deploy "investiture" and "divestiture" tactics vis-à-vis their members. Through investiture tactics, organizations acknowledge individual members' prior personal characteristics (including their morals). By using divestiture tactics, organizations aim to strip members of their prior characteristics and instill new ones. See John Van Maanen and Edgar H. Schein, "Toward a Theory of Organizational Socialization," in *Research in Organizational Behavior*, ed. B. Staw and L. Cummings (Greenwich, CT: JAI Press, 1979).
12. For example, studies of "self-managed teams" have focused on individuals' submission to the collective (i.e., the pressure to perform) rather than individuals' relative latitude within teams. See James R. Barker, "Tightening the Iron Cage: Concertive Control in Self-Managing Teams," *Administrative Science Quarterly* 38, no. 3 (1993).

13. Gideon Kunda, *Engineering Culture: Control and Commitment in High-Tech Corporation* (Philadelphia: Temple University Press, 1992), 12.

14. For organizations' members to "consent" to being controlled, an individual's independent sense of self is needed. Thus, some restraint from shaping members' "souls" too forcefully via routines is probably a corollary to the development of "engaging" forms of control. For discussions of consent and engaging control, see Michael Burawoy, *Manufacturing Consent: Changes in the Labor Process under Monopoly Capitalism* (Chicago: University of Chicago Press, 1979); Steven Peter Vallas, *Work: A Critic* (Cambridge, UK: Polity Press, 2012), 43–59.

15. Alexandra A. Michel, "Transcending Socialization: A Nine-Year Ethnography of the Body's Role in Organizational Control and Knowledge Workers' Transformation," *Administrative Science Quarterly* 56, no. 3 (2011): 328–29.

16. Max Weber, *The Theory of Social and Economic Organization*, ed. Talcott Parsons (New York: Free Press, 1947), 71–72.

17. Frank Dobbin, *Inventing Equal Opportunity* (Princeton, NJ: Princeton University Press, 2009).

18. Jeffrey Cruikshank, *A Delicate Experience: The Harvard Business School, 1908–1945* (Boston: Harvard Business School Press, 1987), 44.

19. Count Wolf Baudissin, "The New German Army," *Foreign Affairs* 34, no. 1 (1955): 9.

20. Wayne C. Thompson and Marc D. Peltier, "The Education of Military Officers in the Federal Republic of Germany," *Armed Forces & Society* 16, no. 4 (1990): 589.

21. Mira Sucharov, "Security Ethics and the Modern Military: The Case of the Israel Defense Forces," *Armed Forces & Society* 31, no. 2 (2005): 181–82.

22. The Catholic church, in particular, appears to offer a less silent alternative. However, past research suggests more silence and flexibility in some Catholic orders than one might expect. See Jean M. Bartunek, "Changing Interpretive Schemes and Organizational Restructuring: The Example of a Religious Order," *Administrative Science Quarterly* 29, no. 3 (1984).

23. Elizabeth Wolfe Morrison and Frances J. Milliken, "Organizational Silence: A Barrier to Change and Development in a Pluralistic World," *Academy of Management Review* 25, no. 4 (2000); Leslie A. Perlow and Nelson Repenning, "The Dynamics of Silencing Conflict," *Research in Organizational Behavior* 29 (2009).

24. The elective course was known as "Interpersonal Behavior." See James F. T. Bugental, "The Silence of the Sky," in *Interpersonal Behavior: Communication and Understanding in Relationships*, ed. Anthony G. Athos and John J. Gabarro (Englewood Cliffs, NJ: Prentice-Hall, 1978).

25. John Van Maanen and Gideon Kunda, "Real Feelings: Emotional Expression and Organizational Culture," in *Research in Organizational Behavior*, ed. Barry M. Staw and L. L. Cummings (Greenwich, CT: JAI Press, 1989).

26. Harrison C. White, "Agency as Control," in *Principals and Agents: The Structure of Business*, ed. John W. Pratt and Richard J. Zeckhauser (Boston: Harvard Business School Press, 1985), 188.

27. Wallace B. Donham, "Report of the President and Treasurer of Harvard College 1924–25," *Official Register of Harvard University* 23, no. 2 (1926): 122.

28. It is no coincidence that *lack* of relevance was historically a major criticism

aimed at US utopian communes. In those instances, relevance was seen as an antidote to the commune's overly focused and exclusive attention on its members. See Rosabeth Moss Kanter, *Commitment and Community: Communes and Utopias in Sociological Perspective* (Cambridge, MA: Harvard University Press, 1972), 224.

29. Cruikshank, *A Delicate Experience*, 44.

30. See Weber, *Protestant Ethic*, 194n11.

31. Bulletin Staff, "Rags to Riches," *HBS Alumni Bulletin*, March 2008.

32. The notion that organizational change does not always require *structural* change challenges many prior conceptions of organizational change. For such a view of change, see Stewart Ranson, Bob Hinings, and Royston Greenwood, "The Structuring of Organizational Structures," *Administrative Science Quarterly* 25, no. 1 (1980).

33. The idea of an "individual victory over one's subjectivity" is formulated by Georges Davy in his introduction to Emile Durkheim's work. See Durkheim, *Leçons de sociologie* (Paris: Presses Universitaires de France, 1950), 24–25. An alternate, non-Durkheimian and perhaps more contemporary view of morals might entail individuals prevailing over the collective.

34. The notion that one commits more to what one discovers oneself was captured by Pascal, who stated that we are in general more convinced by arguments that we have formulated ourselves than by those suggested by others. ("On se persuade mieux, pour l'ordinaire, par les raisons que l'on a soi-même trouvées, que par celles qui sont venues dans l'esprit des autres.") See Blaise Pascal, *Pensées* (Paris: Dezobrie et E. Magdeleine, 1852), 106.

35. For an example of the role of the material world (including the human body) in organizational control, see Michel, "Transcending Socialization."

36. Harrison M. Trice and Janice M. Beyer, *The Cultures of Work Organizations* (Englewoods Cliffs, NJ: Prentice Hall, 1993), 9.

37. Michel Lallement, *Le travail de l'utopie: Godin et le familistère de guise* (Paris: Belles Lettres, 2009), 155–65.

38. As recently as 2008, dean Jay O. Light spoke at the School's centennial celebration about what is needed for sound leadership: "judgment," "communications skills," and "values and integrity." How to teach those attributes of leadership, he added, was the challenge the School had struggled with since its inception. See Light, "Harvard and HBS: The Next 100 Years," in *Centennial Global Business Summit, October 12–14 2008: Executive Summaries* (Boston: President and Fellows of Harvard College, 2009).

39. Jean Bartunek posits that such emotions reside at the core of an organizational change process. See Bartunek, "Changing Interpretive Schemes."

40. That some early ethics course offerings at the School—i.e., "Decision Making and Ethical Values" and "Leadership, Values, and Decision Making"—were intended as much for faculty members' development as for students' socialization partly justifies moving between levels of analysis.

41. Mary C. Gentile, "Engaging the Power and Competence of the Faculty," in *Can Ethics Be Taught? Perspectives, Challenges, and Approaches at Harvard Business School*, ed. Thomas R. Piper, Mary C. Gentile, and Sharon Daloz Parks (Boston: Harvard Business School, 1993), 82.

42. Past debate on what constituted a proper salary level for graduating students

illustrates the limits of the pursuit. In 1923 over three hundred firms tried to hire the School's 168 graduating students: a salary war ensued. Some School administrators, uncomfortable with the salaries that graduates were commanding, suggested that employers impose a "limitation on salaries" paid to MBAs with little or no practical experience. The suggestion never proved feasible. See Cruikshank, *A Delicate Experience*, 149.

43. Ibid., 103.

44. Linda Hill, "Exercising Moral Courage: A Developmental Agenda," in *Moral Leadership: The Theory and Practice of Power, Judgment, and Policy*, ed. Deborah L. Rhode (San Francisco: Jossey Bass, 2006), 267.

45. Cruikshank, *A Delicate Experience*, 168.

46. Max Anderson and Peter Escher, *The MBA Oath: Setting a Higher Standard for Business Leaders* (New York: Portfolio, 2010).

47. Nitin Nohria and Rakesh Khurana, "It's Time to Make Management a True Profession," *Harvard Business Review* 86, no. 10 (2008).

48. Andrew Sridhar, "MBA Oath: An Oath and Its Flaws," *Harbus*, September 28, 2009.

49. Matthew Grayson, "MBA Oath Poll—The Results Are In!" *Harbus*, October 13, 2009.

50. For a social-movement perspective on members' role in promoting change in a different context, see Katherine C. Kellogg, *Challenging Operations: Medical Reform and Resistance in Surgery* (Chicago: University of Chicago Press, 2011).

51. Jay Lorsch and Rakesh Khurana, "The Pay Problem," *Harvard Magazine* 112, no. 5 (2010): 35. For a broader discussion of the disconnect between faculty members' and students' normative views on society, see Neil Gross and Ethan Fosse, "Why Are Professors Liberal?" *Theory & Society* 41 (2012).

52. Magali Sarfatti Larson, *The Rise of Professionalism: A Sociological Analysis* (Berkeley: University of California Press, 1977).

53. Robin Leidner, *Fast Food, Fast Talk: Service Work and the Routinization of Everyday Life* (Berkeley: University of California Press, 1993).

54. Calvin Morrill, Mayer N. Zald, and Hayagreeva Rao, "Covert Political Conflict in Organizations: Challenges from Below," *Annual Review of Sociology* 29 (2003).

55. Harvard University Office of the Senior Vice Provost, "Faculty Development and Diversity, Annual Report 2009" (Cambridge, MA: Presidents and Fellows of Harvard College, 2009), 29–30.

56. The School recently created the position of senior associate dean for culture and community, in part to try to understand gender dynamics on campus.

57. Herbert Gans, *The Levittowners: Ways of Life and Politics in a New Suburban Community* (New York: Vantage, 1967), 409.

58. Burns, *BBC*, 296.

59. The story of stonecutters is taken from the writings of Peter Drucker. Drew Gilpin Faust, "Harvard and HBS: The Next 100 Years," in *The Centennial Global Business Summit, October 12–14, 2008: Executive Summaries* (Cambridge, MA: Presidents and Fellows of Harvard College, 2009).

60. Emile Durkheim, *Sociologie et philosophie* (Paris: Presses Universitaires de France, 2004), 96 (author's translation).

61. Many other sociologists see morals as both a result and a source of collective dynamics. See Michèle Lamont, "The Return of the Moral," in *Handbook of the*

Sociology of Morality, ed. Steven Hitlin and Stephen Vaisey (New York: Springer, 2010), vi.

62. George C. Homans, *The Human Group* (New Brunswick, NJ: Transaction Publishers, 1993), 468.

63. Alain Renaut, *The Era of the Individual: A Contribution to a History of Subjectivity* (Princeton, NJ: Princeton University Press, 1999); Ronen Shamir, "The Age of Responsibilization: On Market-Embedded Morality," *Economy and Society* 37, no. 1 (2008); Louis Dumont, *Essais sur l'individualisme: Une perspective anthropologique sur l'ideologie moderne* (Paris: Seuil, 1983).

64. Durkheim, *Leçons de sociologie*, 24–25.

65. For examples of recent detailed analysis of higher educational settings, see Elizabeth A. Armstrong and Laura T. Hamilton, *Paying for the Party: How College Maintains Inequality* (Cambridge, MA: Harvard University Press, 2013); Amy J. Binder and Kate Wood, *Becoming Right: How Campuses Shape Young Conservatives* (Princeton, NJ: Princeton University Press, 2012); P. F. Kluge, *Alma Mater: A College Homecoming* (Reading, MA: Addison Wesley, 1993); Gaye Tuchman, *Wannabe U: Inside the Corporate University* (Chicago: University of Chicago Press, 2009); Mitchell L. Stevens, *Creating a Class: College Admissions and the Education of Elites* (Cambridge, MA: Harvard University Press, 2007).

66. Scholars such as Neil Gross and Michèle Lamont have examined ways in which professors think, particularly across disciplines. More research is needed, however on how professors think across higher-educational organizational settings. See Gross, "American Academe and the Knowledge-Politics Problem," in *The American Academic Profession: Transformation in Contemporary Higher Education*, ed. Joseph C. Hermanowicz (Baltimore: Johns Hopkins University Press, 2011); Lamont, *How Professors Think: Inside the Curious World of Academic Judgment* (Cambridge, MA: Harvard University Press, 2009).

67. Some critics of business education might view the model as one of stability, aimed at the maintenance of students' class status through education. See Debra J. Schleef, *Managing Elites: Professional Socialization in Law and Business Schools* (Lantham, MD: Rowman & Littefield, 2006), 15.

68. Mitchell L. Stevens, Elizabeth A. Armstrong, and Richard Arum, "Sieve, Incubator, Temple, Hub: Empirical and Theoretical Advances in the Sociology of Higher Education," *Annual Review of Sociology* 34 (2008): 141.

69. Though elite business schools are sometimes depicted pejoratively as "finishing schools," the term also suggests familiarizing students with the norms embraced in corporations, see Schleef, *Managing Elites*.

70. The view of socialization presented in this book is from only one perspective, that of a single faculty member at a given moment in time (see the methodological discussion in the introduction).

71. The Harvard Business School has long been considered a favorite breeding ground for US chief executives, and corporations have long sent their promising employees to the School to develop them into the next elite. See C. Wright Mills, *The Power Elite* (New York: Oxford University Press, 1959), 143.

72. Charles Perrow, *Organizing America: Wealth, Power, and the Origins of Corporate Capitalism* (Princeton, NJ: Princeton University Press, 2002), 10.

73. Recent corporate crises include the 2001 Enron scandal and the 2008 Lehman

Brothers bankruptcy. For a discussion of these crises, see Greta R. Krippner, *Capitalizing on Crisis: The Political Origins of the Rise of Finance* (Cambridge, MA: Harvard University Press, 2011); Michael Lounsbury and Paul Morris Hirsch, *Markets on Trial: The Economic Sociology of the U.S. Financial Crisis*, vol. 30, Research in the Sociology of Organizations (Bingley, UK: Emerald, 2010).

74. Melville Dalton, *Men Who Manage: Fusions of Feeling and Theory in Administration* (New York: John Wiley & Sons, 1959).

75. Robert Jackall, *Moral Mazes: The World of Corporate Managers* (New York: Oxford University Press, 1988).

76. Calvin Morrill, *The Executive Way: Conflict Management in Corporations* (Chicago: University of Chicago Press, 1995); Leslie A. Perlow, "Boundary Control: The Social Ordering of Work and Family Time in a High-Tech Corporation," *Administrative Science Quarterly* 43, no. 2 (1998).

77. Karen Ho, *Liquidated: An Ethnography of Wall Street* (Durham, NC: Duke University Press, 2009), 4–13.

78. Frank C. Pierson, *The Education of American Businessmen: A Study of University-College Programs in Business Administration* (New York: McGraw-Hill, 1959), 92.

79. Calvin Morrill, "Conflict Management, Honor, and Organizational Change," *American Journal of Sociology* 97, no. 3 (1991): 585. The "rules of the game" described by Morrill apply across settings, but some industries operate according to added subrules. For an example of such subrules in the investment banking industry, see Robert G. Eccles and Dwight B. Crane, *Doing Deals: Investment Banks at Work* (Boston: Harvard Business School Press, 1988).

80. Durkheim, *Leçons de sociologie*, 49.

81. Past research suggests how members of lower-status groups "consent" to unequal social arrangements, but a similar process might apply to higher-status groups as well. See Paul Willis, *Learning to Labor: How Working Class Kids Get Working Class Jobs* (New York: Columbia University Press, 1977); Pierre Bourdieu, *The Logic of Practice* (Stanford, CA: Stanford University Press, 1990).

82. Some teaching notes focus on the role of luck or context in a protagonist's success or failure, but most do not comment on these factors.

83. Srikant M. Datar, David A. Garvin, and Patrick Cullen, *Rethinking the MBA: Business Education at a Crossroads* (Boston: Harvard Business Press, 2010), 162.

84. Charles I. Gragg, *Because Wisdom Can't Be Told* (HBSP Case 9-451-005) (Cambridge, MA: President and Fellows of Harvard College, 1940), 3–5.

85. The citations are taken from Sandra J. Sucher, *Action Planning: An LCA Perspective*. Harvard Business School Module Note 605-079 (Boston: Presidents and Fellows of Harvard College, 2011), 3; Lynn Sharp Paine, *Instructor's Guide to Leadership and Corporate Accountability (LCA)* (HBSP Note 5-307-032) (Cambridge, MA: President and Fellows of Harvard College, 2006), 5. Another School teaching note posits that managers' actions build on "personal, family, and cultural values, tenets of our religious beliefs and personal philosophies, past experiences, prior knowledge, and general understanding of what morality means," but again steers clear of articulating what such morals might entail. See Sandra J. Sucher and Nien-hê Hsieh, *A Framework for Ethical Reasoning*. Harvard Business School Background Note 610-050 (Boston: Presidents and

Fellows of Harvard College, 2011), 1. A new course introduced in 2013 by Re-
becca Henderson and titled "Reimagining Capitalism" seeks, however, to better
articulate what these morals might entail.

86. Durkheim, *Leçons de sociologie*, 49.

Postscript

1. I partly followed colleagues' advice and began another project (now published)
on commerce in cadavers for medical education and research.

2. Bronislaw Malinowski, *A Diary in the Strict Sense of the Term* (Stanford, CA:
Stanford University Press, 1989), 107.

Appendix

1. Walter Benjamin, "Romans de servantes du siècle précédent," in *Je déballe ma
bibliothèque* (Paris: Editions Payots et Rivages, 2000).

2. Daniel J. Boorstin, *The Americans: The Colonial Experience* (New York: Random
House, 1958), 169–88.

3. See Scott Snook, "Transformational Leader Development" (paper presented at
the Conference on Research on Positive Organizational Scholarship, University
of Michigan, December 7, 2006).

4. Kai T. Erikson, "A Comment on Disguised Observation in Sociology," *Social
Problems* 14, no. 4 (1967): 368.

5. Howard S. Becker et al., *Boys in White: Student Culture in Medical School* (Chicago: University of Chicago Press, 1961), 17.

6. Michael Taussig, *Walter Benjamin's Grave* (Chicago: University of Chicago
Press, 2006), 62.

7. Peggy Reeves Sanday, "The Ethnographic Paradigm(s)," *Administrative Science
Quarterly* 24, no. 4 (1979): 527.

8. Clifford Geertz, *Works and Lives: The Anthropologist as Author* (Stanford, CA:
Stanford University Press, 1988).

9. Robert E. Park and Ernest W. Burgess, *The City: Suggestions for Investigation of
Human Behavior in the Urban Environment* (Chicago: University of Chicago
Press, 1984), 12.

10. Peter Moskos describes a similar "flattening-out" of his learning curve after one
year in the field. Moskos, *Cop in the Hood: My Year Policing Baltimore's Eastern
District* (Princeton, NJ: Princeton University Press, 2008), 194.

11. For similar methodological challenges, see ibid., 12.

12. Gaye Tuchman, *Wannabe U: Inside the Corporate University* (Chicago: University
of Chicago Press, 2009), 18.

13. John Van Maanen and Deborah Kolb, "The Professional Apprentice: Observa-
tions on Fieldwork Roles in Two Organizational Settings," in *Research in the
Sociology of Organizations*, ed. S. B. Bacharach and S. M. Mitchell (Greenwich,
CT: JAI Press, 1985), 4–5.

14. I do not compare, for instance, the School's practices on course delivery to
those described by recent British scholars of higher education. See Dennis

Hayes and Robin Wynyard, *The McDonaldization of Higher Education* (Westport, CT: Bergin & Garvey, 2002).

15. Roderick D. McKenzie, "The Ecological Approach to the Study of the Human Community," in Park and Burgess, *City*, 67.

16. Ibid., 68.

17. Rakesh Khurana, *From Higher Aims to Hired Hands: The Social Transformation of American Business Schools and the Unfulfilled Promise of Management as a Profession* (Princeton, NJ: Princeton University Press, 2007).

18. Robert M. Emerson, *Contemporary Field Research: Perspectives and Formulations*, 2nd ed. (Long Grove, IL: Waveland Press, 2001), 113–52; Robert R. Faulkner and Howard S. Becker, "Studying Something You Are Part Of: The View from the Bandstand," *Ethnologie française* 38, no. 1 (2008).

19. Sanday, "Ethnographic Paradigm(s)," 528.

20. My history may have prepared me, before I knew it, for ethnographic pursuits. I encountered French society growing up in Paris in a first-generation immigrant family, lived as a "foreigner" in Asia for extended periods of time during my youth, and share my life with a same-sex partner in a society where heterosexual relationships prevail.

21. Robert A. Georges and Michael O. Jones, *People Studying People: The Human Element in Fieldwork* (Berkeley: University of California Press, 1980), 3.

22. For an exception, see Martha S. Feldman, Jeannine Bell, and Michele Tracy Berger, *Gaining Access: A Practical and Theoretical Guide for Qualitative Researchers* (Walnut Creek, CA: AltaMira Press, 2003).

23. Sanday, "Ethnographic Paradigm(s)."

24. Carolyn Ellis and Michael Flaherty, *Investigating Subjectivity: Research on Lived Experience* (Newbury Park, CA: Sage, 1992).

25. Kenneth E. Read, *The High Valley* (New York: Columbia University Press, 1980), ix.

26. Ibid., 250.

27. Pierre Bourdieu and Loïc Wacquant, *Réponses: Pour une anthropologie réflexive* (Paris: Seuil, 1992); Paul Rabinow, *Reflections on Fieldwork in Morocco* (Berkeley: University of California Press, 1977); George E. Marcus and Michael F. Fischer, *Anthropology as Cultural Critique: An Experimental Moment in the Human Sciences* (Chicago: University of Chicago Press, 1986). Also see Raymond Firth's introduction to Bronislaw Malinowski's diaries in Malinowski, *A Diary in the Strict Sense of the Term* (Stanford, CA: Stanford University Press, 1989), xviii.

28. Elenore Smith Bowen, *Return to Laughter: An Anthropological Novel* (New York: Harper, 1954).

29. Some classical examples are Rabinow, *Reflections on Fieldwork*; Jean-Paul Dumont, *The Headman and I* (Austin: University of Texas Press, 1978); Vincent Crapanzano, *Tuhami: Portrait of a Moroccan* (Chicago: University of Chicago Press, 1980).

30. Loïc Wacquant, *Body and Soul: Ethnographic Notebooks of an Apprentice Boxer* (New York: Oxford University Press, 2003); Jeanne Favret-Saada, *Deadly Words: Witchcraft in the Bocage* (Cambridge, UK: Cambridge University Press, 1980); Kay Kaufman Shelemay, *A Song of Longing: An Ethiopian Journey* (Urbana: University of Illinois Press, 1991).

31. Carolyn Ellis, *Final Negotiations: A Story of Love, Loss, and Chronic Illness* (Philadelphia: Temple University Press, 1995).

32. George E. Marcus and Dick Kushman, "Ethnographies as Text," *Annual Review of Anthropology* 11 (1982): 26. For a discussion of the difference between confessional and reflexive ethnographies, see Kamala Visweswaran, *Fictions of Feminist Ethnography* (Minneapolis: University of Minnesota Press, 1994), 21–23.

33. Visweswaran, *Fictions of Feminist Ethnography*. Ethnography more generally is also often seen as an important lens to study issues of power. See Lilla Abu-Lughod, "Locating Ethnography," *Ethnography* 1, no. 2 (2000): 266.

34. Wacquant, *Body and Soul*, xi.

35. According to Jeanne Favret-Saada (2009), these four criteria define a type of ethnography that permits the researcher to trust his or her feelings and emotions. See Jeanne Favret-Saada, *Désorceler* (Paris: Editions de l'Olivier, 2009), 145–61.

36. Gary Alan Fine, "Field Labor and Ethnographic Reality," *Journal of Contemporary Ethnography* 28, no. 5 (1999): 534.

37. Cited in Geertz, *Works and Lives*, 62.

38. The term is used by Herbert Gans, who adapted it from Buford Junker. See Gans, *The Levittowners: Ways of Life and Politics in a New Suburban Community* (New York: Vantage, 1967), 440; Buford H. Junker, *Field Work* (Chicago: University of Chicago Press, 1960), 35–40. (A third role is that of the "total researcher," who "observes events" without participating.)

39. Sallie Westwood, *All Day, Every Day: Factory and Family in the Making of Women's Lives* (Urbana: University of Illinois Press, 1984), and Moskos, *Cop in the Hood*.

40. Moskos, *Cop in the Hood*, 13–14.

41. Rachel Sherman, *Class Acts: Service and Inequality in Luxury Hotels* (Berkeley: University of California Press, 2007); Matthew Desmond, *On the Fireline: Living and Dying with Wildland Firefighters* (Chicago: University of Chicago Press, 2007), 284. For more covert examples, see Donald Roy, "Banana Time: Job Satisfaction and Informal Interaction," *Human Organization* 18, no. 4 (1959); Michael Burawoy, *Manufacturing Consent: Changes in the Labor Process under Monopoly Capitalism* (Chicago: University of Chicago Press, 1979).

42. For examples of role conflict, see Gans, *Levittowners*, 441–42.

43. Nels Anderson, *The Hobo: The Sociology of the Homeless Man* (Chicago: University of Chicago Press, 1961), xiii.

44. Michèle Lamont, *How Professors Think: Inside the Curious World of Academic Judgment* (Cambridge, MA: Harvard University Press, 2009).

45. For examples, see Richard C. Hodgson, Daniel J. Levinson, and Abraham Zaleznik, *The Executive Role Constellation: An Analysis of Personality and Role Relations in Management* (Boston: Harvard University, Division of Research, Graduate School of Business Administration, 1965); Lisa Capps and Elinor Ochs, *Constructing Panic: The Discourse of Agoraphobia* (Cambridge, MA: Harvard University Press, 1995); Sara Lawrence-Lightfoot, *The Art and Science of Portraiture* (San Francisco: Jossey-Bass, 1997).

46. Florence Weber provides another example of a desynchronized disclosure. See Weber, *Manuel de l'éthnographe* (Paris: Presses Universitaires de France, 2008).

47. Talcott Parsons and Gerald M. Platt referred to this danger in their study of the US university system, noting that they were "active participants" and came

"perilously close to setting ourselves up as judges in our own cases." The solution lay, in their opinion, in exposing their findings and themselves to the judgment of their peers. See Parsons and Platt, *The American University* (Cambridge, MA: Harvard University Press, 1973), 28.

48. This project is technically my third in-depth field project.

49. Cara E. Richards, *Man in Perspective* (New York: Random House, 1972), 299.

50. As the authors of an early study of universities remarked, "A university is an institution which applies systematic research to almost everything under the sun—except itself," see University of Pennsylvania, "Report of the Educational Survey, the First Year," (1955).

51. For a discussion of field research issues related to intimacy and autonomy, see Michel Anteby, "Relaxing the Taboo on Telling Our Own Stories: Upholding Professional Distance *and* Personal Involvement," *Organization Science*, forthcoming, doi: 10.1287/orsc.1120.0777, 2012.

52. Jean M. Bartunek and Meryl R. Louis, *Insider/Outsider Team Research* (Thousand Oaks, CA: Sage, 1996).

53. Rabinow, *Reflections on Fieldwork*, 155–61.

54. Furthermore, those without power in a situation typically seek "diagnostic information" and can therefore be ideal observers. See Susan T. Fiske and Eric Dépret, "Control, Interdependance and Power: Understanding Social Cognition in Its Social Context," *European Review of Social Psychology* 7 (1996).

55. The confusion echoed moments when Laura Bohannen was labeled a witch because she breached social norms (such as approaching water thought to breed disease). See Bowen, *Return to Laughter*, 248–50.

56. John Van Maanen, *Tales of the Field: On Writing Ethnography* (Chicago: University of Chicago Press, 1988), 35.

57. Theodore Caplow and Reece J. McGee, *The Academic Marketplace* (New York: Basic Books, 1958), 6.

58. Cited in Robin Leidner, *Fast Food, Fast Talk: Service Work and the Routinization of Everyday Life* (Berkeley: University of California Press, 1993), 236.

59. Van Maanen and Kolb, "Professional Apprentice," 24.

60. Everett C. Hughes, "Who Studies Whom?" *Human Organization* 33 (1974). For an example of such reactions, see Nancy Scheper-Hughes, *Saints, Scholars, and Schizophrenics: Mental Illness in Rural Ireland* (Berkeley: University of California Press, 2001), 311.

61. Pierre Bourdieu, *Homo Academicus* (Paris: Editions de Minuit, 1984), 12 (author's translation).

62. Irving Goldman, cited in Taussig, *Walter Benjamin's Grave*, 145.

63. Ibid., *What Color Is the Sacred?* 64.

64. Rabinow, *Reflections on Fieldwork*, 3.

65. Anthony Forge, "The Lonely Anthropologist," *New Society* 10 (1967).

66. Peter Moskos, "In Defense of Doing Nothing: The Methodological Utility of Introversion," in *New Directions in Sociology: Essays on Theory and Methodology in the 21st Century*, ed. Ieva Zake and Michael DeCesare (Jefferson, NC: McFarland, 2011).

67. Parsons and Platt, *American University*, 29.

68. Frances R. Donovan, *The Schoolma'am* (New York: Fredericks A. Stockes, 1938), xi.

69. Mitchell L. Stevens, *Creating a Class: College Admissions and the Education of Elites* (Cambridge, MA: Harvard University Press, 2007); Tuchman, *Wannabe U*; Lamont, *How Professors Think.*

70. University of Pennsylvania, "Report of the Educational Survey."

71. Unauthorized accounts of unnamed academic settings seem fairly rare. For an example, see Rebekah Nathan, *My Freshman Year: What a Professor Learned by Becoming a Student* (Ithaca, NY: Cornell University Press, 2005). Another example that seems to have gotten its author fired is *Academy X*, a "fictional" account of an elite private school. Andrew Trees, *Academy X* (New York: Bloomsbury, 2006); Allen Salkin, "Private School, Public Fuss," *New York Times*, November 18, 2007.

72. Jacques Siracusa, *Vacances sociologiques: Enseigner la sociologie à l'université* (Saint Denis, France: Presses Universitaires de Vincennes, 2008); Shamus Rahman Khan, *Privilege: The Making of an Adolescent Elite at St. Paul's School* (Princeton, NJ: Princeton University Press, 2010); Atul Gawande, *Complications: A Surgeon's Notes on an Imperfect Science* (New York: Henry Holt, 2002); Henry Rosovsky, *The University: An Owner's Manual* (New York: W. W. Norton, 1990); Byron J. Good, *Medicine, Rationality and Experience: An Anthropological Perspective* (Cambridge, UK: Cambridge University Press, 1994).

73. See for examples: David W. Ewing, *Inside the Harvard Business School: Strategies and Lessons of America's Leading Business School* (New York: Times, 1990); Srikant M. Datar, David A. Garvin, and Patrick Cullen, *Rethinking the MBA: Business Education at a Crossroads* (Boston: Harvard Business Press, 2010).

74. Jeffrey Cruikshank, *A Delicate Experience: The Harvard Business School, 1908–1945* (Boston: Harvard Business School Press, 1987).

75. Fritz J. Roethlisberger, *The Elusive Phenomena: An Autobiographical Account of My Work in the Field of Organizational Behavior at the Harvard Business School,* ed. George F. F. Lombard (Boston: Harvard University Press, 1977); Melvin T. Copeland, *And Mark an Era: The Story of the Harvard Business School* (New York: Little, Brown, 1958).

76. Charles D. Orth, *Social Structure and Learning Climate: The First Year at the Harvard Business School* (Boston: Division of Research, Graduate School of Business Administration, Harvard University, 1963).

77. Melvin Konner, *Becoming a Doctor: A Journey of Initiation in Medical School* (New York: Viking, 1987). Melvin D. Williams, *The Ethography of an Anthropology Department (1959–1979): An Academic Village* (Lewiston, NY: Edwin Mellen Press, 2002).

78. Ruben Gaztambide-Fernandez, *The Best of the Best: Becoming Elite at an American Boarding School* (Cambridge, MA: Harvard University Press, 2009); Tuchman, *Wannabe U.*

79. Amy J. Binder and Kate Wood, *Becoming Right: How Campuses Shape Young Conservatives* (Princeton, NJ: Princeton University Press, 2012); Elizabeth A. Armstrong and Laura T. Hamilton, *Paying for the Party: How College Maintains Inequality* (Cambridge, MA: Harvard University Press, 2013).

80. Joel Seligman, *The High Citadel: The Influence of Harvard Law School* (Boston: Houghton Mifflin, 1978).

81. A typical example is J. Paul Mark, *The Empire Builders: Inside the Harvard Business School* (New York: William Morrow, 1987). An unusual example, a crime

novel set at the School, also fits the subgenre. See Jeffrey Cruikshank, *Murder at the B-School* (New York: Mysterious Press/Time Warner Books, 2004).

82. John Van Maanen, "Golden Passports: Managerial Socialization and Graduate Education," *Review of Higher Education* 6, no. 4 (1983).

83. Jeffrey W. Riemer, "Varieties of Opportunistic Research," *Journal of Contemporary Ethnography* 5, no. 4 (1977).

84. Philip Delves Broughton, *Ahead of the Curve: Two Years at the Harvard Business School* (New York: Penguin, 2008).

85. Fran Worden Henry, *Toughing It Out at Harvard: The Making of a Woman MBA* (New York: G. P. Putnam's Sons, 1983).

86. Authenticity, plausibility, and criticality have been identified as three crucial qualities of "convincing" ethnographic texts. Karen Golden-Biddle and Karen Locke, "Appealing Work: An Investigation of How Ethnographic Texts Convince," *Organization Science* 4, no. 4 (1993).

87. Kenton W. Elderkin, Mutiny on the Harvard Bounty: The Harvard Business School and the Decline of the Nation (Mansfield, OH: Elderkin Associates, 1996).

References

AACSB. "Average Faculty Salaries at U.S. AACSB International Member Schools." http://www.aacsb.edu/dataandresearch/salaries.asp (accessed April 1, 2010).

Abbott, Andrew. "Status and Status Strain in the Professions." *American Journal of Sociology* 86, no. 4 (1981): 819–35.

———. *The System of Professions: An Essay on the Division of Expert Labor.* Chicago: University of Chicago Press, 1988.

Abend, Gabriel. "The Origins of Business Ethics in American Universities, 1902–1936." *Business Ethics Quarterly* 23, no. 2 (2013): 171–205.

Abu-Lughod, Lilla. "Locating Ethnography." *Ethnography* 1, no. 2 (2000): 261–67.

Adler, Patricia, and Peter Adler. "The Identity Career of the Graduate Student: Professional Socialization to Academic Sociology." *American Sociologist* 36, no. 2 (2005): 11–27.

Adler, Paul S., and Bryan Borys. "Two Types of Bureaucracy: Enabling and Coercive." *Administrative Science Quarterly* 41, no. 1 (1996): 61–89.

Amburgey, Terry L., Dawn Kelly, and William P. Barnett. "The Dynamics of Organizational Change and Failure." *Administrative Science Quarterly* 38 (1993): 51–73.

Anderson, Max, and Peter Escher. *The MBA Oath: Setting a Higher Standard for Business Leaders.* New York: Portfolio, 2010.

Anderson, Nels. *The Hobo: The Sociology of the Homeless Man.* Chicago: University of Chicago Press, 1961.

Anteby, Michel. "Relaxing the Taboo on Telling Our Own Stories: Upholding Professional Distance *and* Personal Involvement." *Organization Science.* Forthcoming, doi: 10.1287/orsc.1120.0777, 2012.

Armstrong, Elizabeth A., and Laura T. Hamilton. *Paying for the Party: How College Maintains Inequality.* Cambridge, MA: Harvard University Press, 2013.

Augier, Mie, and James G. March. *The Roots, Rituals, and Rhetorics of Change: North American Business Schools after the Second World War.* Stanford, CA: Stanford University Press, 2011.

Bailey, Frederick G. *Morality and Expediency: The Folklore of Academic Politics.* Chicago: Aldine, 1977.

Barker, James R. "Tightening the Iron Cage: Concertive Control in Self-Managing Teams." *Administrative Science Quarterly* 38, no. 3 (1993): 408–37.

Barley, Stephen R. "Technology as an Occasion for Structuring: Evidence from Observation of CT Scanners and the Social Order of Radiology Departments." *Administrative Science Quarterly* 31, no. 1 (1986): 78–108.

Barley, Stephen R., and Gideon Kunda. "Bringing Work Back In." *Organization Science* 12, no. 1 (2001): 76–95.

Barlow, Andrew L. "Coordination and Control: The Rise of Harvard University, 1825–1910." Doctoral dissertation, Harvard University, 1979.

Barnes, Louis B., C. Roland Christensen, and Abby J. Hansen. *Teaching and the Case Method.* Boston: Harvard Business School Press, 1994.

Bartunek, Jean M. "Changing Interpretive Schemes and Organizational Restructuring: The Example of a Religious Order." *Administrative Science Quarterly* 29, no. 3 (1984): 355–72.

Bartunek, Jean M., and Meryl R. Louis. *Insider/Outsider Team Research.* Thousand Oaks, CA: Sage, 1996.

Bartunek, Jean M., and Sara L. Rynes. "The Construction and Contributions of 'Implications for Practice': What's in Them and What Might They Offer?" *Academy of Management Learning and Education* 9, no. 1 (2010): 100–117.

Bateman, Patrick. "Two Parables of the Wild Turkey." *Harbus*, November 16, 2007, 13.

Baudissin, Count Wolf. "The New German Army." *Foreign Affairs* 34, no. 1 (1955): 1–13.

Bechky, Beth. "Object Lessons: Workplace Artifacts as Representations of Occupational Jurisdiction." *American Journal of Sociology* 109, no. 3 (2003): 720–52.

Becker, Howard S. *Outsiders: Studies in the Sociology of Deviance.* London: Free Press, 1963.

Becker, Howard S., Blanche Geer, Everett C. Hughes, and Strauss L. Anselm. *Boys in White: Student Culture in Medical School.* Chicago: University of Chicago Press, 1961.

Beer, Michael. *High Commitment, High Performance: How to Build a Resilient Organization for Sustained Advantage.* San Francisco: Jossey-Bass, 2009.

Bellah, R. N., R. Madsen, W. M. Sullivan, A. Swidler, and S. M. Tipton. *Habits of the Heart: Individualism and Commitment in American Life.* New York: Harper and Row, 1985.

Bellamy, Edward. *Looking Backward, 2000–1887.* New York: Grosset and Dunlap, 1888.

Benford, Robert D., and David A. Snow. "Framing Processes and Social Movements: An Overview and Assessment." *American Sociological Review* 26 (2000): 611–39.

Benjamin, Walter. *The Arcades Project.* Translated by H. Eiland and K. McLaughlin. Cambridge, MA: Harvard University Press, 1999.

———. "Romans de servantes du siècle précédent." In *Je déballe ma bibliothèque*, 77–84. Paris: Editions Payots et Rivages, 2000.

Berelson, Bernard. *Graduate Education in the United States.* New York: McGraw-Hill, 1960.

Beyer, Janice M., and Harrison M. Trice. "The Communication of Power Relations in Organizations through Cultural Rites." In *Inside Organizations: Understanding the Human Dimension*, edited by Michael Owen Jones, Michael Dane Moore and Richard Christopher Snyder, 141–57. Newbury Park, CA: Sage, 1988.

Beyer Blinder Belle (Architects & Planners LLP). "Campus Plan Executive Report." 2007.

Biggart, Nicole Woolsey. *Charismatic Capitalism: Direct Selling Organizations in America.* Chicago: University of Chicago Press, 1989.

Binder, Amy J., and Kate Wood. *Becoming Right: How Campuses Shape Young Conservatives*. Princeton, NJ: Princeton University Press, 2012.

Boltanski, Luc, and Eve Chiapello. *Le nouvel esprit du capitalisme*. Paris: Gallimard, 1999.

Boorstin, Daniel J. *The Americans: The Colonial Experience*. New York: Random House, 1958.

Both, Anne. *Les managers et leurs discours: Anthropology de la rhéthorique managériale*. Bordeaux: Presses Universitaires de Bordeaux, 2008.

Bourdieu, Pierre. *Homo academicus*. Paris: Editions de Minuit, 1984.

———. *The Logic of Practice*. Stanford, CA: Stanford University Press, 1990.

———. *Méditations Pascaliennes*. Paris: Editions du Seuil, 1997.

———. "Remarques provisoires sur la perception sociale du corps." *Actes de la recherche en sciences sociales* 14, no. 1 (1977): 51–54.

Bourdieu, Pierre, and Jean-Claude Passeron. *Reproduction in Education, Society, and Culture*. London: Sage, 1990.

Bourdieu, Pierre, and Loïc Wacquant, J.D. *Réponses: Pour une anthropologie réflexive*. Paris: Seuil, 1992.

Bowen, Elenore Smith. *Return to Laughter: An Anthropological Novel*. New York: Harper, 1954.

Bradney, Philip. "The Joking Relationship in Industry." *Human Relations* 10, no. 2 (1957): 179–87.

Bradt, Steve. "After 78 Years at Harvard, Danilov Bells Will Return to Russia." *Harvard University Gazette*, May 29, 2008.

Bugental, James F. T. "The Silence of the Sky." In *Interpersonal Behavior: Communication and Understanding in Relationships*, edited by Anthony G. Athos and John J. Gabarro, 176–85. Englewood Cliffs, NJ: Prentice-Hall, 1978.

Bulletin Staff. "Hi-Ho, Hi-Ho: Class of 2007 Goes to Work." *HBS Alumni Bulletin*, 2007, 11.

———. "Rags to Riches." *HBS Alumni Bulletin*, March 2008, 48.

———. "Where Are They Now?" *HBS Alumni Bulletin*, 2007, 14.

Burawoy, Michael. "For Public Sociology." *American Sociological Review* 70 (2005): 4–28.

———. *Manufacturing Consent: Changes in the Labor Process under Monopoly Capitalism*. Chicago: University of Chicago Press, 1979.

Burns, Tom. *The BBC: Public Institution and Private World*. London: MacMillan Press, 1977.

Camic, Charles, Neil Gross, and Michèle Lamont. *Social Knowledge in the Making*. Chicago: University of Chicago Press, 2011.

Caplow, Theodore, and Reece J. McGee. *The Academic Marketplace*. New York: Basic Books, 1958.

Capps, Lisa, and Elinor Ochs. *Constructing Panic: The Discourse of Agoraphobia*. Cambridge, MA: Harvard University Press, 1995.

Carlile, Paul R. "Using Artifacts to Interpret and Negotiate Knowledge across Domains." In *Artifacts and Organizations*, edited by Anat Rafaeli and Michael Pratt. Mahwah, NJ: Lawrence Erlbaum, 2004.

Chan, Cheris Shun-ching. "Invigorating the Content in Social Embeddedness: An Ethnography of Life Insurance Transactions in China." *American Journal of Sociology* 115, no. 3 (2009): 712–54.

Chandler, Alfred D. *The Visible Hand: The Managerial Revolution in American Business.* Cambridge, MA: Harvard University Press, 1977.

Chatman, Jennifer. "Matching People and Organizations: Selection and Socialization in Public Accounting Firms." *Administrative Science Quarterly* 36 (1991): 459–484.

Christensen, C. Roland, David A. Garvin, and Ann Sweet, eds. *Education for Judgment: The Artistry of Discussion Leadership.* Boston: Harvard Business School Press, 1991.

Christensen, Clayton M. "If Harvard Business School Were a Religion, It Could Be Mormonism." http://www.washingtonpost.com/national/on-leadership/if-harvard-business-school-were-a-religion-it-could-be-mormonism/2012/05/11/gIQA04biIU_story.html (accessed July 30, 2012).

Cohen, Michael D., and Paul Bacdayan. "Organizational Routines Are Stored as Procedural Memory: Evidence from a Laboratory Study." *Organization Science* 5, no. 4 (1994): 554–68.

Cohen, Peter. *The Gospel According to the Harvard Business School: The Education of America's Managerial Elite.* Baltimore: Penguin, 1973.

Copeland, Melvin T. *And Mark an Era: The Story of the Harvard Business School.* New York: Little, Brown, 1958.

Crane, Diana. *Invisible Colleges: Diffusion of Knowledge in Scientific Communities.* Chicago: University of Chicago Press, 1972.

Crapanzano, Vincent. *Tuhami: Portrait of a Moroccan.* Chicago: University of Chicago Press, 1980.

Cruikshank, Jeffrey. *A Delicate Experience: The Harvard Business School, 1908–1945.* Boston: Harvard Business School Press, 1987.

———. "A Force for Good." *HBS Alumni Bulletin,* December 2008, 31–37.

———. *Murder at the B-School.* New York: Mysterious Press/Time Warner Books, 2004.

Dalton, Melville. *Men Who Manage: Fusions of Feeling and Theory in Administration.* New York: John Wiley & Sons, 1959.

Datar, Srikant M., David A. Garvin, and Patrick Cullen. *Rethinking the MBA: Business Education at a Crossroads.* Boston: Harvard Business Press, 2010.

Delves Broughton, Philip. *Ahead of the Curve: Two Years at the Harvard Business School.* New York: Penguin, 2008.

Densley, James A. "Street Gang Recruitment: Signaling, Screening, and Selection." *Social Problems* 59, no. 3 (2011): 301–21.

Desmond, Matthew. *On the Fireline: Living and Dying with Wildland Firefighters.* Chicago: University of Chicago Press, 2007.

Dobbin, Frank. *Inventing Equal Opportunity.* Princeton, NJ: Princeton University Press, 2009.

Dober Lidsky Craig and Associates. "Harvard University, Graduate School of Business Administration: Campus Master Plan." 1996.

Donham, Wallace B. "Report of the President and Treasurer of Harvard College 1924–25." *Official Register of Harvard University* 23, no. 2 (1926): 117–24.

Donovan, Frances R. *The Schoolma'am.* New York: Fredericks A. Stockes, 1938.

Douglas, Mary. *How Institutions Think.* Syracuse, NY: Syracuse University Press, 1986.

———. *Purity and Danger: An Analysis of Concepts of Pollution and Taboo.* New York: Routledge Classics, 2002.

Dumont, Jean-Paul. *The Headman and I.* Austin: University of Texas Press, 1978.

Dumont, Louis. *Essais sur l'individualisme: Une perspective anthropologique sur l'idéologie moderne.* Paris: Seuil, 1983.

Duneier, Mitchell. *Sidewalk.* New York: Farrar, Straus and Giroux, 1999.

———. *Slim's Table: Race, Respectability, and Masculinity.* Chicago: University of Chicago Press, 1992.

Durkheim, Emile. *The Division of Labor in Society.* Glencoe, IL: Free Press, 1964.

———. *Emile Durkheim on Morality and Society.* Edited by Robert N. Bellah. Chicago: University of Chicago Press, 1973.

———. *Leçons de sociologie.* Paris: Presses Universitaires de France, 1950.

———. *Sociologie et philosophie.* Paris: Presses Universitaires de France, 2004.

Durkheim, Emile, and Marcel Mauss. "De quelques formes primitives de classification: Contribution à l'étude des représentations collectives." *Année sociologique* 6 (1903): 1–72.

Eccles, Robert G., and Dwight B. Crane. *Doing Deals: Investment Banks at Work.* Boston: Harvard Business School Press, 1988.

Eisenberg, Theodore, and Martin T. Wells. "Inbreeding in Law School Hiring: Assessing the Performance of Faculty Hired from Within." *Journal of Legal Studies* 29, no. 1 (2000): 369–88.

Elderkin, Kenton W. *Mutiny on the Harvard Bounty: The Harvard Business School and the Decline of the Nation.* Mansfield, OH: Elderkin Associates, 1996.

Elias, Norbert. *The Civilizing Process: Sociogenetic and Psychogenetic Investigations.* Oxford, UK: Blackwell, 2000.

———. *The Court Society.* New York: Pantheon Books, 1983.

———. *The Genesis of the Naval Profession.* Edited by René Moelker and Stephen Mennell. Dublin: University College Dublin Press, 2007.

Ellis, Carolyn. *Final Negotiations: A Story of Love, Loss, and Chronic Illness.* Philadelphia: Temple University Press, 1995.

Ellis, Carolyn, and Michael Flaherty. *Investigating Subjectivity: Research on Lived Experience.* Newbury Park, CA: Sage, 1992.

Emerson, Robert M. *Contemporary Field Research: Perspectives and Formulations.* 2nd ed. Long Grove, IL: Waveland Press, 2001.

Erikson, Kai T. "A Comment on Disguised Observation in Sociology." *Social Problems* 14, no. 4 (1967): 366–73.

Espeland, Wendy Nelson, and Mitchell L. Stevens. "Commensuration as a Social Process." *Annual Review of Sociology* 24 (1998): 313–44.

Ewing, David W. *Inside the Harvard Business School: Strategies and Lessons of America's Leading Business School.* New York: Times, 1990.

Faulkner, Robert R., and Howard S. Becker. "Studying Something You Are Part Of: The View from the Bandstand." *Ethnologie française* 38, no. 1 (2008): 15–21.

Faust, Drew Gilpin. "Harvard and HBS: The Next 100 Years." In *The Centennial Global Business Summit, October 12–14, 2008: Executive Summaries,* 14–15. Cambridge, MA: Presidents and Fellows of Harvard College, 2009.

Favret-Saada, Jeanne. *Deadly Words: Witchcraft in the Bocage.* Cambridge, UK: Cambridge University Press, 1980.

———. *Désorceler.* Paris: Editions de l'Olivier, 2009.

Feldman, Martha S. "Organizational Routines as a Source of Continuous Change." *Organization Science* 11, no. 6 (2000): 611–29.

Feldman, Martha S., Jeannine Bell, and Michele Tracy Berger. *Gaining Access: A Prac-*

tical and Theoretical Guide for Qualitative Researchers. Walnut Creek, CA: AltaMira Press, 2003.

Feldman, Martha S., and Wanda J. Orlikowski. "Practicing Theory and Theorizing Practice." *Organization Science* 22, no. 5 (2011): 1240–53.

Feldman, Martha S., and Brian T. Pentland. "Reconceptualizing Organizational Routines as a Source of Flexibility and Change." *Administrative Science Quarterly* 48 (2003): 94–118.

Fine, Gary Alan. "Field Labor and Ethnographic Reality." *Journal of Contemporary Ethnography* 28, no. 5 (1999): 532–39.

Fiske, Susan T., and Eric Dépret. "Control, Interdependance and Power: Understanding Social Cognition in Its Social Context." *European Review of Social Psychology* 7 (1996): 31–61.

Flexner, Abraham. *Universities: American, English, German.* New York: Oxford University Press, 1930.

Forge, Anthony. "The Lonely Anthropologist." *New Society* 10 (1967): 221–23.

Fox, Renée C. *Experiment Perilous: Physicians and Patients Facing the Unknown.* Glencoe, IL: Free Press, 1959.

Freidson, Eliot. *Professional Powers: A Study in the Institutionalization of Formal Knowledge.* Chicago: University of Chicago Press, 1986.

Frisch-Gauthier, Jacqueline. "Le rire dans les relations de travail." *Revue francaise de sociologie* 2 (1961): 292–303.

Fung, Abby. "Crime Drops in Cambridge." *Harvard Crimson*, June 5, 1997, x.

Galeota, William R. "Class Attendance Falls Drastically as Harvard Observes Moratorium." *Harvard Crimson*, October 16, 1969, 1.

Gambetta, Diego. *Codes of the Underworld: How Criminals Communicate.* Princeton, NJ: Princeton University Press, 2009.

Gambetta, Diego, and Heather Hamill. *Streetwise: How Taxi Drivers Establish Their Customers' Trustworthiness.* New York: Russell Sage Foundation, 2005.

Gans, Herbert. *The Levittowners: Ways of Life and Politics in a New Suburban Community.* New York: Vantage, 1967.

Garfinkel, Harold. *Studies in Ethnomethodology.* Englewood Cliffs, NJ: Prentice Hall, 1967.

Gawande, Atul. *Complications: A Surgeon's Notes on an Imperfect Science.* New York: Henry Holt, 2002.

Gaztambide-Fernandez, Ruben. *The Best of the Best: Becoming Elite at an American Boarding School.* Cambridge, MA: Harvard University Press, 2009.

Geertz, Clifford. *Works and Lives: The Anthropologist as Author.* Stanford, CA: Stanford University Press, 1988.

Gentile, Mary C. "Engaging the Power and Competence of the Faculty." In *Can Ethics Be Taught? Perspectives, Challenges, and Approaches at Harvard Business School*, edited by Thomas R. Piper, Mary C. Gentile and Sharon Daloz Parks, 73–115. Boston: Harvard Business School Press, 1993.

Georges, Robert A., and Michael O. Jones. *People Studying People: The Human Element in Fieldwork.* Berkeley: University of California Press, 1980.

Ghaziani, Amin, and Delia Baldassarri. "Cultural Anchors and the Organization of Differences: A Multi-Method Analysis of LGBT Marches on Washington." *American Sociological Review* 76, no. 2 (2011): 179–206.

Ghoshal, Sumantra. "Bad Management Theories Are Destroying Good Management Practices." *Academy of Management Learning & Education* 4, no. 1 (2005): 75–91.

Gintis, Herbert, and Rakesh Khurana. "Corporate Honesty and Business Education: A Behavioral Model." In *Moral Markets: The Critical Role of Values in the Economy*, edited by Paul J. Zak, 300–327. Princeton, NJ: Princeton University Press, 2008.

Glaser, Barney, and Anselm L. Strauss. *The Discovery of Grounded Theory*. Chicago: Aldine, 1967.

Godden, Alex. "Feathered Friends." *Harbus*, November 5, 2007, 8.

Golden-Biddle, Karen, and Karen Locke. "Appealing Work: An Investigation of How Ethnographic Texts Convince." *Organization Science* 4, no. 4 (1993): 595–616.

Good, Byron J. *Medicine, Rationality and Experience: An Anthropological Perspective*. Cambridge, UK: Cambridge University Press, 1994.

Gouldner, Alvin W. "Cosmopolitans and Locals: Toward an Analysis of Latent Social Rules." *Administrative Science Quarterly* 2 (1957): 281–307.

Gragg, Charles I. *Because Wisdom Can't Be Told*. (HBSP Case 9-451-005.) Cambridge, MA: President and Fellows of Harvard College, 1940.

Granfield, Robert. *Making Elite Lawyers: Visions of Law at Harvard and Beyond*. London: Routledge, 1992.

Grayson, Matthew. "MBA Oath Poll—The Results Are In!" *Harbus*, October 13, 2009, 4.

Gross, Neil. "American Academe and the Knowledge-Politics Problem." In *The American Academic Profession: Transformation in Contemporary Higher Education*, edited by Joseph C. Hermanowicz, 111–41. Baltimore: Johns Hopkins University Press, 2011.

Gross, Neil, and Ethan Fosse. "Why Are Professors Liberal?" *Theory & Society* 41 (2012): 127–68.

Guillén, Mauro F. "Scientific Management's Lost Aesthetic: Architecture, Organization, and the Taylorized Beauty of the Mechanical." *Administrative Science Quarterly* 42, no. 4 (1997): 682–715.

———. *The Taylorized Beauty of the Mechanical: Scientific Management and the Rise of Modernist Architecture*. Princeton, NJ: Princeton University Press, 2006.

Hallett, Tim, and Marc J. Ventresca. "Inhabited Institutions: Social Interactions and Organizational Forms in Gouldner's Patterns of Industrial Bureaucracy." *Theory and Society* 35, no. 2 (2006): 213–36.

Halpern, Greg. *Harvard Works Because We Do*. New York: Quantuck Lane Press, 2003.

Halvorson Company. "The Original Landscape Design of the Harvard Business School, 1925–1927: A Review and Analysis of the Works of Olmsted Brothers, Landscape Architects." 2000.

Harbus staff. "This Month from Baker: Tips and Tidbits from Baker Staff." *Harbus*, April 2, 2007, 4.

Harvard Business School. "Community Values, Spring Report." Boston: Harvard Business School, 2007.

———. "Harvard Business School Annual Report." Cambridge, MA: President and Fellows of Harvard College, 2007.

Harvard Magazine staff. "Baker Re-Belled." *Harvard Magazine* 108, no. 2 (2007): 79.

Harvard University Graduate School of Business Administration. "Information for Research Assistants." Baker Library Historical Collections. E75B.42, 1931.

———. "Information for Research Assistants." Baker Library Historical Collections. E75B.42, 1950.

———. "Nuts and Bolts: A Guide to HBS Services for Research Assistants." Baker Library Historical Collections. E75B.62, 1982.

Harvard University Office of the Senior Vice Provost. "Faculty Development and Diversity, Annual Report 2009." Cambridge, MA: Presidents and Fellows of Harvard College, 2009.

Hayes, Dennis, and Robin Wynyard. *The McDonaldization of Higher Education.* Westport, CT: Bergin & Garvey, 2002.

Heimer, Carol A. "The Unstable Alliance of Law and Morality." In *Handbook of the Sociology of Morality,* edited by Steven Hitlin and Stephen Vaisey, 179–202. New York: Springer, 2010.

Heimer, Carol A., and Lisa R. Staffen. *For the Sake of the Children: The Social Organization of Responsibility in the Hospital and the Home.* Chicago: Chicago University Press, 1998.

Henry, Fran Worden. *Toughing It Out at Harvard: The Making of a Woman MBA.* New York: G. P. Putnam's Sons, 1983.

Heritage, John. *Garfinkel and Ethnomethodology.* Cambridge, UK: Polity Press, 1984.

Hermanowicz, Joseph C. *Lives in Science: How Institutions Affect Academic Careers.* Chicago: University of Chicago Press, 2009.

Hill, Linda. "Exercising Moral Courage: A Developmental Agenda." In *Moral Leadership: The Theory and Practice of Power, Judgment, and Policy,* edited by Deborah L. Rhode, 267–90. San Francisco: Jossey Bass, 2006.

Hill-Popper Besharov, Marya. "Mission Goes Corporate: Understanding Employee Behavior in a Mission-Driven Business." Doctoral dissertation, Harvard University, 2008.

Hitlin, Steven, and Stephen Vaisey. "Back to the Future." In *Handbook of the Sociology of Morality,* edited by Steven Hitlin and Stephen Vaisey, 3–14. New York: Springer, 2010.

Ho, Karen. *Liquidated: An Ethnography of Wall Street.* Durham, NC: Duke University Press, 2009.

Hodgson, Richard C., Daniel J. Levinson, and Abraham Zaleznik. *The Executive Role Constellation: An Analysis of Personality and Role Relations in Management.* Boston: Harvard University, Division of Research, Graduate School of Business Administration, 1965.

Hollingshead, A. B. "Ingroup Membership and Academic Selection." *American Sociological Review* 3, no. 6 (1938): 826–33.

Homans, George C. *The Human Group.* New Brunswick, NJ: Transaction Publishers, 1993.

Hughes, Everett C. *Men and Their Work.* London, UK: Collier-Macmillan, 1958.

———. "Who Studies Whom?" *Human Organization* 33 (1974): 327–34.

———. "Work and Self." In *The Sociological Eye: Selected Papers,* 338–47. Chicago: Aldine-Atherton, 1971.

Huising, Ruthanne, and Susan S. Silbey. "Governing the Gap: Forging Safe Science through Relational Regulation." *Regulation and Governance* 5, no. 1 (2011): 14–42.

Ibarra, Herminia. "Provisional Selves: Experimenting with Image and Identity in Professional Adaptation." *Administrative Science Quarterly* 44, no. 4 (1999): 764–91.

Jackall, Robert. "Morality in Organizations." In *Handbook of the Sociology of Morality*, edited by Steven Hitlin and Stephen Vaisey, 203–10. New York: Springer, 2010.
———. *Moral Mazes: The World of Corporate Managers*. New York: Oxford University Press, 1988.
Jensen, Michael C., and William H. Meckling. "Theory of the Firm: Managerial Behavior, Agency Costs and Ownership Structure." *Journal of Financial Economics* 3, no. 4 (1976): 305–60.
Johnson, Victoria. *Backstage at the Revolution: How the Royal Paris Opera Survived the End of the Old Regime*. Chicago: University of Chicago Press, 2008.
Jones, Graham M. *Trade of the Tricks: Inside the Magician's Craft*. Berkeley: University of California Press, 2011.
Junker, Buford H. *Field Work*. Chicago: University of Chicago Press, 1960.
Kabak, Victoria. "HBS Rings in New Russian Bell." *Harvard Crimson*, October 2, 2007, 1.
Kanter, Rosabeth Moss. *Commitment and Community: Communes and Utopias in Sociological Perspective*. Cambridge, MA: Harvard University Press, 1972.
Katz, Jack. "On the Rhetoric and Politics of Ethnographic Methodology." *Annals of the American Academy of Political and Social Science* 595 (2004): 280–308.
Kelleher, Caren. "Do Grades Matter at HBS?" *Harbus*, September 14, 2009, 1–2.
Kellogg, Katherine C. *Challenging Operations: Medical Reform and Resistance in Surgery*. Chicago: University of Chicago Press, 2011.
Keohane, Nannerl O. *Higher Ground: Ethics and Leadership in the Modern University*. Durham, NC: Duke University Press, 2006.
Kerr, Clark. *The Uses of the University*. 5th ed. Cambridge, MA: Harvard University Press, 2001.
Khan, Jamil. "On-Campus Interview Series: A Spangler Squirrel." *Harbus*, May 10, 2004, 10.
Khan, Shamus Rahman. *Privilege: The Making of an Adolescent Elite at St. Paul's School*. Princeton, NJ: Princeton University Press, 2010.
Khurana, Rakesh. *From Higher Aims to Hired Hands: The Social Transformation of American Business Schools and the Unfulfilled Promise of Management as a Profession*. Princeton, NJ: Princeton University Press, 2007.
Killam, Charles W. "Harvard Graduate School of Business Administration." *Architectural Forum* 47, no. 4 (1927): 305–32.
Kleinman, Arthur. *Writing at the Margin: Discourse between Anthropology and Medicine*. Berkeley: University of California Press, 1997.
Kluge, P. F. *Alma Mater: A College Homecoming*. Reading, MA: Addison Wesley, 1993.
Konner, Melvin. *Becoming a Doctor: A Journey of Initiation in Medical School*. New York: Viking, 1987.
Krippner, Greta R. *Capitalizing on Crisis: The Political Origins of the Rise of Finance*. Cambridge, MA: Harvard University Press, 2011.
Kunda, Gideon. *Engineering Culture: Control and Commitment in High-Tech Corporation*. Philadelphia: Temple University Press, 1992.
Lallement, Michel. *Le travail de l'utopie: Godin et le familistère de guise*. Paris: Belles Lettres, 2009.
Lamont, Michèle. *The Dignity of Working Men: Moralities and the Boundaries of Race, Class, and Immigration*. New York: Russell Sage Foundation, 2000.

———. *How Professors Think: Inside the Curious World of Academic Judgment.* Cambridge, MA: Harvard University Press, 2009.

———. "The Return of the Moral." In *Handbook of the Sociology of Morality*, edited by Steven Hitlin and Stephen Vaisey, v–iix. New York: Springer, 2010.

Lawrence-Lightfoot, Sara. *The Art and Science of Portraiture.* San Francisco: Jossey-Bass, 1997.

Leidner, Robin. *Fast Food, Fast Talk: Service Work and the Routinization of Everyday Life.* Berkeley: University of California Press, 1993.

Light, Jay O. "Harvard and HBS: The Next 100 Years." In *Centennial Global Business Summit, October 12–14 2008: Executive Summaries*, 12–13. Boston: President and Fellows of Harvard College, 2009.

Lorsch, Jay, and Rakesh Khurana. "The Pay Problem." *Harvard Magazine* 112, no. 5 (2010): 30–35.

Lounsbury, Michael, and Paul Morris Hirsch. *Markets on Trial: The Economic Sociology of the U.S. Financial Crisis.* Vol. 30, Research in the Sociology of Organizations. Bingley, UK: Emerald, 2010.

Lynd, Robert S., and Helen Merrell Lynd. *Middletown: A Study in Modern American Culture.* New York: Harcourt Brace, 1929.

Malinowski, Bronislaw. *Argonauts of the Western Pacific: An Account of the Native Enterprise and Adventure in the Archipelagoes of Melanesian New Guinea.* Long Grove, IL: Waveland Press, 1984.

———. *A Diary in the Strict Sense of the Term.* Stanford, CA: Stanford University Press, 1989.

Manohar, Lavanya. "Getting It Right!" *Harbus*, September 29, 2009, 5.

Marcus, George E., and Michael F. Fischer. *Anthropology as Cultural Critique: An Experimental Moment in the Human Sciences.* Chicago: University of Chicago Press, 1986.

Marcus, George E., and Dick Kushman. "Ethnographies as Text." *Annual Review of Anthropology* 11 (1982): 25–69.

Margolis, Joshua D. "Responsibility in Organizational Context." *Business Ethics Quarterly* 11, no. 4 (2001): 431–54.

Mark, J. Paul. *The Empire Builders: Inside the Harvard Business School.* New York: William Morrow, 1987.

Martin, Joanne. *Cultures in Organizations: Three Perspectives.* New York: Oxford University Press, 1992.

Marwell, Nicole P. *Bargaining for Brooklyn: Community Organizations in the Entrepreneurial City.* Chicago: University of Chicago Press, 2007.

Mauss, Marcel. *Manuel d'éthnographie.* Paris: Editions Payot, 1967.

McArthur, John H. "Foreword." In *Principals and Agents: The Structure of Business*, edited by John W. Pratt and Richard J. Zeckhauser, vii-viii. Boston: Harvard Business School Press, 1985.

McKenzie, Roderick D. "The Ecological Approach to the Study of the Human Community." In *The City: Suggestions for Investigation of Human Behavior in the Urban Environment*, edited by Robert E. Park and Ernest W. Burgess, 63–79. Chicago: University of Chicago Press, 1984.

Mead, George H. *Mind, Self and Society from the Standpoint of a Social Behaviorist.* Chicago, IL: University of Chicago Press, 1934.

Menand, Louis. "The Ph.D. Problem: On the Professionalization of Faculty Life, Doctoral Training, and the Academy's Self-Renewal." *Harvard Magazine* III, no. 2 (2009): 28–31, 91.

Michel, Alexandra A. "Transcending Socialization: A Nine-Year Ethnography of the Body's Role in Organizational Control and Knowledge Workers' Transformation." *Administrative Science Quarterly* 56, no. 3 (2011): 325–68.

Mills, C. Wright. *The Power Elite.* New York: Oxford University Press, 1959.

————. *White Collar: The American Middle Classes.* New York: Oxford University Press, 1951.

Mitchell, Stephanie. "Harvard Center Shanghai." *Harvard Magazine* 112, no. 5 (2010): 53.

Morrill, Calvin. "Conflict Management, Honor, and Organizational Change." *American Journal of Sociology* 97, no. 3 (1991): 585–621.

————. "Culture and Organization Theory." *Annals of the American Academy of Political and Social Science* 619, no. 1 (2008): 15–40.

————. *The Executive Way: Conflict Management in Corporations.* Chicago: University of Chicago Press, 1995.

Morrill, Calvin, and David A. Snow. "The Study of Personal Relations in Public Places." In *Together Alone: Personal Relationships in Public Spaces,* edited by Calvin Morrill, David A. Snow and Cindy H. White, 1–22. Berkeley: University of California Press, 2005.

Morrill, Calvin, Mayer N. Zald, and Hayagreeva Rao. "Covert Political Conflict in Organizations: Challenges from Below." *Annual Review of Sociology* 29 (2003): 391–415.

Morrison, Elizabeth Wolfe, and Frances J. Milliken. "Organizational Silence: A Barrier to Change and Development in a Pluralistic World." *Academy of Management Review* 25, no. 4 (2000): 706–25.

Moshe Safdie and Associates. "Harvard Business School Master Plan: Preliminary Design Decisions." 1984.

Moskos, Peter. *Cop in the Hood: My Year Policing Baltimore's Eastern District.* Princeton, NJ: Princeton University Press, 2008.

————. "In Defense of Doing Nothing: The Methodological Utility of Introversion." In *New Directions in Sociology: Essays on Theory and Methodology in the 21st Century,* edited by Ieva Zake and Michael DeCesare, 160–71. Jefferson, NC: McFarland, 2011.

Mukerji, Chandra. *Territorial Ambitions and the Gardens of Versailles.* Cambridge, UK: Cambridge University Press, 1997.

Musselin, Christine. *The Market for Academics.* New York: Routledge, 2009.

Musselin, Christine, and Catherine Paradeise. "France: From Incremental Transition to Institutional Change." In *University Governance: Western European Comparative Perspectives,* edited by Catherine Paradeise, Emanuela Reale, Ivar Bleiklie and Ewan Ferlie, 21–50. Dordrecht: Springer, 2009.

Nathan, Rebekah. *My Freshman Year: What a Professor Learned by Becoming a Student.* Ithaca, NY: Cornell University Press, 2005.

Needham, Rodney. *Right and Left: Essays on Dual Classification.* Chicago: University of Chicago Press, 1973.

Newman, Katherine S. *Falling from Grace: Downward Mobility in the Age of Affluence.* Berkeley: University of California Press, 1988.

Nicolai, Alexander, and David Seidl. "That's Relevant! Different Forms of Practical Relevance in Management Science." *Organization Studies* 31 (2010): 1257–85.

Nohria, Nitin, and Rakesh Khurana. "It's Time to Make Management a True Profession." *Harvard Business Review* 86, no. 10 (2008): 70–77.

O'Reilly, Charles, and Jennifer Chatman. "Culture as Social Control: Corporations, Cults, and Commitment." In *Research in Organizational Behavior*, edited by B. Staw and L. Cummings, 157–200. Greenwich, CT: JAI Press, 1996.

Orr, Julian E. *Talking about Machines: An Ethnography of a Modern Job*. Ithaca, NY: Cornell University Press, 1996.

Orth, Charles D. *Social Structure and Learning Climate: The First Year at the Harvard Business School*. Boston: Division of Research, Graduate School of Business Administration, Harvard University, 1963.

Padgett, John, and Ansell Christopher. "Robust Action and the Rise of the Medici, 1400–1434." *American Journal of Sociology* 98, no. 6 (1993): 1259–1319.

Paine, Lynn Sharp. *Instructor's Guide to Leadership and Corporate Accountability (LCA)*. (HBSP Note 5-307-032.) Cambridge, MA: President and Fellows of Harvard College, 2006.

Paradeise, Catherine, Stéphanie Mignot-Gérard, Jean-Claude Thoenig, Emilie Biland, Aurélie Delemarle, and Gaële Goastellec. "Practical Relevance and Academic Excellence: Four Business Schools in Context." In *The Transformation of Higher Education Institutions and Business Schools*, edited by Andrew Pettigrew. Oxford: Oxford University Press, forthcoming.

Park, Robert E., and Ernest W. Burgess. *The City: Suggestions for Investigation of Human Behavior in the Urban Environment*. Chicago: University of Chicago Press, 1984.

Parks, Sharon Daloz. "Young Adults and the Formation of Professional Ethics." In *Can Ethics Be Taught? Perspectives, Challenges, and Approaches at Harvard Business School*, edited by Thomas R. Piper, Mary C. Gentile and Sharon Daloz Parks, 13–72. Boston: Harvard Business School Press, 1993.

Parsons, Talcott, and Gerald M. Platt. *The American University*. Cambridge, MA: Harvard University Press, 1973.

Pascal, Blaise. *Pensées*. Paris: Dezobrie et E. Magdeleine, 1852.

Patterson, Orlando. "Taking Culture Seriously: A Framework and an Afro-American Illustration." In *Culture Matters: How Values Shape Human Progress*, edited by Lawrence E. Harrison and Samuel P. Huntington, 202–18. New York: Basic Books, 2001.

Paugam, Serge. "Introduction." In *De la division du travail social*. Paris: Presses Universitaires de France, 2007.

Peixotto, Jessica B. *Getting and Spending at the Professional Standard of Living: A Study of the Costs of Living an Academic Life*. New York: Macmillan, 1927.

Perlow, Leslie A. "Boundary Control: The Social Ordering of Work and Family Time in a High-Tech Corporation." *Administrative Science Quarterly* 43, no. 2 (1998): 328–57.

Perlow, Leslie A., and Nelson Repenning. "The Dynamics of Silencing Conflict." *Research in Organizational Behavior* 29 (2009): 195–223.

Perrow, Charles. *Organizing America: Wealth, Power, and the Origins of Corporate Capitalism*. Princeton, NJ: Princeton University Press, 2002.

Perry, Nancy O. "A Job with a Future." *HBS Bulletin* (1990): 3–10.

Petriglieri, Gianpiero, and Jennifer Louise Petriglieri. "Identity Workspaces: The Case of Business Schools." *Academy of Management Learning and Education* 9, no. 1 (2010): 44–60.

Pfeffer, Jeffrey. "A Modest Proposal: How We Might Change the Process and Product of Managerial Research." *Academy of Management Journal* 50, no. 6 (2007): 1334–43.

Pierson, Frank C. *The Education of American Businessmen: A Study of University-College Programs in Business Administration.* New York: McGraw-Hill, 1959.

Piper, Thomas R., Mary C. Gentile, and Sharon Daloz Parks. *Can Ethics Be Taught? Perspectives, Challenges, and Approaches at Harvard Business School.* Boston: Harvard Business School Press, 1993.

Polzer, Jeffrey T., Ranjay Gulati, Rakesh Khurana, and Michael L. Tushman. "Crossing Boundaries to Increase Relevance in Organizational Research." *Journal of Management Inquiry* 18, no. 4 (2009): 280–86.

Pratt, Michael G. "The Good, the Bad, and the Ambivalent: Managing Identification among Amway Distributors." *Administrative Science Quarterly* 45, no. 3 (2000): 456–93.

Primus, V. "Tough Turkeys." *Harvard Magazine* 110, no. 4 (2008): 76.

"Proposed Foot Bridge across the Charles, Named for Weeks, to Link Harvard Groups." *New York Times,* November 9, 1925, 1.

Rabinow, Paul. *Reflections on Fieldwork in Morocco.* Berkeley: University of California Press, 1977.

Ranson, Stewart, Bob Hinings, and Royston Greenwood. "The Structuring of Organizational Structures." *Administrative Science Quarterly* 25, no. 1 (1980): 1–17.

Read, Kenneth E. *The High Valley.* New York: Columbia University Press, 1980.

Reid, Robert. *Year One: An Intimate Look inside Harvard Business School.* New York: Avon, 1994.

Renaut, Alain. *The Era of the Individual: A Contribution to a History of Subjectivity.* Princeton, NJ: Princeton University Press, 1999.

Reuben, Julie A. *The Making of the Modern University: Intellectual Transformation and the Marginalization of Morality.* Chicago: University of Chicago Press, 1996.

Richards, Cara E. *Man in Perspective.* New York: Random House, 1972.

Riemer, Jeffrey W. "Varieties of Opportunistic Research." *Journal of Contemporary Ethnography* 5, no. 4 (1977): 467–77.

Riesman, David. *Constraint and Variety in American Education.* Lincoln: University of Nebraska Press, 1956.

Ritzer, George. *The McDonaldization of Society: An Investigation into the Changing Character of Contemporary Social Life.* Newbury Park, CA: Pine Forge Press, 1993.

Roethlisberger, Fritz J. *The Elusive Phenomena: An Autobiographical Account of My Work in the Field of Organizational Behavior at the Harvard Business School.* Edited by George F. F. Lombard. Boston: Harvard University Press, 1977.

Rosenberg, John S. "An Education in Ethics: Teaching Business Students Life Lessons in Leadership." *Harvard Magazine* 109, no. 1 (2006): 42–49, 102–3.

Rosovsky, Henry. *The University: An Owner's Manual.* New York: W. W. Norton, 1990.

Rosso, Brent D., Kathryn H. Dekas, and Amy Wrzesniewski. "On the Meaning of Work: A Theoretical Integration and Review." *Research in Organizational Behavior* 30 (2010): 91–127.

Roy, Donald. "Banana Time: Job Satisfaction and Informal Interaction." *Human Organization* 18, no. 4 (1959): 158–68.

Ruef, Martin. *The Entrepreneurial Group: Social Identities, Relations, and Collective Action.* Princeton, NJ: Princeton University Press, 2010.

————. "From Higher Aims to Hired Hands: The Social Transformation of American Business Schools and the Unfulfilled Promise of Management as a Profession (Review)." *Administrative Science Quarterly* 53 (2008): 745–52.

Salancik, Gerald R. "Commitment Is Too Easy!" *Organizational Dynamics* 6, no. 1 (1977): 62–80.

Salkin, Allen. "Private School, Public Fuss." *New York Times*, November 18, 2007, ST1–2.

Sanday, Peggy Reeves. "The Ethnographic Paradigm(s)." *Administrative Science Quarterly* 24, no. 4 (1979): 527–38.

Sarfatti Larson, Magali. *The Rise of Professionalism: A Sociological Analysis*. Berkeley: University of California Press, 1977.

Sarfaty, Galit. *Values in Translation: Human Rights and the Culture of the World Bank*. Stanford, CA: Stanford University Press, 2012.

Schein, Edgar H., Inge Shneier, and Curtis H. Barker. *Coercive Persuasion: A Socio-Psychological Analysis of the "Brainwashing" of American Civilian Prisoners by the Chinese Communists*. New York: W. W. Norton, 1961.

Scheper-Hughes, Nancy. *Saints, Scholars, and Schizophrenics: Mental Illness in Rural Ireland*. Berkeley: University of California Press, 2001.

Schleef, Debra J. *Managing Elites: Professional Socialization in Law and Business Schools*. Lantham, MD: Rowman & Littlefield, 2006.

Seligman, Joel. *The High Citadel: The Influence of Harvard Law School*. Boston: Houghton Mifflin, 1978.

Sewell, William Hamilton. *Logics of History: Social Theory and Social Transformation*. Chicago: University of Chicago Press, 2005.

Shamir, Ronen. "The Age of Responsibilization: On Market-Embedded Morality." *Economy and Society* 37, no. 1 (2008): 1–19.

Sharone, Ofer. "Chemistry or Specs: Comparing Job Search Games and Subjective Responses to Unemployment." Paper presented at the International Sociological Association Annual Conference, Gothenburg, Sweden, July 16, 2010.

Shelemay, Kay Kaufman. *A Song of Longing: An Ethiopian Journey*. Urbana: University of Illinois Press, 1991.

"Sherman Hall History." Archives Resource Files (Facilities), HBS Archives, Baker Library Historical Collections, 2008.

Sherman, Rachel. *Class Acts: Service and Inequality in Luxury Hotels*. Berkeley: University of California Press, 2007.

————. "'Time Is Our Commodity': Gender and the Struggle for Occupational Legitimacy among Personal Concierges." *Work and Occupations* 37, no. 1 (2010): 81–114.

Silbey, Susan S. "Taming Prometheus: Talk of Safety and Culture." *Annual Review of Sociology* 35 (2009): 341–69.

Siracusa, Jacques. *Vacances sociologiques: Enseigner la sociologie à l'université*. Saint Denis, France: Presses Universitaires de Vincennes, 2008.

Small, Mario Luis. *Villa Victoria: The Transformation of Social Capital in a Boston Barrio*. Chicago: University of Chicago Press, 2004.

Smelser, Neil J. *Reflections on the University of California: From the Free Speech Movement to the Global University*. Berkeley: University of California Press, 2010.

Smith, Adam. *An Inquiry into the Nature and Causes of the Wealth of Nations*. Dublin: Whitestone, 1776.

Smith, Vicky. *Managing in the Corporate Interest: Control and Resistance in an American Bank.* Berkeley: University of California Press, 1990.

Snook, Scott. "Transformational Leader Development." Paper presented at the Conference on Research on Positive Organizational Scholarship, University of Michigan, December 7, 2006.

Sridhar, Andrew. "MBA Oath: An Oath and Its Flaws." *Harbus,* September 28, 2009, 1, 4.

Stark, David. *The Sense of Dissonance: Accounts of Worth in Economic Life.* Princeton, NJ: Princeton University Press, 2009.

Stevens, Mitchell L. *Creating a Class: College Admissions and the Education of Elites.* Cambridge, MA: Harvard University Press, 2007.

Stevens, Mitchell L., Elizabeth A. Armstrong, and Richard Arum. "Sieve, Incubator, Temple, Hub: Empirical and Theoretical Advances in the Sociology of Higher Education." *Annual Review of Sociology* 34 (2008): 127–51.

Stinchcombe, Arthur L. *Constructing Social Theories.* New York: Harcourt, Brace & World, 1968.

———. *Information and Organizations.* Berkeley: University of California Press, 1990.

———. "Monopolistic Competition as a Mechanism." In *Social Mechanisms: An Analytical Approach to Social Theory,* edited by Peter Hedström and Richard Swedberg, 268–305. Cambridge, UK: Cambridge University Press, 1998.

———. "Social Structure and Organizations." In *Handbook of Organizations,* edited by James G. March, 142–93. Chicago: Rand McNally, 1965.

Subrahmanyam, Sanjay. "One for the Money, Two for the Show." *L'homme* 187–188 (2008): 93–104.

Sucharov, Mira. "Security Ethics and the Modern Military: The Case of the Israel Defense Forces." *Armed Forces & Society* 31, no. 2 (2005): 169–99.

Sucher, Sandra J. *Action Planning: An LCA Perspective.* Harvard Business School Module Note 605-079. Boston: Presidents and Fellows of Harvard College, 2011.

———. *Teaching the Moral Leader: A Literature-Based Leadership Course.* New York: Routledge, 2007.

Sucher, Sandra J., and Nien-hê Hsieh. *A Framework for Ethical Reasoning.* Harvard Business School Background Note 610-050. Boston: Presidents and Fellows of Harvard College, 2011.

Taussig, Michael. *Walter Benjamin's Grave.* Chicago: University of Chicago Press, 2006.

———. *What Color Is the Sacred?* Chicago: University of Chicago Press, 2009.

Thompson, Wayne C., and Marc D. Peltier. "The Education of Military Officers in the Federal Republic of Germany." *Armed Forces & Society* 16, no. 4 (1990): 587–606.

"Timeline." Harvard Business School Institutional Memory website, http://institutional memory.hbs.edu/timeline/1943/h063sc/navy_supply_corps_midshipmen-officers _school_launched.html (accessed November 10, 2008).

Trees, Andrew. *Academy X.* New York: Bloomsbury, 2006.

Trice, Harrison M., and Janice M. Beyer. *The Cultures of Work Organizations.* Englewoods Cliffs, NJ: Prentice Hall, 1993.

Tuchman, Gaye. *Wannabe U: Inside the Corporate University.* Chicago: University of Chicago Press, 2009.

University of Pennsylvania. "Report of the Educational Survey, the First Year." 1955.

Vaisey, Stephen. "Motivation and Justification: A Dual-Process Model of Culture in Action." *American Journal of Sociology* 114, no. 6 (2009): 1675–1715.

———. "Structure, Culture, and Community: The Search for Belonging in 50 Urban Communes." *American Sociological Review* 72, no. 6 (2007): 851–73.

Vallas, Steven Peter. *Work: A Critique*. Cambridge, UK: Polity Press, 2012.

———. "Workers, Firms, and the Dominant Ideology: Hegemony and Consciousness in the Monopoly Core." *Sociological Quarterly* 32 (1991): 61–83.

Van Gennep, Arnold. *The Rites of Passage*. Chicago: University of Chicago Press, 1960.

Van Maanen, John. "Displacing Disney: Some Notes on the Flow of Culture." *Qualitative Sociology* 15, no. 1 (1992): 5–36.

———. "Golden Passports: Managerial Socialization and Graduate Education." *Review of Higher Education* 6, no. 4 (1983): 435–55.

———. "Observations on the Making of Policemen." *Human Organization* 32, no. 4 (1973): 407–18.

———. *Tales of the Field: On Writing Ethnography*. Chicago: University of Chicago Press, 1988.

Van Maanen, John, and Deborah Kolb. "The Professional Apprentice: Observations on Fieldwork Roles in Two Organizational Settings." In *Research in the Sociology of Organizations*, edited by S. B. Bacharach and S. M. Mitchell, 1–33. Greenwich, CT: JAI Press, 1985.

Van Maanen, John, and Gideon Kunda. "Real Feelings: Emotional Expression and Organizational Culture." In *Research in Organizational Behavior*, edited by Barry M. Staw and L. L. Cummings, 43–103. Greenwich, CT: JAI Press, 1989.

Van Maanen, John, and Brian T. Pentland. "Cops and Auditors." In *The Legalistic Organization*, edited by S. Sitkin and R. Bies, 53–90. Beverly Hills, CA: Sage, 1994.

Van Maanen, John, and Edgar H. Schein. "Toward a Theory of Organizational Socialization." In *Research in Organizational Behavior*, edited by B. Staw and L. Cummings, 209–64. Greenwich, CT: JAI Press, 1979.

Vaughan, Diane. "Autonomy, Interdependence, and Social Control: NASA and the Space Shuttle Challenger." *Administrative Science Quarterly* 35, no. 2 (1990): 225–57.

———. *The Challenger Launch Decision: Risky Technology, Culture, and Deviance at NASA*. Chicago: University of Chicago Press, 1996.

———. "The Dark Side of Organizations: Mistake, Misconduct, and Disaster." *Annual Review of Sociology* 25 (1999): 271–305.

———. "Theorizing Disaster: Analogy, Historical Ethnography, and the *Challenger* Accident." *Ethnography* 5 (2004): 313–45.

Veblen, Thorstein. *The Higher Learning in America: A Memorandum on the Conduct of Universities by Businessmen*. New York: B. W. Huebsch, 1918.

Visweswaran, Kamala. *Fictions of Feminist Ethnography*. Minneapolis: University of Minnesota Press, 1994.

Wacquant, Loïc. *Body and Soul: Ethnographic Notebooks of an Apprentice Boxer*. New York: Oxford University Press, 2003.

Wademan, Daisy. *Remember Who You Are: Life Stories That Inspire the Heart and Mind*. Boston: Harvard Business School Press, 2004.

Walsh, James P. "Embracing the Sacred in Our Secular Scholarly World." *Academy of Management Journal* 36, no. 2 (2011): 215–34.

Weber, Florence. *Manuel de l'éthnographe*. Paris: Presses Universitaires de France, 2008.

Weber, Max. *Economy and Society: An Outline of Interpretative Sociology.* Berkeley: University of California Press, 1978.

———. *The Protestant Ethic and the Spirit of Capitalism.* San Francisco: Jossey-Bass, 1958.

———. *The Theory of Social and Economic Organization.* Edited by Talcott Parsons. New York: Free Press, 1947.

Weeks, John. *Unpopular Culture: The Ritual of Complaint in a British Bank.* Chicago, IL: University of Chicago Press, 2004.

Westwood, Sallie. *All Day, Every Day: Factory and Family in the Making of Women's Lives.* Urbana: University of Illinois Press, 1984.

"Where the Women Are—and Aren't." *Harvard Magazine* 113, no. 3 (2011): 47.

White, Harrison C. "Agency as Control." In *Principals and Agents: The Structure of Business,* edited by John W. Pratt and Richard J. Zeckhauser, 187–232. Boston: Harvard Business School Press, 1985.

———. "Innovation in Style." Paper presented at the Instituting and Institutions Conference, University of California, Santa Barbara, March 7, 2003.

Whyte, William F. *Street Corner Society: The Social Structure of an Italian Slum.* Chicago: University of Chicago Press, 1943.

Wickersham, Joan. "What Gets Built at Harvard, What Doesn't, and Why?" *Harvard Magazine* 110, no. 1 (2007): 50–58.

Williams, Melvin D. *The Ethography of an Anthropology Department (1959–1979): An Academic Village.* Lewiston, NY: Edwin Mellen Press, 2002.

Willis, Paul. *Learning to Labor: How Working Class Kids Get Working Class Jobs.* New York: Columbia University Press, 1977.

Wrzesniewski, Amy. "Finding Positive Meaning in Work." In *Positive Organizational Scholarship: Foundations of a New Discipline,* edited by K. S. Cameron, J. E. Dutton and R. E. Quinn, 296–308. San Francisco: Berrett-Koehler, 2003.

Young, Michael F. D., ed. *Knowledge and Control: New Directions for the Sociology of Education.* London: Collier-Macmillan, 1971.

Zelizer, Viviana A. *Economic Lives: How Culture Shapes the Economy.* Princeton, NJ: Princeton University Press, 2010.

———. *Morals and Markets. The Development of Life Insurance in the United States.* New York: Columbia University Press, 1979.

Index

Abbott, Andrew, 181n3
absence, notifications of, 94
Academic Performance Committee, 97
academic purity: Abbott's definition of, 181n3; competing definitions of, 48; HBS reshapes definition of, 13, 36–37, 39, 48, 49
Academy X (Trees), 204n71
"Administrative Practices" course, 38, 182n12
aesthetics, social orders associated with, 19
affirmative-action policies, mainstreaming and routinization of, 127
alumni: become chief executives, 190n71; buy-in, 129–30; evolving composition of, 135; faculty transmit organizational perspective to, 6; fields in which they work, 172n39; in socialization of students, 173n35
Anderson, Nels, 157, 158
athletic facilities, 30–31, 179n53

Bailey, F. G., 43
Baker, George F., 11–12, 18–19, 48
Baker Scholars, 100, 106
Barlow, Andrew L., 176n82
Baudissin, Wolf, 127
"Because Wisdom Can't Be Told" (Gragg), 142
Becker, Howard S., 150, 160, 163
Bellamy, Edward, 35, 37
Benjamin, Walter, 180n57
Berelson, Bernard, 112
"better business standards" narrative, 12, 85, 124, 129

bias, personal, 156
Bohannan, Laura, 155
Boorstin, Daniel, 10
Boston Brahmins, 175n78
Bourdieu, Pierre, 6–7, 117, 125, 160, 168n13
Boys in White (Becker), 150
Briggs, Asa, 124
British Broadcasting Corporation (BBC), 124, 137
Bugental, James, 128
Burns, Tom, 137
business schools: average faculty salary, 104, 191n30; medical and business students compared, 78; in monopolistic competition, 174n62; recruit from quantitative fields and social sciences, 113; seen as finishing schools, 198n69; socialization in university-based, 10–11; tension with disciplinary faculty, 47. *See also* Harvard Business School

Campanella, Tommaso, 89
Caplow, Theodore, 48–49, 118, 119, 160
cases, 53; "cracking the case," 59; digesting to teach well, 72; figuring out how to best teach, 60; former faculty names on, 120; method does not focus on answers, 73; as most conspicuous organizational artifact, 86; producing new, 66–68, 86; requests for more information about, 65; research associates write, 114; reviewing before a session, 56; teaching notes on high stakes of, 78, 81, 82, 87; tracking the day's discussion of, 60